SAVING THE CORPORATE BOARD

Why Boards Fail and How to Fix Them

Ralph D. Ward

WILEY

John Wiley & Sons, Inc.

This book is printed on acid-free paper. ∞

Copyright © 2003 by John Wiley & Sons, Inc. All rights reserved.

Published by John Wiley & Sons, Inc., Hoboken, New Jersey.
Published simultaneously in Canada.

For general information on our other products and services, or technical support, please contact our Customer Care Department within the United States at 800-762-2974, outside the United States at 317-572-3993 or fax 317-572-4002.

Wiley also publishes its books in a variety of electronic formats. Some content that appears in print may not be available in electronic books.

For more information about Wiley products, visit our web site at www.wiley.com.

Library of Congress Cataloging-in-Publication Data

Ward, Ralph D.
  Saving the corporate board : why boards fail and how to fix them / by Ralph Ward.
    p. cm.
  ISBN 0-471-43383-7
  1. Boards of directors--United States.   2. Directors of corporations--United States.   3. Corporate governance--United States.   I. Title.
  HD2745.W377 2003
  658.4'22--dc21

                                                                          2003000579

Printed in the United States of America.

10 9 8 7 6 5 4 3 2 1

Preface

It was a breakthrough moment in the history of U.S., and even world, corporate governance, when the way our top corporations govern themselves suddenly burst through to become a wide public policy issue. Best of all, it came from a wholly unexpected quarter. On February 26, 2002, the *National Enquirer*, America's gold standard of supermarket tabloid trash journalism, made the Enron scandal its front-page story. "Enron: Adultery, Greed, How They Ripped off Americans!" screamed the cover headline, with plenty of juicy details inside.[1] No celebrity scandals, much less aliens or Elvis sightings . . . nope, we've lived to see tabloid headlines grabbed by a *corporate governance failure*.

Meanwhile, major TV news media, not just C-SPAN but also CNN and CNBC, gave us live coverage of congressional hearings into the Enron mess (including company board members in the media hot seat). As someone who has written about corporate governance for over a decade, such a turn of events is astonishing. Corporate oversight, fiduciary duties, and the role of the board were topics for academic journals and public pension fund manifestos. Governance change, whether through new laws or shifts in corporate strategy, advanced at the pace of a glacier melt. Governance reform was too obtuse and unthreatening even for corporate chieftains to bother opposing. Certainly in the massive 1990s stock market runup, good governance concerns seemed as quaint as value investing.

But now the world has been turned upside down. Americans have learned that people hate us enough to treat us as living missiles and targets for mass murder. The tech stock meltdown, market turmoil, and recession have drained billions in shareholder value from even the best

---

[1] *The National Enquirer*, 26 February, 2002.

of companies. And at a few of the past decade's highest-flying, new-concept companies, overt corporate fraud destroyed shareholder value utterly, turning investors and employees from millionaires to paupers.

Corporate names, over the last year, have invaded the mainstream news: Enron, Tyco, Global Crossing, WorldCom, and Adelphia are the most noted. The cancer has spread to other firms, corrupting and destroying the once-respected auditor Arthur Andersen, and staining many of Wall Street's most noted investment, legal, and banking firms. Xerox and Kmart face their own investigations for audit, revenue, and executive pay shams. Even General Electric, revered for the benchmark value creation of chairman Jack Welch, faced withering criticism for the munificent retirement package it gave Welch on his way out the door. And I won't even mention Martha Stewart.

As noted, our national conniption over business fraud has targeted not just corporate greed, but specifically (and perhaps for the first time) the board of directors. This is a major change in what has been the American order of things. The board of directors has long been to business what the electoral college was to presidential politics. Both, according to musty old documents, were technically the true powers in their spheres of influence, but had long since faded to irrelevance, merely rubber stamping decisions made by more famous figures. The U.S. presidential elections of 2000 suddenly brought the electoral college into the spotlight—unfortunately as a negative relic that triggered a crisis in American democracy. The corporate fraud meltdowns of 2002 likewise thrust the musty role of the board of directors onto the public stage. I'll leave it to you to decide which was the more disastrous.

It's both the blessing and the curse of the Anglo-Saxon corporate governance model that it has enormous staying power. The corporate board is a concept cobbled together centuries ago to control modest joint stock companies. If it has been able to thrive, grow, and adapt to see a new millennium, we should assume that a few corporate crooks and ticked-off investors won't be able to kill it now. The corporate board, like capitalism itself, has proven a hardy perennial. The downside of this is that we have been wholly unable to create any other mechanism for governing corporations.

This book springs from a 2002 essay I wrote titled "Ten Reasons Why Corporate Boards Suck." This homely, Anglo-Saxon characterization may be the best diagnosis of the board's failings. The corporate board model, as practiced in advanced economies, is not "troubled," nor is it facing a "crisis of faith." The board simply sucks as a tool for fiduciary oversight of the modern corporation. But the reasons for this failure are complex and often missed even by governance critics.

After completing my original essay, I realized that it was not enough to simply diagnose these failings; solutions were also needed. In talking with people who have first-hand experience in making boards work, and in reviewing recent issues of my *BoardroomINSIDER* online newsletter, I found that the best, most usable boardroom advice all seemed to fit under one of these 10 headings. I have organized the book in this manner.

Ralph D. Ward
The Farm
Riverdale, Michigan
February 2003

To Hazel Ward (1917–2002)—

my mother, and a great storyteller.

Contents

The Data Disaster: Boards Receive Too Little, Too Much (or Just Plain Bad) Information

Board meeting books go by different names, such as the "Fed–Ex lump" or the "board meeting info dump," but for many board members, the effect is the same: an indigestible overload of information. A week or two before the board meeting, directors may receive several hundred pages of financials, spreadsheets, analyses, reports, graphs, letters, legal opinions, and memos on the company. Even the savviest business professional then faces the intimidating task of winnowing through this bundle to find the most relevant numbers, snapshot measures that show key trends, and any red flags. He or she ultimately learns to sift out some of what matters, but in a way, it's like a diet of junk food—fattening, but with too few essential nutrients. Worse, if a bomb is ticking away somewhere deep within the bundle —a potential lawsuit, an audit fraud, or an operating ratio that's headed south—it has many places to hide.

But if feast is a problem, so is famine. Even in this age of toughened governance standards, some directors still tell of not receiving their board info until the moment they file into the board meeting. This is one way CEOs keep directors on a need-to-know basis. Another way is to simply limit how much goes into the board package; a few basic financial statements, an agenda, committee reports, and that's it. Then the CEO will say that directors can have further data . . . "All they have to do is ask." Of course, this puts the burden on the already overburdened board (and assumes that they'll know what they need to see without seeing it first).

We like to think that the corporations caught up in the past year's business scandals kept their directors in the dark when it came to company information. Research suggests otherwise; the boards at Enron, Tyco, and Global Crossing received data that was as timely and complete as that sent to most large company boards (indeed, probably better). Whether the

1

context and implications of the board information were fully understood is another matter. Most infamous were the board members at Enron, who voted to waive Enron's own conflict of interest rules to allow CFO Andrew Fastow to make self-dealing transactions. The U.S. Senate's August 2002 report on Enron found that the board was fully aware of questionable corporate policies and "approved an awful lot of what happened" according to Senator Carl Levin (D–Michigan).

Such oversight "oversights" demand to be seen within the context of all the scandal companies. Were key financials, audit and legal opinions, and approvals buried in the middle of fat board books? Were the dangers and alternatives to policies fully explained (or were they presented by the same execs who would profit from them)? Was enough information on the downside potential of strategic moves and policy changes offered? Did the board investigate, or did it let management investigate for them?

Yet the board's disinformation problems go beyond just the data it receives. How the corporation preserves and respects its corporate data has now become a criminal matter. Enron audit firm Arthur Andersen worked overtime to shred incriminating evidence as the scandal broke out early in 2002, and the destruction of awkward info was alleged at most of the other scandal companies. The U.S. Sarbanes–Oxley audit reform law, hastily passed in the summer of 2002, addresses this issue in draconian terms. Section 1102 of the law makes the shredding or alteration of potential evidence a felony in itself, with huge fines and prison terms up to 20 years (I'll discuss the specifics of Sarbanes–Oxley later). The board of directors thus takes on an added duty when it comes to information. Directors must do more than just keep themselves intelligently informed on the company. They must also act as conservators of that information, guardians who ensure that data remains preserved and untainted.

For too long, corporate boards have been satisfied with a junk food information diet that management was all too willing to serve. Today, we're all paying for the health consequences. The following are ideas for radically improving a board's information policies, most using the common sense demanded for any effective diet. Start by taking control of the quality and quantity of intake. Learn more about the ingredients. Don't overindulge (or undernourish). And take a good look behind the kitchen door.

Bringing Yourself up to Speed

Among the few people who belong in any boardroom hall of fame, a place would definitely be reserved for Robert Lear. Recently retired from

Columbia University, retired chair of Schaefer Corporation, and chairman of the advisory board of *Chief Executive* magazine, Lear holds wide respect as a sharp governance writer—and practitioner. He offered me some good observations on what boards do right—and wrong—when it comes to boardroom information:

- "One of the biggest boardroom headaches I've seen is when the company presents a full agenda with no room for discussion. You have 2 hours of slides and presentations, and you've received 20 pounds of reports the day before the meeting, so there's no time to digest it. This happens all the time."

- "Full participation on all items is vital, with no one afraid to tell the CEO he's wrong. This means good board quality, with a balance of understanding in markets, finance, technology, research, and the operations of a company. You can't get this discussion if you have two or three large shareholders represented in the boardroom dominating the conversation."

- "I hate getting the agenda 5 minutes before the meeting. You need time to call in and ask questions. Otherwise, there are too many hurried situations. Having material ready for the meeting is an overall problem. They'll say we're sorry, we don't have it done, and Old Joe even stayed up all night to get it finished."

- Lear sees this dollar-short-and-a-day-late board info problem as most common, and serious, during mergers. "When an acquisition is under way, things are changing up to the last minute, so there's some reason for it. But the board has a thousand questions, yet it can't get a clear picture, and the result is some of the great mistakes that happen during acquisitions."

It isn't often that an individual board member makes the business news, but that's what happened in 2000 when Shirley Young quit (or was pushed from) the board at Bank of America (BofA). A May 2000 *Business Week* article slammed the strongly top-down BofA boardroom culture nurtured by CEO and chair Hugh McColl, a culture that clashed with the governance ideals of Young. A noted former vice president at General Motors, who also serves on the board of Bell Atlantic, Young makes strong, open information flow a first principle in her board service. I asked this boardroom pro about her governance must-haves and she says:

- First, the board must receive "key information relating to corporate strategy. . . not necessarily operational info, but key indicators of strategy, including financial data, the debt situation, short- and long-term revenue projections, and other numbers vital to the business, like market share." If these data are skimpy, late, or fudged, directors are flying blind—and forced to do their own digging.

- The board meeting must have both agenda time and an atmosphere that encourages open discussion. "Management must be willing to take questions and show respect for the board's role. The agenda must also support this, not [be] laid out like a military drill with directors having to dig through 27 items." The CEO needs to respect and encourage board questions on the firm's long- and short-term success measures—and have good answers.

- Young reiterates the point that management's view of the board sets the whole governance atmosphere—for good or bad. "Is the management attitude that the board is there to enlighten the process? Are they accepting of board inquiries? Do they encourage members to speak up, or discourage them? Do they view their board as a constructive force? Or do they act like kids avoiding the truant office at school?"

- CEOs who diss their boards often view board info and parliamentary procedures as things to be followed or gamed, depending on what's convenient. "There has to be respect for the intent of process. The rules are there so everyone on the board has a true understanding of the governance process and to encourage fairness." If your board bends the rules to keep "friendly" directors on, while enforcing them to the letter to shut out someone who asks too many questions, beware.

Learning about your company and your exploding governance responsibilities will require you to do more than just tapping inside sources. Recent years have seen a boom in excellent online resources:

- The Corporate Library (www.thecorporatelibrary.com) is veteran governance activist Nell Minow's omnibus governance page. It continues to add more and more goodies, including the latest worldwide governance news, reviews, and summaries of major governance reports and academic papers. It also offers a searchable database of board members and CEO contracts.

Some premium items now go for a fee, but this site definitely belongs among your governance bookmarks.

- Boardseat.com is an online director search service and more. Any qualified board wannabe should look into registering with the Boardseat database, which also offers useful clues on what sort of talent the boards are seeking. Boardseat also includes a collection of recent articles with specific tips on how boards and directors can be more effective.

- Virtual-Board.com is the web page of frequent *Boardroom-INSIDER* contributor Ed Merino, whose Office of the Chairman firm in California offers excellent board search and consulting services. It is especially valuable on advisory board topics.

- Don't forget to stop by the pioneer of online governance sources, the Corporate Governance web site (www.corpgov .net). Editor Jim McRitchie keeps adding new links and news items on a huge range of governance, activism, and social responsibility topics.

- The Institute of Directors (www.iod.com) is an international source for global governance codes, news, and resources based in Great Britain. This is especially valuable for country-by-country governance info.

Taking Charge of the Board Book

The next step in shaping up your board information should be a close look at what goes into your board books. I asked some of our most seasoned corporate directors, "What should go into the ideal board book?" Robert Lear, quoted earlier, complains that "sometimes minutes of the committee meetings aren't included, and I like to have them. Also, better background on items in the agenda. If there is an agenda item on Joe, I want to see info in the book on Joe. And I'd like to see a report on capital spending projects a year after we approved the project . . . did it stay on budget and things like that?" Other experienced directors share their own board book wish lists, as follows.

Charles Elson of the University of Delaware Center for Corporate Governance was one of the directors spoken to. "I want an agenda and info that will give me a good sense of everything that's going to come up at the meeting," Elson said. "If there's going to be a presentation, I'd like an advanced summary. I also like to read analyst's reports on the company—what they're saying is always helpful."

Walter Wriston, retired chair of Citicorp, remarked, "I don't think board books are exceedingly useful anyway. Obviously, when a company is going into some major new venture, a major project like a new factory or data project, we want full information at that point. But too often management sends out 50 pages of stuff with all the useful information concealed in the data. The total size of a board book should be limited to 30, 40 pages."

Of course, talking about the board *book* limits board info to dead-tree technology from the start. Over the past decade, online and digital communications technology has become a standard tool of business at every level of the corporation, except the boardroom. There, paper remains the medium of choice, and directors have proven themselves classic tech "late adapters."

But more boards are getting the message that technology will not only make their lives easier, but also improve the quality of their governance. Entergy Corporation has moved its 14-member board exclusively to digital media over the last couple of years. This includes sending *all* info to directors on CD, plus a password-protected board web site. Entergy corporate secretary Chris Screen describes how the firm not only got its directors wired, but made them eager for more:

- Start by solving a specific board info problem. "Boards always get a foot-high stack of paper for meetings, and nobody likes to carry something like that around," says Screen. The Entergy board web site was launched to meet this need by "posting things we normally mail, including the board agenda and presentations, plus agendas and exhibits for committee meetings." The site is a high-security password environment, but remains very easy to use. "Directors can view all the material needed for a board meeting, and print out any items they choose."

- Be ready to move on. "The web site is popular with the board, but directors like being able to bring board materials along with them to the meeting to review on the flight." Printing everything out, though, brings you back to the foot-high stack problem again, so . . .

- Put your board mailing on a CD. "We provide directors with a laptop with built-in password protection, and put all the board materials on a CD that we mail out 9 days before the board meeting." Board members can browse the board package on their flight, and during the actual board meeting, "we have 14 laptops open." Plus, burning a CD takes a lot less time than "making 50 two-sided color copies and spiral binding them" notes Screen, so the secretary's office requires less lead time (plus hassle and expense) to assemble the board mailing.

- Ease into the technology. Audit committees typically have the biggest paper load to wrestle with, so they were the first to try the CD board book format. Entergy "started by sending their material on a CD, and it proved very popular, especially for audit's big annual review of 10K filings." Other directors liked what they saw and started clamoring for all board info on disk.

- Screen also notes some potential downsides to avoid. "Tech is wonderful, but limit what you give the directors to *real* board needs. Make sure it's user driven, not techie driven. Maybe the software can tell you the temperature in Nome, Alaska, but who cares?" Make the software interface practical and graphic, with lots of hyperlinks to referenced material. "If the agenda mentions the February minutes, the director can click on the link and review those minutes. . . . Get input from the IT people at the director's end of things [typically their own tech staff]. You may make the director happy, but if you irritate his IT person, you shoot yourself in the foot."

Finally, make sure your internal IT staff is *very* responsive to any director questions. Think of your own last telephone tech support experience, and ask if you'd want to put one of your board members through such an ordeal.

Making Board Presentations More Effective (and Less Scary)

Boardroom chemistry involves more than just discussion. For directors or members of staff who give presentations to the board, knowing your dog-and-pony etiquette is vital. Business careers have been made (and broken) depending on how well a rising executive impresses the board. Marjorie

Brody, president of communications consulting firm Brody Communications, has some specific tips to make board presentations more informative and less scary:

- Do some research on the individuals who make up the board. "Know their individual motivators, learn who they are, and how to talk their language. Think of it this way: You're there to help *them* make a decision."

- Boards "are bottom-line driven and don't have a lot of time." This means not subjecting them to a long windup before reaching your conclusion. "Give them your conclusion up front and then back it up with one page of bullet points. Have more documentation, though, in case they want it."

- Directors don't like to sleep through presentations, so don't make them. "Shorter is better on visuals . . . I call it death by PowerPoint," says Brody. "I suggest more time for questions and less for the presentation. It gets the directors more involved . . . they like to have this control."

- Keep It Simple, Stupid (KISS). Or, to be more businesslike, the board just doesn't have time for details. "Understand the knowledge and sophistication of your board members. You may be used to presenting ideas in excruciating detail, but the board doesn't have time for all that."

Although directors should be supplied with all the background they request, they must be able to debate and judge proposals based on big ideas, not details, says Brody. "They're not experts on the subject, and they've got maybe 15 minutes to decide." Learn to probe into specific details because they're crucial, as opposed to a desire to prove how savvy you are.

Even among fellow directors, trying to pitch a viewpoint or committee findings to the board can be difficult. Rob Sherman, head of Sherman Leadership consulting, counsels on presentation skills and offers these director-to-director boardroom showtime tips:

- One of the most common errors Sherman sees when a director presents to fellow board members is a lack of preparation. "Directors tend to think that they're among peers, so they don't have to practice, but that just won't do. Don't try to wing it."

- One difference between your board and management presentations is that most top managers have a feel for how their fellow execs will respond, who's for and who's against, and what sort of questions to expect. With the board, though, you'll face more wildcards, so be prepared. "Sometimes board members are not as well informed, so expect some off-the-wall questions." Also, you work with fellow execs day to day, but the board meets, decides, and then disperses, so "you can't answer a question by saying I'll get back to you. You'll have to address the issue right there."

- Smart CEOs (those who keep their jobs) know how vital it is to build support among individual board members before pitching an idea. Anyone presenting to the board should practice this as well. "Know the positions of those on the board going in, and presell some allies." Another good idea is to practice your presentation in advance with some folks who can serve as board proxies.

There Are No Stupid Questions in the Boardroom

Board information problems cover more than just input and digestibility. What does the board *do* with the information it receives, particularly when it concerns a major strategic issue? Before they became engulfed in scandal, companies such as WorldCom and particularly Tyco were most famous as serial acquirers, gobbling companies at a ferocious rate. Were their directors able to intelligently weigh all these acquisitions, ask penetrating questions, and get straight info on potential downsides? In instances when a deal or strategy would benefit a company officer, did directors know all the facts? (Tyco director Frank E. Walsh, Jr. pleaded guilty in December 2002 for failing to tell fellow directors about a $20 million fee he received for helping arrange Tyco's takeover of CIT Group.)

Major corporate decisions that the board makes affecting corporate value—mergers, buybacks, spin-offs, acquisitions, and going private—should include an objective *fairness opinion*. This is similar to a notary public's seal for a major deal, examining price, terms, legality, and potential conflicts in relation to similar transactions. It's "almost like an insurance policy, telling the shareholders that what the board is doing is fair," observes Barry Steiner of the Florida firm Capitalink.

Like an insurance policy, a fairness opinion helps protect boards from later embarrassments and legal second-guessing on their decisions. The fairness opinion typically won't tell the board if something is strategically wise, merely whether it meets legal minimums. It is a black and white finding, stating either that the deal as presented seems fair or unfair, with no shadings in between. The way an opinion is assembled and how it's then reviewed by the board, however, make a real difference in how well it stands up to a legal challenge. What should a board demand from a fairness opinion?

- Look for the essentials that make a fairness opinion *fair.* Basic due diligence, analysis of risks, deal structure, pricing, potential conflicts, comparable benchmark transactions, and timeliness.

- Tighten standards depending on whether the concept of fairness is being stretched. "The transaction may involve an interested board member who's somehow affiliated with the company in the deal," notes Steiner. In these cases, bulletproof the opinion with a solid paper trail of the board member recusing him- or herself from review of the deal and by assuring that all aspects of the potential conflict are examined in the opinion. If a company executive is involved, the standard may be even higher—and if it can't be met, shouldn't that tell you just how fair the deal really is?

- Be aware of what things "are *not* included in a fairness opinion," counsels Ben Buettell, managing director with Houlihan Lokey Howard & Zukin investment bankers. "We're not being asked to find a better deal or the best price, just that the price is fair." Any tricky legal ramifications of a deal (antitrust, foreign trade, etc.) also won't be considered. Finally, the quality of data and the time allowed for analysis affect the quality of the final opinion. Thus, some situations (dealing with a secretive, privately held deal partner, lack of full data on the deal, or a rush effort) may cause later problems.

- Directors must be inquisitive. "This is not just a letter to the board, but an opportunity for directors to ask questions," says Steiner. "If I'm later asked by a judge or arbiter whether the board asked questions on the opinion, the answer had better be yes." Do we know who all of the interested parties are, and what their interests really are? Are there any competitive companies left out of the comparisons, and if so, why? Are projections verified, and do they seem reasonable? Are discounts needed for certain factors (such as a lack of trading in the company's stock, etc.)?

10

One handicap directors face in judging strategic deals is that the board usually doesn't come into the process until late in the game, often during the final approval stages. But that doesn't mean the board can't play a vital last-minute role. Asking some smart questions before the deal closes can improve the terms and in some cases prevent a disaster. Jim Rowe and Jim Mintz are snoops at the James Mintz Group, a firm of consultants and due diligence investigators, and make a specialty of uncovering closeted skeletons at merger and acquisition (M&A) prospects. What questions do they suggest your board asks before the "deal of the century" closes?

- Mintz notes that due diligence pays too little attention to the top executives and owners of the target. "Do some digging in the public records. Prior criminal convictions are obviously relevant, but so are civil cases, which are more likely." If the person tends to be litigious, someone who sues at the drop of a hat, that tells you a few things about how he or she handles disputes (which could include merger misunderstandings).

- This civil litigation history (both for individual officers and the company as a whole) can cut both ways. "They may pursue a win at all costs, scorched-earth strategy, but they may take a policy of avoiding litigation and throwing money at plaintiffs to make them go away," says Mintz. This could mean that the target company has a reputation as a target in another sense: easily shaken down for settlements. Also, it might be eye opening to find out what the company or its officers have agreed to in settling such cases (settlements that you as an acquirer will inherit).

- "Ask the company what we'll hear if we ask others about their legal, civil, and business issues," says Rowe. Check their answers against public records. Mintz and Rowe find many cases where a target's executives describe a business or legal dispute as no big deal, but it turns out to be a very serious issue indeed.

- How about the target's extended "family?" "What are their relations with labor unions and employees?" asks Rowe. "Have there been recent layoffs or plant closings? How much employee turnover is there?" He notes that most companies have a cadre of employees who have no use for the firm, and a contentious cutback can make them "both noisy and disloyal." The infamous disgruntled former employee may blow the whistle about company misdeeds after you've said "I do."

- Some surprises are "not as bad as they first look," observes Rowe. "Some industries will just get sued a lot, and a level that seems high at first may not really be such a big thing." He cites property management as a field where lawsuits are common.

Despite uncovering discrepancies on a regular basis, Rowe and Mintz note that few finds are actual dealbreakers, but "usually the acquirer changes the terms of the deal." Your due diligence duty as a board is to ensure that you don't pay prime property prices for a corporate fixer upper.

When the Board Isn't Satisfied: Digging Deeper

The standard for being an "informed" director has risen several notches over the past year, and at times the techniques mentioned, even if well practiced, may not be enough. Note that these tips remain *passive*, based on improving, questioning, and sharpening info that comes to the board. Should you and your board take a more active role, demanding more information, sidestepping the CEO's office, and launching your own investigations? At times, you may have little choice. I'll offer more information on how you can build board links to staff and shareholders in a later chapter, but here are some ideas on sleuthing from the boardroom when something in the corporation just doesn't smell right.

For example, let's say you receive some bad news. The CEO tells your board that improper (maybe even illegal) actions may have taken place within the company. The matter is serious enough that the board itself needs to look into affairs. Board investigations have become a much more urgent topic with Sarbanes-Oxley and subsequent stock exchange and Securities and Exchange Commission (SEC) rules. New laws place the board in a position of info nexus and investigator, especially for finance-related issues. This is odd, given that boards have already proven to be pretty awful as auditors, pay consultants, and CEO hall monitors. Now we want them to play sleuth, too. But how do you proceed?

Start by asking yourself if an investigation is warranted. Has a government regulator or prosecutor started seeking evidence? Would the potential wrongdoing be serious enough to rise to the level of board oversight? What damages could occur in a worst-case scenario? If outside board members feel uneasy about a situation, go with your group gut instinct, even if the CEO assures you that the whole thing will blow over. (Remember how Enron CEO Ken Lay conducted an investigation into financial mischief at the company, with his first mention of it to the board being that nothing was amiss?)

A distinct committee of the board should launch the investigation, which should be chartered by the board as a whole with a specific mandate, powers, and timeline. Although you can empower your current audit or governance committee, Charles Demonico, a partner with the law firm of Dickie McCamey & Chilcote and a board consultant, suggests that you form "a subcommittee of the board, called compliance and audit or such." A custom committee lets you shape membership to address the unique problem at hand.

That having been said, the board committee should *not* do its own investigating. Go first to corporate counsel to structure the investigation for maximum legal protection against later forced discovery of evidence. Counsel (either inside or an attorney from outside the firm) should then be charged by the board to do the actual digging. "Work hand in hand with counsel and your corporate compliance officer to decide whether they should do the investigation internally, or go through outside counsel," says Demonico. "The board should keep its hands out of the actual investigating." Demonico favors hiring an outside counsel for your inquiry. "He has less of a bias on the outcome, and it makes a claim of privilege easier."

After counsel looks into the matter, it should then "report back to the committee." The sleuthing counsel should not be reporting to management or even bring it into the loop at this stage. The committee then reports to the full board, which may question the committee and counsel at a full board meeting. "The board should ask probing questions of those who make the report," notes Demonico. Remember that the real goal of the investigation is to inform the board so it can proceed.

Assuming the investigation turns up some mischief, the board and inside counsel will face some tough questions. Do you make voluntary disclosures to the government in hope of leniency? How much do you disclose and when? Counsel can then help you make these tricky calls, but at least you'll go in knowing all the facts.

But how well do you handle the boardroom info you *do* receive? The security and retention of vital board info has never been much of an issue until recent debacles made the business headlines and court dockets. In 2001, Irwin Jacobs, savvy, long-time CEO at Qualcomm, let a laptop full of vital company info slip away from him at a conference, and he probably still hasn't lived it down. Awkward fumbles like this will only grow more common as more and more sensitive info goes to directors and officers electronically. What can your board do to ensure that stray hard drives, disks, and email don't slip between the boardroom cracks?

- Take a need-to-know approach. Every member of the board doesn't need access to every bit of touchy data, notes R.J. Heffernan, an info security consultant. "Typically, boards try to limit the number of directors who look at info." In reviewing takeover prospects, for example, directors often won't know specifics until management has winnowed the field to final candidates. This also makes board info programs more efficient and manageable.

- Set a board data-handling policy, and make sure directors take it seriously. "Have directors sign agreements as to their handling of proprietary info, similar to a nondisclosure agreement," counsels Heffernan. "Frankly, more boards need to understand their obligations. Directors themselves are proving to be a weak link." Careful handling of the company's secrets is a basic fiduciary responsibility, and letting them slip is a violation of that duty.

- Treat board members like anyone else when it comes to confidential info. Corporations have grown willing to set tough policies for employee access to privileged data, but who's going to tell corporate directors what they can and can't do? The board itself, that's who. "It's absolutely wrong to set policies that won't apply with equal force to the board," warns Mark Rasch, vice president of cyberlaw for Global Integrity Corporation. "If a board member calls up and demands access to info and the corporate secretary says no, rather than firing the secretary, you should promote him."

- Try building info security *into* the data that goes to directors. Encryption programs that are both simple and highly secure can be built into your software, even reencrypting data after a director accesses it. Auto-delete and electronic "shredder" programs can give directors access to the info they need and then auto-destroy it after use. "Make it easy, even automatic, for directors to comply with security," counsels Rasch.

- Keep the info safe at home whenever possible. "Some companies have their own extranets allowing director access, secured with firewalls and encryption passwords," says Kapua Rice, corporate secretary of Niagara Mohawk Power and head of the American Society of Corporate Secretaries Technology Committee. "Directors can go to the sites when they need to and access them from anywhere in the world." Directors don't download the data to their machines, but can securely obtain all the goodies they need.

Policies and schedules for the retention of documents (both paper and electronic) have become standards at most corporations, especially those in sensitive sectors (finance, defense, multinationals, etc.) Yet few boards have taken a close look at how well they function, much less whether they meet the new legal demands of Sarbanes-Oxley. Worse, even fewer boards realize how document retention issues directly hit them in the boardroom. What you as a board member keep or toss is not wholly your decision, and missteps can prove costly.

The board should start with a review of the company's overall info retention policy. Review the policy, who is responsible for its enforcement, what retention schedules are required, and what control systems are used to enforce it. What are your company's particular vulnerabilities for info loss or tampering? Has a full review and inventory been made of corporate data caches? Remember that any retention policy even a year old is already outdated.

After assuring that company policies are up-to-speed, take on the trickier task of shaping your board's own policies. These should be based on the company's overall retention procedures, which bring several benefits. First, it keeps board members from pleading ignorance. Basing the board policy on overall company plans also forces board info to interface more smoothly with management systems, and it raises awareness of all the media (email, personal notes, etc.) that must be considered.

Yes, I said your *personal* notes as a board member. "*All* your board records, including handwritten notes, are potentially discoverable," counsels Patricia Eyres, head of the Litigation Management consulting firm in California. Remember the tale of a director under cross-examination in a strike suit trial? He swore that the board had heartily supported a motion, just as the minutes said it did, but was then presented with his copy of the meeting agenda, his own handwritten note, "Who came up with this stupid idea?" next to the item. Even a director's circled items or question marks beside a number have been food for plaintiff attorneys.

Your policy should be customized to meet the unique data issues of a board. Making sure that info is retained and then shredded on schedule is tricky enough when limited to employees and company computer nets, but directors add a wildcard. Many boards collect board info packs for disposal as soon as the meeting adjourns. This can work, but what about a director who received the info, but then missed the meeting? His bundle of sensitive info, complete with any notes he may have made in the margins, is then a time bomb ticking away in his desk.

Email retention has become an issue, and again the far-flung independence of your directors brings danger. Email to your directors "may end up on their home computers or the networks at their own workplace," warns Eyres. In the latter case, the email may then go onto *their* company's backups, further complicating matters. In case of legal action, document purging must be halted and all principals must identify where their records are. Since directors rarely think about document backups, you could be perjuring yourself without even knowing it.

In conclusion, you can use some practical tools to cope with board shredding headaches: Set a board retention policy, make sure everyone knows about it, and check up regularly. Know where all of your board info and email end up, and limit caches as much as possible. Don't tape-record board or committee meetings, and destroy all notes used in writing the minutes as soon as the minutes are completed.

The Boardroom Leadership Gap: The Board Oversees (at the Same Time It Is Led by) the CEO

The combined position of CEO and board chairman is such a universal part of America's boardroom furniture that we don't appreciate just how odd the concept looks to the rest of the world. In most business cultures, especially in Europe, the roles of chair and chief executive are typically divided, with a wise elder statesman serving as chairman of the board who collectively supervises management. The U.S. model seems an obvious case of being allowed to grade one's own report card. Since the CEO knows far more about the company than the board's outsiders (and bosses its insiders), the temptation to defer to his or her judgment is hard to resist. This old-style CEO overlord was summed up for me a few years ago when I interviewed Lee Iacocca shortly before he retired as chairman of Chrysler. When discussing the automaker's board, he didn't refer to the group in a neutral way as "the" board—and he sure didn't use any big group-hug term like "our" board. For Lido, the Chrysler board was "my" board. "These are my guys," he said, between puffs on his cigar, and made it clear that nothing happened in his boardroom that wasn't his idea.

A striking symptom of all the recent corporate scandals is how unquestioned and powerful the bosses' leadership was. Ken Lay, Bernie Ebbers, Dennis Kozlowski, John Rigas—all of them were, if not founders, then certainly the men who personally shaped their empires with obsessive drive and little respect for the rules. These patriarchs *were* the company, and the line between themselves and the corporation was hard to define. The most extreme cases may have been Kozlowski's Tyco and Rigas' Adelphia, where the company essentially served as the CEO's personal bank.

The past year's corporate scandals have been so traumatic that even the most sacred of corporate cows, the combined CEO/chair, is under attack.

The last few years have brought open boardroom warfare at Walt Disney Co. over the Magic Kingdom's fading fortunes. In September 2002, a shareholder group led by Providence Capital's Herbert Denton targeted Disney specifically for its bad governance practices, particularly its lack of board independence. One of Denton's Magic Wishes, however, went straight to the top; he wanted Disney CEO/Chair Michael Eisner to give up one of his titles. The idea was not dismissed out of hand. As *Fortune* writer Marc Gunther noted, "Disney will be one of the first high-profile companies to address questions that CEOs and directors face in a post-Enron world. How will corporate power be wielded? Will CEOs work for boards, or will they dominate them as they have in the past?"[1]

In the U.S. business world, we've long viewed a split at the top as a sign of CEO weakness and board hubris, and it remains uncommon. Non-CEO chairs "don't have a clue what's going on" a respected turnaround CEO once told me. Unfortunately, that CEO was "Chainsaw Al" Dunlap. His fall, along with those of Lay, Ebbers, and so on, has suddenly made the omnipotent boss seem dangerous. Further, the rising tide of reforms has made leadership of the board less a ceremonial perk and more of a role with real powers. In January 2003, corporate America's ultimate status quo, The Conference Board, cautiously endorsed splitting the CEO and chairman roles in a report from its Blue Ribbon Commission on public trust and private enterprise. At last, the job of separate chairman may finally be one worth having.

The following fixes for the CEO/board power mismatch cover a broad spectrum, ranging from the idealistic to the gritty. Here is how the board can establish its own power through strong board leadership and administration, how (for lack of a better term) the board can let the chief executive know who's in charge, and how the board can hire and nurture CEOs for a sound balance of power. But tips are also included on how smart CEOs work with their board to lead strategic change and establish their own rightful executive powers—because both the board *and* the CEO are most effective when they stay out of each other's turf.

Teaching Your Board to Lead

A valuable voice of experience on returning leadership to the boardroom is Walter Wriston. Former chair of Citicorp, leader of the banking revolution that put ATMs on every street, member of many boards, and the defining

---

[1] Marc Gunther, "The Directors," *Fortune,* 14 October, 2002: 132.

business insider, Wriston is the go-to guy for boardroom insight. Though now 83, Wriston remains active on the boards of several young companies, including high-tech startups. Here are his first-hand views on how a chairman should lead a boardroom:

- Every director brings unique strengths to the boardroom, so learn them and tap them. "If I'm on a biotech company board, for instance, I may know how engineered proteins work. Each member should be very value added," says Wriston.

- Assume that directors want (and may need) to learn more. "At Citibank, it occurred to me one day that the directors didn't really understand the bank's accounting issues," relates Wriston. "I asked the board if they'd like to come an hour early to the next board meeting for a presentation on how bank accounting works, and every one of them signed up immediately." A smart chairman doesn't wait for the directors to ask for help. "You can sense whether or not what you're saying makes sense to them."

- The board will give you input one way or another, so try to make it positive. "Some chairmen may ask directors, 'What do you think of this idea?' and they'll tell you it's lousy, but at least that starts a dialogue. The major thing is open discussion. I've never seen a proposal that went before the board that didn't come out better."

- Still, Wriston notes that seeking board input *doesn't* mean asking them what you should do. "You wouldn't bring an idea to the board if you didn't know what you wanted done. You have to be able to go in saying this is what we want to do, and why it makes sense. For a chair to go around the boardroom asking what he should do, that's very rare."

- You'll have to be good at reading people before you can read directors. "Mostly, if a chair senses that directors will consider an idea dumb, he just sends it back to the laundry."

- What's the quickest way for a board chairman to become ineffective? "Not telling the truth. Once that happens, the chairman is out of there. The integrity of the chair is the most important thing, and what you say has to be accurate to the best of your knowledge." Even nudging the envelope here will get you in trouble. "I had a recent case where the chairman was being truthful, but you had to be a district attorney to ask him the right question. It's crucial to be forthcoming with your board. None of that 'no controlling legal authority' stuff —that's absolutely out."

Speaking of top execs putting one over on the board, what role did board deception play in the recent corporate scandals? For that, let's talk to another boardroom veteran who's seen it all before—the good and the bad. Hicks Waldron, emeritus chair and cofounder of the Boardroom Consultants search firm in New York, was once chair of Avon and Heublein. He's also served on 13 corporate boards over the decades, including Hewlett-Packard and Westinghouse. Now retired, Hicks tells me that the past year's board scandals are nothing new, and that a few wise director countermeasures could have headed off disaster.

- "At these scandal companies, you run into a situation where there is a headstrong CEO or a founder, Kozlowski at Tyco, Ken Lay at Enron—someone who's a heavy, dominant person." The result, says Waldron, can be the deadly mix of a deferential board and a CEO convinced that he *is* the company. So what are effective governance countermeasures? "Name a lead director and executive sessions of the board at every meeting [without the CEO present]. That's just common sense."

- Smart directors have grown far choosier about board offers they accept, and tough directors are more willing to walk out on a board when they smell danger. Waldron told me of a Fortune 500 company whose board he joined. "I went to four board meetings and quit. It was a one-man show, with the board just approving things the CEO had already approved." The company ultimately failed. Yes, a name director dumping the board of a name company draws some negative attention and not too long ago was viewed as unseemly. But that was then, and this is now. "Directors are more willing to say 'I quit.'"

- Directors must watch out for groupthink and other breakdowns that can lead to a later "what the hell were we thinking?" response. "Some of this just infuriates me, when directors go off the deep end," says Waldron. "I read of one board approving a CEO loan for $380 million and thought there had to be a decimal point off. I can't imagine sitting on a board and approving this."

Try this experiment: Look over the last year's worth of your firm's board minutes and imagine that they refer to a company that's now melting down in fraud and is under close examination. Would any of *your* yes votes now prompt a "what was he thinking?" response?

A first step in board leadership is for the board to actually *have* a true leader. This requires an effective board chair (or lead director) and crafting a board structure able to meet the new demands of governance. If we look at chairing the corporate board as a distinct job, what are some of the best practice elements that go into its job description? According to people who work with boards for a living, the effective chair should:

- Both set and stick to the board agenda. "The chair must be the one who actually sets the board's agenda for the meeting, but *after* soliciting other directors on what they want to see covered," says Stephanie Joseph of the Director's Network in New York. For the combined CEO/chair, this means knowing who your informal lead director is and valuing his or her views. "The lead director is the voice of the independent board member," Joseph remarks. "[Y]ou need to make sure they are being considered."

- Be able to move beyond details. Corporate operations is, of course, the domain of the CEO, the company's top manager. But the chairman must have an ability to disengage from this day to day for a short while to speak in the more strategic, detached mindframe of the other board members. "The excellent chair has an ability to stay above detail, to think at the big-picture, strategic level," says Louise Corver, president of Corporate Learning and Development consultants. "They keep strategic vision, but can also get their hands dirty if need be, knowing both the vision and how to fulfill it." Balancing this almost schizophrenic split is one of the CEO/chair's toughest roles.

- Build unique relationships with each board member, and use them to shape consensus. Corporate directors are proven achievers and may have egos to match, so "individual communication is important," says Dee Soder, founder of the CEO Perspective Group. "But even more, each director must feel

21

that he or she is receiving individual communication from the chair, which can be two different things." Try handwritten follow-up notes or personal calls to directors. "Tell them that you know they'd want to discuss this, or that you wanted to run this or that by them."

You hear plenty about your board duties and responsibilities, but how about your *rights* as a board member? Good governance guidelines tend to focus on what the board and its members must do, but they pay little attention to what directors should demand in the way of tools and powers to do it.

I recently sat in at a board retreat that included a novel (and good) idea: a list of "rights of a board member." This list, originally developed by the Williams Young accounting/consulting firm of Madison, Wisconsin, is targeted to the nonprofit board member, but some items from their "bill of rights" are valuable to the members of any board. These include the right:

- To request that a vote be taken in a particular manner (roll call, show of hands, voice, or secret ballot)

- To request added information on any subject brought before the board, and to personally question anyone who presents to the board, before a vote is called

- To request changes in minutes before their approval, and to have changes made that accurately reflect what actually happened

- To have personal opposition to an item passed by majority vote be reflected in the minutes

- To move to defer action on any item of business to a later date (this, of course, must still be approved by a majority vote)

- To request a summary of internal policies and procedures that the board has developed through its history

Such a director's Magna Carta would be a useful addition to any board's governance guidelines, but it should also include items specific to your corporation, its membership, and its committee structure (audit committee members should have a right to specific financials, for example). Empowered boards need a list of these rights.

Q: I'm an outside director with a midsized industrial company here on the East Coast. Our CEO and board chair is a good guy, but has always been a bit strong-handed in dealing with the board—not a bully, but he makes it clear who's in charge when it comes to steering the company. However, with the changes and reforms that are going on in business now, a few of us directors feel we need to reassert our powers as a board. How do we subtly send a message to the CEO that a change is needed without sparking a face-off?

A: Strong boards are a wave of the future, but the CEOs who most need them are usually the last to want one. William George, retired CEO of success story (and governance leader) Medtronic Corporation, has seen the issue of board power from both sides and believes that "boards already have the power, but don't exercise it and have ceded it to the CEO." Any attempt to strengthen the board's hand begins with strengthening the board itself. "First, the outside members of the board need to organize themselves as independent directors. Start by writing corporate governance principles that you'll need to operate." Next, since your CEO is also board chair, "the board needs to have a leader of its own, a lead director so outside board members can meet on their own."

George notes that lead directors or separate chairs are in the process of being mandated anyway by the stock exchanges, so naming such a board leader should not be viewed by the CEO as a shot across the bow. "This should not be threatening to the CEO. If it is, it shows a problem on the CEO's part."

Although many CEOs and boards view the current rush to reform governance as a threat, it can also be a golden opportunity for boards who are seeking to tip the balance of power back without rocking the boat. The wave of new rules from regulators and stock exchanges leaves boards little choice but to review their independence, oversight of management, and level of authority. Make it clear to the CEO that questions on the board/management power mix must be asked. But then be sure to follow through by honestly asking them.

Ed Vick, chairman of mega-ad agency Young & Rubicam, offers some good first-hand advice on the qualities that make a successful board chairman. "Being the board's leader and being *perceived* as the leader are two different things. The board is typically made up of very successful people, so they want to know that, if you're chair, you're going to show leadership." Vick sees leading a board as demanding its own "tough love" aspects. "A board is like a high-powered family. In one way, they don't want to be told what to do, but in another, they do. If it's a good board, they want to see that the chair is in control."

The smart chair never forgets one rule: *communicate* with the board. "The head of the board must be a good communicator, able to clearly express to directors where he wants the company to go, to be persuasive and able to get them on board," counsels Vick. "But you also need active listening skills, and the ability to have an honest dialogue.

"The board meeting should have no surprises," he continues, "even good ones. If I surprise the board members, it says that I wasn't communicating with them ahead of time, or worse, I was taken by surprise. You should have the nuts and bolts well buttoned up in advance, and communicate them to the board ahead of time." *Author's note*: A seasoned CEO once told me that knowing you'll win a board vote in advance isn't enough. You need to be able to predict the *exact* vote, or you're out of touch.

As you should gather from the previous discussion, "80 to 90 percent of the chairman's role happens outside of board meetings. It's a poor chairman who tries to make everything happen inside the meeting room."

When is an emeritus board chairman *not* an emeritus board chairman? When he's now the lead director. That's the boardroom equation at Wolverine World Wide, a Michigan-based shoe manufacturer best known as the maker of Hush Puppies casual shoes. California-based investor Phillip Matthews served as separate chairman of the company for four years in the 1990s, but in 1996 Wolverine CEO Geoffrey Bloom added the chair's seat. Rather than fade away, though, Matthews stayed onboard and shaped a whole new function as Wolverine's lead director. "The board decided it wanted an outside director to facilitate, and I'd been doing that as chairman anyway," says Matthews.

What did this board seek in a lead director? "I work with the outside directors to establish an agenda, raise issues to be discussed, and consolidate their viewpoints," Matthews explains. "I also facilitate our private meetings of the outside board members." (These are held once or twice a year.) Matthews also coordinates the Wolverine board's director evaluation program, which is held every other year. "We survey our directors for feedback on meetings, lead director performance, and overall board evaluation."

His status as former chairman gives Matthews credibility with current chair Bloom when serving as the outside directors' liaison. "I spend more time alone with the CEO, making sure that major issues are on the agenda, and letting him know what the outside directors want to be involved in."

So has the lead director role worked for the Wolverine board? "Definitely," says Matthews. "The major improvement I see is that a combined chair and CEO has a lot of things on his mind in running the business. The lead director can focus on improving the board process itself. Significant opportunities can be missed here because the chair/CEO is just too busy."

But does *your* board need a formal lead director? Maybe not. "You don't have to name a lead director," observes Matthews. "[Y]ou just need a senior director who can serve as a focal point for things that need communication. But it doesn't need to be formal. It's the *role* that needs to exist."

Q: The founder/chairman/CEO of our company is backing out of his management role, and we're hiring our first full-time CEO from the outside. The founder will continue to serve as chairman of the board, though. My question is, how do you pay the separate chairman of the board as a distinct position?

A: Although most experts agree that you don't compensate the board chair as just another member of the board, how (and how much) you should pay a separate chair will depend on how the job came about. An emeritus chair such as yours may be eased out with his previous year's total pay extended for a brief period.

"Usually you pay them the same salary for the rest of the fiscal year," advises J. Richard, president of J. Richard Consulting. "But even then, the role can vary a lot depending on whether the former CEO/chair just slams the gavel down at board meetings or is more active in guiding and mentoring the CEO." A first step is to gain a good fix on the amount of time the separate chair devotes to specific board duties, and then compare this to the time required of other board members. This could help you shape a new pay model based on a new board structure, rather than the old CEO model.

Hard numbers are available on how separate chairs are paid, but these vary as much as the positions themselves. Pearl Meyer & Partners, pay consultants in New York, find that, at the Fortune 200 level, non-CEO chairs are paid an average of 63 percent more than the outside directors. But "only three of these companies have an outside chair," notes PM consultant Rhoda Edelman, so this figure is shaky and may include consulting fees.

Lower down in the corporate food chain, separate chairs are more common. At companies with $1 billion to $3 billion in revenues, the separate chair averages 85 percent more than other directors, and between $200 and $600 million, 142 percent more. "Generally, the smaller the corporation, the more the separate chair is paid compared to other directors," observes Edelman.

Why It's Not the Board *versus* the CEO

After the board shapes its own leadership, it needs to establish with the CEO how that leadership will be asserted. This can lead to two obvious pitfalls. The first is a board manifesto to the CEO saying, in effect, we're the bosses here, and don't you forget it. This boardroom insurrection is less than likely, and such an overt challenge would probably weaken the CEO's ability to get the job done anyway. At the other extreme (and more common) is a board too timid to assert its rightful powers. This group feels it must ask executive permission before acting as an active shareholder fiduciary.

Both boardroom rebellion and masochism can be avoided if the board approaches empowerment as *procedures* rather than philosophy. As we've seen, most board communication is one way: from the exec to the boardroom. Your board can be more active in building bridges back to the CEO, in communicating the leadership values required in today's corporation, and in coaching and nurturing CEOs who want a partner rather than a chorus. Also, you can treat the inevitable trend toward effective board evaluation of the CEO as a strategic opportunity (rather than an executive threat).

When it comes to building leaders (as well as great boardroom practices), the place to start must be General Electric. Under Jack Welch, GE became North America's "Starfleet Academy" for nurturing top executive talent. Not only did this approach pay off by shaping a cadre of leaders at other corporations, but it gave GE a talent like Jeffrey Immelt, who continues to lead the firm to growth in a down market.

The GE boardroom is a key part of this leadership effort, through its Management Development and Compensation committee. A GE spokesman told me that the committee, chaired by retired Illinois Tool Works CEO Silas Cathcart, is "charged with overseeing executive compensation plans and policies, and all key changes in executive assignments." Whenever a GE hi-pot is promoted to the executive level, the committee keeps tabs on his or her progress and performance. The GE spokesman explains that the committee "is exposed to talent within GE, and members are required to go out several times a year" to meet the managers. As part of GE's succession horse race, Jack Welch made sure that coming talent attended board meetings to present ideas (and themselves). Board members are also "encouraged to talk with executives on their own." The CEO does not orchestrate the committee's agenda, and indeed, the committee often makes it a point to meet without CEO Immelt or other inside members present to discuss their findings.

The committee has plenty of opportunities to meet on its own. In the run up to Welch's retirement, it held 10 scheduled meetings yearly, more than any other GE board committee.

Board evaluation of the chief executive has gone from being a good idea to a must, but that doesn't mean that your board is grading the CEO *effectively*. Tough evaluation does not require a hostile approach by the board, but bad CEO reviewing is not usually caused by the other extreme: a board kowtowing to the boss. Rather, boards fumble CEO evaluation through a lax, path-of-least-effort approach says Dick Marty, boss at the Execucounsel.com board consulting service. His first-hand take on how boards get CEO evaluation wrong is as follows:

- Boards give too little thought to the precise criteria that measure exec performance and end up with "too many indicators that can't be well defined or tracked properly," according to Marty. The result is a mind-numbing pile of indicators that directors would rather not dig into (and which a sly CEO can manipulate). Better for your board to put some debate into "identifying the 10 best indicators of CEO performance" long before you ever try evaluating by them.

- This "keep It Simple" approach to evaluation criteria also helps your board take more frequent looks at the CEO's performance, which Marty sees as a serious need. "Evaluation tracking isn't done frequently enough. If you check in every year or 6 months, you won't find out there's a problem until it's too late." By sticking to a list of 10 or so key markers, "directors can check performance quarterly or even monthly, and it doesn't take long, perhaps 20 minutes at each [board] meeting."

- Boards too often end up dogging it on the overall evaluation process. "They really don't want to bother that much, so the CEO ends up providing all the support information and is involved in ways that aren't appropriate," says Marty. The more your board lets the CEO handle his or her own evaluation legwork, the less the value of the final product.

- Although a committee of independent directors needs to handle the CEO evaluation, Marty wants the committee to be "reporting and accountable to the full board. The other directors should have the same information as the committee. It's more convenient to have the committee handle everything, but I feel it's a serious mistake." Everyone needs to stay informed on a matter like this.

- One final (but crucial) CEO review tip. The board should heavily communicate the evaluation process and structure (but *not* the results) to shareholders and other stakeholders. "Communication between the board and stakeholders is usually not very effective, but transparency here is vital," Marty adds.

Q: Our current CEO is finally getting serious about a succession plan, although we'd like to keep our options open through the process. There's a sense that we need some change here, and we want to consider outside as well and internal CEO candidates. I've never seen anything on how you really judge a potential CEO successor, though. If we don't want just a clone of the incumbent, what specific things should our board weigh?

A: It sounds like you have some boardroom dissatisfaction with the present chief, so the outside members of your board may want to convene and discuss both the similarities and differences you'll seek in a candidate. Try not to skew this process toward a favored internal candidate; view it as a fresh job description. This approach should also help steer you toward specifics and away from generalities in setting CEO criteria. You don't want to measure leadership or corporate vision, but instead what a prospect has achieved and what this suggests for future accomplishments.

"Explore how you're really going to work together," suggests Beverly Lieberman of Halbrecht Lieberman Associates, an executive search firm. "Have the candidate outline a strategic plan for the company going forward." What would the candidate's 90-day plan be? The board should also do some benchmarking of the candidate against peers in the industry. Track the candidate's records against those peers, and do a gap analysis.

For internal CEO prospects, directors may want to do some subtle, deep-background checking with those who know the candidate: the CFO, the heads of strategic planning and marketing, or divisional heads. This will be subjective and tricky, though—use caution.

Who's in Charge (or Should Be) of CEO Pay?

Sure, CEOs have been effective at leading their bosses in the boardroom, but when it comes to nudging the board process of CEO paysetting, chief executives have been downright brilliant. The recent corporate scandals may have been about keeping stock prices up and losses hidden, but those were only a means toward the shifty CEO's real concerns: stock, bonuses, loans, investment deals, and perks. Yet executive manipulation of the board on pay goes far beyond the headline meltdown companies. Pay plans have grown astonishingly complex, often in response to tax and regulatory policy, and are far beyond the ken of most board compensation committees. But, needless to say, the effect of this bafflement has not been to make CEO pay more reasonable or performance based. The past decade's explosion in top executive pay warrants a book in itself, but a board can take certain steps to regain control.

Q: Our board's compensation committee is at work on the annual exercise of putting together the CEO's pay package, and as usual, I feel that the deck is stacked against us. For instance, in our business sector, it's hard to get realistic CEO compensation benchmarks, so it often seems as if one set of numbers is just as good as any other. Any advice on finding real-world CEO pay levels?

A: You're right in finding executive pay benchmarks vapory, and the problem is worse in some sectors than in others. Fast growth companies, the young tech startups, heavily international firms, and unique areas as nonprofits often require such specialized CEO talents that benchmarks may not even exist.

But this doesn't mean the comp committee's job is hopeless. One of the quickest rules of thumb is to ask "what would it cost to replace him," according to Arnold Ross, president of the Ross

Companies, a pay consultant firm. "If you went to a search firm with this particular job description, along with a particular board mission, say, growing the company or tightening controls, they'll tell you what it would take to get a new guy." Still, this is an iffy use of a search firm. Also, since it always costs more to hire a new person than keep the old one, you're building in some inflation (though you might be able to factor it out later).

Be willing to look outside your specific industry for benchmarks based on the company's size, goals, and challenges. "For a new company, build [pay] around the stages of funding," suggests Ken Kaleza of ExecuComp Systems. "Are you at the first or second round, or pre- or post-IPO?" Pay consultants will often have defensible numbers for these stages of funding that will translate into your sector.

Or try doing your own comp survey. Target some similar firms that are not necessarily competitors and tap their public filings. For an even simpler approach, have a member of your committee call up some of their top pay people (or the head of their comp committee) to swap notes. A board member carries the clout to get through in these cases, and other firms may be surprisingly willing to pool pay info with you if they get your numbers in return. Their board may be facing the same CEO pay quandary as yours.

Boards face grief not only for what they pay their CEOs to stick around, but also for what they offer as a goodbye gift. When Dynergy was poised to acquire the troubled Enron in the spring of 2002, CEO Ken Lay announced that he would not take the $60 million severance package he would have been allowed. Given the collapse of Enron's stock price into pennies with failure of the Dynergy deal, and ultimately the fall of Lay's company itself, such *noblesse* now seems like chutzpah. Even at General Electric, the nearest thing to an American Corporate Mother Church, the board was slammed in 2002 over Jack Welch's rich severance package. How should boards reevaluate their severance and golden parachute deals with the CEO in light of the new era?

- Take a sensible pay stand on the CEO's way *in*. If the board is trying to lure outside talent on board, the temptation is to view a too-puffy future departure package as a minor detail, setting generous terms or easy standards. "I've seen boards get rushed; they're so antsy to get someone in the CEO's position," says Steven Currall, a professor at the Jones School of Management at Rice University. As with rushing into any marriage, it's wise to stay cool long enough for a good pre-nup.

- Build smart CEO evaluation into severance terms. Too many boards are already softies when it comes to setting tough CEO standards for pay, much less for severance. "What other reference companies are we using, how far above industry averages do we want to go, and what time frames should we use?" are a few board queries suggested by Currall. For setting severance, don't be afraid to weight performance toward the *end* of the CEO's tenure. Currall cites CEO Jill Barad's ouster from Mattel in February 2000, complete with a generous severance package, despite poor results. "The board rationalized a generous severance package by saying she'd added a lot of corporate value early." Too often, though, boards are willing to overlook value *destroyed* late in the CEO's term in their eagerness to move on.

- Apply the smell factor. When negotiating CEO severance, both going in and at departure, ask how the outcome will look to investors, employees, and analysts. "What concerns will there be, and what is the timing of the announcement?" asks Currall. Announcing a premium parachute package at the same time as major layoffs or plant closings is asking for trouble.

- Stand firm. Assuming the contract severance terms you set with the CEO were fair, resist the temptation to sweeten the deal when he or she leaves, even if the CEO wants to play tough. "CEOs use whatever tactics they can, including guilt and the threat of litigation," says Currall. Although you'd think departing CEOs (especially those with performance problems) have zero leverage, the *threat* of hardball tactics often does the job of bringing a richer payoff. Directors should be good poker players and stick by the CEO's original terms.

- As to golden parachute plans, these were taking on some tougher terms even before the discontents of the past year, says Howard Golden of William M. Mercer. "The past few years

31

have seen increased use of a double trigger for benefits," Mercer comments. Under a traditional *single trigger*, parachute benefits for the CEO or other exec would kick in with a change in control of the company. A *double trigger* requires both a change in control *and* a change in the exec's employment status. A modified single trigger (giving the exec a time window after a change in control) is more common.

- "A major issue for boards is gross-ups," says Golden, referring to added severance payments to offset taxes on the face amount. Although the formula used is complex, the IRS imposes "excess" taxes on compensation beyond some baseline amount. The penalty faced by the exec is tough (taxes on the full payment plus 20 percent on the excess), and the corporation can't deduct the excess. Boards can help out by adding a "gross-up" amount to the plan that makes the exec whole. "This is a very important decision for the board, since obviously any gross-up amount itself is an excess, non-deductible expense," Golden explains. Still, gross-ups are growing in popularity, he says, from being used at 50 percent of major firms a few years ago to 72 percent today.

- Changes in parachute and severance plans are not speedy processes, but Golden is seeing some anecdotal shifts in how board views are changing. "The standards for granting parachute payments seem to be growing more stringent. Boards are taking a long, hard look now at things like the definition of cause or effective termination in ending employment." The trend has been toward a more generous definition of "cause," such as a top executive getting a lesser position in a merged firm. Now though, tougher times may "see a contraction in the definition of cause."

Flashpoints in the Board/CEO Relationship

Building your board's internal leadership and laying out its relationship with the CEO are crucial, but they only serve as preparation. The real test comes when "flashpoint" issues arise between the board and chief executive, disputes ranging from the mundane to the traumatic. How these issues are handled by the board (as opposed to how the CEO suggests they be handled) will be crucial to shaping your new board leadership model.

Perhaps the most obvious of these defining moments (though I hope your board will be spared) is firing the CEO. The modern era of board empowerment began a decade ago when General Motors directors rose up to oust CEO Robert Stempel and has continued, up to October 2001, when Ford CEO Jacques Nassar was edged out by the company's board, making way for Chairman Bill Ford to take over as chief executive. (By the way, over the past century in Dearborn, Michigan, the script of "top Ford exec gets on the wrong side of the family and is sacked by the board" has played out at least once a generation.) But broader corporate patterns apply when a board of directors gives its CEO the boot. Most boardroom coups have several shared features:

- The CEO's personal chemistry with the board and his or her performance are inseparable. Too many underperforming CEOs still hang on via their tight bond with directors, while competent chiefs who fumble the boardroom relationship do not last. Or as Henry Ford II said when sacking his successful president Lee Iaccoca in 1978, "Sometimes you just don't like someone."

- The board needs a sparkplug director to lead the coup. Typically, this is the outside lead director (John Smale of General Motors in GM's 1992 board rising is the classic example), a major investor, or a retired chair. Usually, this coup leader arises spontaneously among the directors. This ad hoc approach is less common among companies with strong governance policies and an established lead director (where the need to sack the CEO seems less likely to begin with).

- Outside voices make their discontent known to the board. Most often these are major investor blocks or, in some industries, labor (as happened in 2001 when James Godwin was ousted as CEO at United Airlines). Boards today are more likely to listen to these voices, and the CEO who still thinks in boardroom "us-versus-them" terms may end up on the wrong side of the equation.

Q: I'm an outside director on the board of a major regional retailer. Our CEO has been on board for several years, and for most of that time he's proven very effective. In the last couple of quarters, though, some key numbers have slipped, and we've been hit by some nasty market and legal surprises. Some of these problems have good excuses, and our CEO seems to be coping so far, but I also know that this is how corporate failures can start. How do you tell when to stick with your CEO, or if it's time for a change?

A: Consider judging your CEO the way analysts do: Is he reliable? That's not to ask if he's lying, but do his projections tend to work out? "If you indicate that your earnings will be X, then they'd better be X," says Ben Boissevain, managing partner with Agile Equity, LLC, in New York. Also, set your company's key must-have metrics (revenue projections, financials, etc.) in advance, making sure they're known to all, and arrive at the fudge factors (if any) you can live with. "Is it one quarter or several? Has he missed by 5 or 25 percent?" asks Boissevain. Your retailing sector, and some others (particularly technology and e-business) allow less time for a wait-and-see attitude.

Such make-or-break situations make an insightful CEO evaluation process all the more vital. Such evaluation should not just be a yearly event, observes Dr. Richard Furr, president of CCG consultants in Greensboro, North Carolina. "You need an evaluation process that's ongoing and descriptive," suggests Furr. Good CEO evaluation does more than take a snapshot; it builds a mechanism for continuous appraisal of the CEO, building benchmarks that indicate any sudden decline.

Such ongoing evaluation will also give immediate intelligence beyond raw numbers on how investors, customers, employees, and the markets view the CEO. "What's triggering the board's concerns?" asks Furr. "Is it coming from inside or from customers?" If the metrics are uncertain, such a board pipeline to the CEO's "publics" can either confirm or disprove your gut concerns.

Finally, in a jam like this, expect the CEO to be heavily lobbying and reassuring the board. A CEO's effectiveness at such tasks can actually be a good sign. If directors are persuadable, it suggests they still haven't lost faith in the CEO. Also, if the CEO isn't trying to work the board as much as he is the metrics, this could be a sign that he has a tin ear and isn't even aware of the trouble.

The trend toward faster CEO turnover is making the board's relationship with the chief less stable and patient. These shakeups have also left more boards dealing with a new issue: how to work effectively with an interim CEO.

Hiring interim chief executives as part of a turnaround, spin-off, or succession search has become a fact of life in corporate America. Shorter CEO life spans bring a greater need for temporary talent, with terms ranging from a few months to a couple of years. But an effective interim CEO is just as vital as an effective permanent CEO, and at times more so. How does your board choose a good fill-in, build an effective relationship, and obtain strong results?

- Set a solid mandate from the start, and keep it simple. What the CEO is expected to do varies greatly by circumstances. Do you need a turnaround artist or a placekeeper while a CEO search is under way? Permanent CEOs need multiyear goals, but "your goals here may only be 2 or 6 months," says Paul Dinte, head of the Dinte Resources CEO placement firm in Virginia. This means setting few and basic goals, with immediate impact and measures—turn a loss into a profit, unload that division, maintain the current strategy, and so forth.

- The biggest problem between boards and interim chiefs is too little authority for the CEO. Any CEO must have full powers and board support, even if he is just a caretaker. "We insist on a board resolution giving the CEO full authority," says Richard Brenner, head of the Brenner Group, a consulting firm in California that places interim CEOs in Silicon Valley. "If the board's not ready to commit full authority, that's a bad sign. . . . the board has to provide the autonomy and P&L responsibility necessary to run the company."

- Internal executive politics could work against the temp CEO, so Dinte says the smart board will "identify the top one, two, or three key people reporting to [the interim CEO]. Let them know he has the board's blessing and why." The last thing you'll want is to have subordinates undermining the interim chief for their own career agendas. (Note: It's vital that the board show a united front here. Disgruntled top execs plus one or two directors who dislike the temp CEO could easily trigger a collapse.)

- Another big reason for interim (and then overall company) failure is that boards are not fully candid with the temp CEO

35

from the start. Directors may prefer to hide a few skeletons (legal, financial, or product surprises) in the closet, particularly in turnaround or CEO firing situations. "In a turnaround especially, the board has to have an open kimono with the CEO," warns Dinte. Short-term execs already have enough to handle. Don't add any messy secrets that will throw them off stride and destroy your relationship when they surface (and they always do).

- A new full-time CEO usually gets to make some boardroom changes to suit his style, but an interim CEO won't be there long enough and frankly, the power balance differs. "The interim's role is to oversee, to do the job, and get out," says Dinte. This means, unlike most CEOs, the interim should not serve as board leader (which means giving a trusted director the chairman's slot). This also means that directors should plan on devoting more time to the company for the duration of the CEO's tenure. Yes, an interim CEO needs enough power to run the company (as noted previously), but the board should continue to run the board.

Since an interim CEO tends to call for greater director involvement anyway, more boards are simply cutting out the middleman and putting one of their own outside directors in charge. Recent boardroom pinch hitters at several of the scandal companies (plus Henry Schacht at Lucent, Leonard Hadley at Maytag, and John Creighton at UAL) are just a few instances of a board member slipping into the driver's seat in an emergency. But such a move remains tricky for any board. Which director will take over? How much power for change is needed? And is the director still truly a member of the board—or a member of management?

When the board puts one of its own in the top slot, it can be a positive sign that the board is on top of the situation, but more likely it means that the board has let problems drag on until a hasty fix is needed. "All too often boards have waited too long, hoping things will improve," observes Dee Soder of the CEO Perspective Group in New York, "and then time runs out." Failed CEO strategy and leadership are ultimately a failure of board oversight, so the impulse to boot the CEO and put a director in charge could be prompted by boardroom guilt, leaving investors unimpressed.

Which member of the board should take command? "It's almost always one of the strongest outside directors, one who's familiar with the business," says Soder. Indeed, this is why if a retired chair of the company stays on the board, he's often drafted. The candidate is not usually a consensus pick of the board, but is rather the lead director (one who often sparked the ousting of the CEO).

Most CEO replacements from the boardroom are short-term measures, often when the company needs a turnaround. Despite demands for haste, the board should still ensure solid ground rules for the director/CEO from the start. First, the new chief and the board need to decide the director's tenure at the helm, based on either time or strategic goals. The new chief's mandate will also tie into this. Is he to serve as a caretaker until a new CEO is recruited, or are solid turnaround moves to be made? "Make sure the acting CEO is not left without input from the board," warns Soder. "Too often, the other directors will say, 'okay, now it's your problem,' and then back away."

Don Perkins, who found himself in the interim slot at Kmart a few years ago, finds that the smart director/CEO "bends over backwards to communicate with the board." After moving up to the CEO's slot, though, "it's almost impossible to go back to being one of the guys in the boardroom."

As boards face growing responsibility for the quality and results of the corporation as a whole, they've had to look deeper into the CEO's organization chart. One quick test of your corporate structure is to ask how many people report to the CEO. Two decades of flattening organizations have left many titles with a direct line to the CEO's office. But are there *too* many? How do you judge if your CEO is overstretched?

Start by getting a handle on the company's total strategy. "If you see a lot of synergies between the company's business areas, such as in a financial services firm, then a smaller span of control can cut across the firm," says Mark Cecere, a vice president at Giga Information Group in Massachusetts. "But if it's a broad global firm without the synergies, then you need broader staff control for the CEO." Whether the corporate structure is aligned by major customer groups or by business processes is another factor.

How can you tell from the boardroom if your CEO has too many or too few direct reports (*before* disasters can arise)? "There are some danger signs," observes Cecere. "If the CEO talks a lot about company administration or personnel issues, or is not well versed on the competition—in short, if he's not externally focused, but mired in administrivia—that could mean that the maturity of people reporting to the CEO is very weak." The CEO is too busy with internals to give attention to the outside big picture. Corporate size, structure, and industry make it hard to set CEO reporting standards, but "as a rule of thumb, anything beyond six to eight direct CEO reports can be a problem," says Cecere. "In a very stable business, with very mature managers and a simple corporate structure, though, you can have more reports."

Cecere sees a common error among boards when it comes to CEO succession and the company's current top executive structure: expecting the new CEO to fit with what you've got. "Boards assume the person they hire has to be able to handle this span of control. They want a flat organization, so they have 12 people report to the CEO, regardless of whether the new CEO would work better with fewer reports." Whether you expect the new CEO or the reporting system to be the one to change is up to your board, but consider this crucial factor in succession.

Movement toward fewer CEO direct reports is growing. In the 1990s, greater corporate complexity and the rush to flatten the organization chart pushed up the CEO's span of control, but the Web, info technology, and corporate consolidation are again narrowing the A-list of who has the CEO's ear.

And for the CEO Dealing with the Board . . .

What is it about board members that *really* drives CEOs nuts? Ask Katherine Catlin. As president of the top management consulting firm the Catlin Group, she's worked with hundreds of chief executives over the years and has heard "tons of complaints about board members." Her view of directors from the CEO's end of the board table is provocative and should give both directors and managers some food for thought:

- "CEOs complain about directors who show up at the board meeting to give advice, then go away, and the CEO doesn't hear a thing from them until the next board meeting." Then the director comes back a couple of months later to spout off again, sometimes contradicting the advice he or she gave on the first go-around. "CEOs actually want some communication from directors between board meetings," says Catlin. Today's overstretched executives too often view a board seat as a hat that they only wear every couple of months, ignoring the firm the rest of the time.

- But then there's the opposite extreme. "Some CEOs have a board member who calls them up every other day, sinking too much into operating details rather than looking at strategy. They ask things like, why are we spending this $10,000 here rather than there?" By micromanaging, these directors simply aren't delivering the governance value that they should.

- The sad truth is that many directors, even if they're venture people invested in the firm, have a shallow knowledge of the industry, and too often it shows. "They bring a herd mentality to the board. . . . they read in *The Wall Street Journal* that dot coms are dropping, for instance, and panic, telling the CEO that we've got to cut back and so on, rather than really examining the company's strategy," says Catlin. Such dilettante directors end up not only failing as a CEO resource, but become one more hand-holding headache for the chief, along with customers, suppliers, lenders, and so on.

- CEOs can get general advice from anyone, but look to their boards for "specific examples from other companies they work with," Catlin emphasizes. "A VC on the board, for instance, can tell how an issue was handled at other companies in the portfolio." Directors: Be sure your examples *really* apply and bring value. Don't start every other sentence with "Well, at our company, we used to . . ."

- All directors are not created equal, and CEOs find "unevenness in competency" on the board frustrating, according to Catlin. A venture firm that invests, for instance, may put a junior partner on the board as a representative, but a lack of competence and background in the industry often makes them the class dunce. Meetings then slow down (if not dumb down) to the Lowest Common Director level, weakening the quality of governance and irritating everyone in the boardroom.

In a chapter on how boards should retake control, it may seem odd to ask if boards can become *too* powerful, but this is an issue both for boards seeking to reassert themselves and for CEOs trying to cope. As an example, in November 2000, the Coca-Cola Company was in discussions with Quaker Oats about acquiring Quaker, but at the last minute Coke backed out of the deal. Takeovers come undone all the time, but an article in *The*

Wall Street Journal suggested that this deal suffered an unusual boardroom breakdown at the Coca-Cola end.

Coke CEO Robert Daft had worked out the $15.75 billion deal with Quaker and thought that the Coca-Cola board would wave the purchase through as a smart strategic fit. Instead, Coke's board, sparked by its estimable director Warren Buffett, expressed reservations about the deal, particularly the high price and the large amount of Coca-Cola stock that would be traded away in the transaction. What should have been a brief boardroom due diligence presentation turned into an inquisition, and Daft wisely never brought the merger to a formal vote.

Coke's board gained an activist sheen when it edged out CEO Douglas Ivester the previous year, and its actions showed a board taking its duty to shareholders seriously. But the *WSJ* article suggested the downside such a strong board presents for the CEO trying to lead a company. "Nobody can negotiate with Coke now. . .It looks like [the board] runs the company, and Daft is the chief operating officer," said an observer.[2] Daft put the best face on the turndown, pointing out that he actively sought input from the board: "My job is not to dictate to them, but to involve them." This example offers no good guys or bad guys, only a warning to all that even the best board reforms carry a price tag.

Bob Neuschel has a solid reputation in both the academic and boardroom worlds, as a business professor at Northwestern University and a member of many boards. He shares a gem of a CEO board communication tip that he finds effective (and, hint-hint, can help make the CEO's job more secure). "I like a CEO who periodically telephones the director, once a week or every other week, so they can chat with each other," comments Neuschel. "The point is just to bring the director up-to-date. The call is fairly short, just a few minutes, usually under five. But it makes me feel so comfortable to get frequent communication like that from the CEO on what's going on, issues that are coming along. . . if there's a problem and we're warned ahead, it doesn't seem so bad."

CEOs: If you were to make a weekly call to every outside director on your board just to catch up, how much time would it take? Perhaps half an

---

[2]"Why Coke Didn't Buy Quaker Oats," *The Wall Street Journal*, 30 November 2000.

hour per week in total? Can you think of any other way you could use a half-hour that pays such benefits?

Q: I'm in line to succeed our company's CEO when he retires later this year, and I'll be taking over as board chairman soon after that. The succession process has worked well here, but as the date grows nearer, I realize that the current CEO has done too little to expose me and other top managers to the board, its members, and workings. What sort of a board-coaching program could you suggest I try to set up for myself?

A: Even well-thought-out CEO succession plans tend to skimp on familiarizing candidates with the company's board. Just be thankful you're not coming in cold from the outside, where you'd also be struggling to learn the names of your new bosses in the boardroom (unfortunately, high CEO turnover means that many new chiefs are in just such a spot).

Make up for lost time by personally building bridges to your board members. "As a rule of thumb, the new CEO should spend about 1 hour a month personally talking to all of the board members, and more with the movers and shakers," says Tom Fitzgerald, head of his own executive coaching firm in Lake Forest, Illinois. Such chats and telephone time forge the personal relationship you'll need. In your position, though, "you might want to make it an hour a week" for a brief period to catch up.

The current CEO should support this, but you may need to start out by building relationships with one or two key directors, and then let them know you feel it's important that you get to know the whole board. This can prompt the board in turn to reach out to you as the incoming CEO (which should have been on their list of priorities in the first place). By "getting to know directors as individuals, their likes and dislikes," you'll gain needed confidence, says Joy McGovern, an executive coach with Manchester Consulting.

Although you'll want to build this open relationship with your directors, new CEOs need to learn when to keep their mouths shut as well. "Especially when a CEO comes in from the outside, he's tempted to tell the board all is well, based on the one-tenth of the business he's been able to get his hands around in the first month," says Tom Fitzgerald. But as the novice CEO digs deeper, problems may be uncovered, and you'll then either have to be evasive or admit to early ignorance.

Q: I'm a finalist for the CEO slot at a fast-growing tech company. The potential here is great, but I have one concern. The present founder/chair/CEO will be leaving the chief executive position but holding onto the board chair slot, and it looks like he intends to stay as chairman permanently. Any tips for dealing with the board as CEO when I won't be its chair?

A: The CEO/chair mix has become a standard in the United States, so much so that we too often assume that a CEO minus the chair's seat is somehow on probation. Yet the latter is growing more acceptable, especially at companies like the one you described, a newer, fast-growing firm where founders and initial investors still hold large chunks of equity.

Since you won't be directly leading the board, your first task is to scope out just what sort of a chair your chair wants to be. "You can't do enough research on the chair/founder," advises Larry Stybel of the search and consulting firm Stybel Peabody. "Get a sense of his business maturity. The founder/chair may not be all that mature and may have control issues with you." Stybel suggests that adding a third leg to the power stool here might be the best approach. "Create a lead director. The chair might actually welcome one, and the role is valuable when the inevitable conflict comes. Two is a bad number in the boardroom."

Also, "does the chairman intend to hold a perfunctory, honorary role, or does he intend to exert real power and influence?" asks Tom Sherwin, founder of the CEO Resources consulting firm. "I can't picture an adversarial relationship here that works for the CEO. That's a risky social disease. Sooner or later, the CEO loses, paying a price in his job, agenda, or compensation."

Rather, make it clear that your chairman can help you better perform the CEO's job by concentrating on his own board duties. "Often, a board chair doesn't know how to be a chair," says Sherwin. Although the CEO needs to know the agendas and priorities of his board members, your chairman should be the expert, "knowing what their priorities are depending on the business they come from, and the lens of experience they view your business through." The chair "positions the board agenda to keep the board at an oversight level," explains Sherwin. Also, the chair is the one who is "in communication with the board members between meetings, or who sits down with a board member over dinner." This turns the separate chair from being a potential turf contender for the CEO into a valuable board liaison tool. The smart CEO in turn works the relationship with the chair, and thus everyone stays happy.

Executive coaching has become one of the hottest fields in management consulting. But at the CEO level, a coach can offer the executive some excellent tips on dealing with the board of directors. What advice are top CEO coaches giving their clients on how to work with and effectively lead their boards?

- "CEOs may come in assuming that the board members know what they don't really know, or at least that they can figure it out on their own," says Thomas McIntosh, a coach affiliated with the Silver Fox advisory group in Houston, Texas. Spell out ideas, options, and issues, and don't just hope for the best.

- "One area where there are a lot of problems is when the CEO comes in to work with a board who are strangers to him," McIntosh remarks. "Try to figure out what their individual agendas are, and how they may conflict with each other. The CEO needs to build a running profile of each member, how to reach them, what sort of communication they want. Some might prefer personal phone calls, while others like a lot of information to read."

- Although some advise that the new CEO ask individual board members for deep background on how to handle the other directors, McIntosh says that "asking members about the board's chemistry can be dangerous at this stage." It brings an air of plotting and conspiracy that the novice CEO should avoid. Better to let the directors bring up such "just between you and me" takes on their own.

- A good coach can serve as a facilitator between the board and its leadership. "The coach can help board members work collaboratively," says Carl Kaestner of Robert Hargrove Consulting. "They can serve as a thinking partner for the CEO. It really is lonely at the top." By turning the board itself into an executive coach, "they become an extraordinary combination, brokers able to create extraordinary relationships."

I'll offer more on the use of advisory boards later, but they can be targeted brains trust that give smart CEOs added board expertise. For example, Jurgen Schrempp, chair of DaimlerChrysler, is in charge of an unwieldy automaking giant that strides the Atlantic from Stuttgart to Auburn Hills, Michigan. But to help him stay ahead of the strategic issues involved, Schrempp has formed a personal advisory board called the Chairman's Council. This 12-member brain trust is chaired by Schrempp himself and offers "advice to management on global business strategy issues," according to a DaimlerChrysler spokesman.

Although six members of the company's supervisory board serve on the panel, five are international business leaders, including IBM's Lou Gerstner, Mitsubishi chair Minoru Makihara, and Nortel chair Lynton Wilson. Schrempp observes that he "uses them as a sounding board." He explains, "I have no hesitation to go in there and say, 'I have an idea . . . how do you see it?'" The panel has no official status, but has proven an invaluable think tank for the chairman.

The Boardroom Amateurs Syndrome: Inadequate Time, Resources, and Expertise for the Job

Here's a tale to consider as we wade through the current flood of board reforms. Decades, even centuries, ago, there was a small town called Businessville. It was a little burg typical of the time, its economy based on small farms, crafts, and trades. A symbol of how things were done in Businessville was the village fire brigade. If flames should erupt at the Dry Goods and Mercantile, a dozen or so volunteers would drop what they were doing, rush to the village fire hall, wheel the hand-pumped "fire engine" to the scene, and squirt away until the blaze was stopped. Simple and amateur were these doughty yeomen, but they were state of the art for the era.

Over the decades, though, Businessville grew and reincorporated into today's massive city of Corpopolis. It sprawls over many square miles of sky-scrapers, factories, financial centers, and business parks. Its infrastructure for finance, trade, communications, transport, law enforcement, and technology is world class. Yet as Corpopolis booms into a new century, one relic of its small-town days remains. Fire protection is *still* provided by a small, part-time group of about a dozen amateur volunteers. Their technology has kept up with the times, of course (look at that shiny new fire truck!), and most of the fire brigade's duties now consist of auditing Corpopolis's private fire-prevention efforts. But this handful of part-time amateurs remains the front-line fire protection for Gotham. Several recent disasters have occurred, however. For instance, a huge energy-trading firm was a near total loss. Apparently, some top managers had embezzled sprinkler system funds. Also, tragedy struck a big telecom conglomerate when all the employee fire doors were kept locked (though top execs were able to escape through their private exits).

Why not give Corpopolis the full-time, professional fire protection it needs? Well, it seems the amateur brigade system is written into law, and no one can quite agree on how to replace it. Those who want to reform the current system are likewise divided on how. Some just want to make the present volunteers sign more forms certifying that they are indeed doing their jobs. Others would even jail these dozen ill-trained amateurs should they find themselves overwhelmed by a high-rise fire.

What to do? Well, first, we admit that the present system is not working. Second, we find ways to improve it.

A 2002 study by Korn/Ferry consultants found that the typical Fortune 1,000 corporate board member devotes about 183 hours per year to a board seat.[1] This is a grand total of about four-and-a-half weeks' work yearly. Within this narrow window of time, those part-time dilettantes on the board are expected to peek into every nook and cranny of the corporate structure where full-time managers might have overlooked (or stashed) something.

Time is only one hobble facing the active board of directors. Directors, intelligent but laypeople in the business world, are expected to sit in judgment on incredibly complex finance, accounting, and legal structures set up by global experts in the field. They have no choice but to accept the assurances of these experts that the things directors sign off on are proper—just as the directors at Enron did.

Moving beyond these brain busters, board members next must study all the audit controls and opinions of the corporation to ensure that they reflect the true numbers and meet the current laws, regulations, and Generally Accepted Accounting Principles (GAAP). These audit rules have recently been turned upside down in pursuit of reform (and their implementation is still being sorted out), so whatever is learned today is likely illegal tomorrow. The board then lightens up by reviewing all 100 pages of the CEO's compensation plan, with its intricate tax, stock, and incentive provisions (again, drafted by experts in the field). To assure that they do this job properly, directors must now hire their own compensation consultant, who produces another 100 pages for review.

These factors all assume that management makes no attempt to deceive the board. If management *is* up to mischief, the board would have to dedicate far more time, effort, and expertise to sleuthing out chicanery, misstatements, and shortfalls. These would be carefully hidden away by the

---

[1]Twenty-ninth Annual Korn/Ferry Board of Directors Survey, Korn/Ferry International, 2002.

executive experts who live, eat, and sleep the corporation, and be verified by skilled audit and legal talent (which is paid by management).

As my teenage daughter observes, "*Riiiiiight . . .*"

Of all the ways our corporate board model sucks, this administrative amateurism is the most obvious. Yet it may also be the one easiest to, if not cure, at least improve. Board members can be better recruited and trained to bring specific skills to work on oversights. And the huge amount of time now being wasted on misgovernance can be redirected.

Let's Get Organized around Here

William Adams is retired chairman of Armstrong World Industries and a member of several corporate boards. He's also a pro on searching out good boardroom procedures. Here he shares some of his observations on good nuts and bolts boardsmanship.

- Help your directors get (and stay) organized with a good three-ring binder with topical tabs. Then your board crew can easily organize monthly mailings under the proper headings. "It helps them get into the zone," says Adams. "And if they don't want to bring the whole book to the board meeting, they can just bring the guts."

- Instead of ticking off lots of agenda items that need board approval but are largely pro forma (extending a line of credit, minor title transfers, etc.), try bundling them into a *consent calendar*. These ephemera aren't usually debated, so you can "send them out for directors to look at in advance, and approve them all together at the meeting." Since "anyone can question an item, you're not sneaking anything by." Bunching minor items in a consent calendar can save valuable agenda time. "I had 11 items in one of these at a board meeting yesterday," says Adams. (The plusses and minuses of consent agendas will be covered in the chapter "Reason #7" on board meetings.)

- Squeezing the maximum value out of meeting time means keeping reasonable limits on discussion, so Adams suggests that the "chair or CEO let directors know what they have in mind for time parameters. Don't regiment things; just say that you'd like to get through Item Four by 10:30 or such." Suggested time points can even be built into the agenda for items, with the understanding that they're expandable if needed. Even if you don't enforce the schedule, it gives the directors an unconscious discipline on time usage, so "someone who wants to raise a question about the color of the company trucks will hold onto it."

- "Put the most important agenda items first. This seems obvious, but few boards do it. I had the chance to help launch a new board recently, so we decided to do things the way they ought to be done. Unless information is needed for a further discussion, we start right out with the important stuff. If we're running out of time for the boilerplate items, we always have the option of working through lunch."

- And don't forget: "One thing we always cry out for in [board] meetings is less on operational reports and more time for discussing the business. On operating reports, staff should learn to boil the information down, to tell a brief story. Then, for the meeting, have them come in to answer questions, rather than just show us PowerPoint presentations on stuff we already read."

Most boards, top execs, and corporate secretaries have spent the past few months sweating out compliance with the new Sarbanes-Oxley requirements. But now that you've bought into governance reform, get ready for the price tag. Your next boardroom headache: board budgeting.

Funds the corporation spends on its board have traditionally come out of the corporate secretary's budget and other line items, befitting the afterthought nature of governance. Now the duties, chores, and liabilities the board must take on its shoulders would blow through that old magpie budget overnight. Your board has gone from spending the leftover budget scraps of other departments to (in some cases) *being* the budget authority over those departments. Where will the board money go now, and how will your company keep a handle on it?

- **Director Fees and Training**   Board members will be putting in more time and effort, and (especially on audit committees) require more specific skills. Fewer candidates qualify, they will be in more demand, and they will face greater personal liability. Basic free-market principles tell you which way this will drive director compensation. Also, the use of options for pay will tighten up, making cash a bigger part of the mix. Since directors will need to know more and stay more up-to-date on laws and accounting policies, their training expenses will soar.

- **D&O Coverage**   The D&O price spike is hitting hard. Coverage for your board members will grow even more costly (if obtainable) as suits from the 2002 corporate scandals are settled.

- **Board Support Services**   The days when the corporate secretary's office could just CC: a bunch of reports sent by other departments are passing. Now the board will demand much more (and more specialized) data that has to be compiled on someone's time. Directors will spend more face and phone time with staffers too, especially finance and legal folks. Though few corporations have a dedicated support person just for the board, the role will become more common, either in the corporate secretary's office or as a stand-alone board ombudsman.

- **Board Contracting**   Much of this is outside consulting work now done at the behest of internal staff: auditing, pay consulting, legal opinions, and investment banking. Reforms will either force or nudge contracting toward the board to assure that this expertise answers only to the board or its committees. Also, new consulting sources must be tapped to meet new oversight and independence demands. The board will require its own budget to hire this talent.

All of this adds up to a whole new governance budget heading, and one that will be large enough to give any CEO ulcers. What can you do to keep the boardroom budget in line while still meeting all the new demands? Here are some preliminaries:

- As noted, consider making the board its own budget item, not just a subitem under the corporate secretary's office (the new Securities and Exchange Commission [SEC] reporting requirements are already gobbling up their funds anyway). By collecting all governance expenses under one heading, they become easier to track and manage.

- Avoid overreacting to the new rules. Although added outside consulting or opinions may be needed in some areas, the business judgment rule still applies: Once you take reasonable steps, further gold plating is not necessary. As Jim Sullivan, an attorney with the Bricker & Ecker law firm observes, "If you were buying a car, six quotes might be needed, but if you're getting a fountain pen, you only need one or two. We see some [consulting] steps being recommended that are appropriate for GM, but not for a small NASDAQ company."

All the new pressures hammering corporate governance lately boil down to one simple (if brutal) operational equation: Less time, plus more oversight, plus more information, plus fewer qualified directors must somehow equal better governance. Yet business in general has been learning to do far more, far faster, and with less over the last decade. How? Smart use of new communications technology. But only now are boards beginning to join the high-tech move to light-speed info flow and decision making.

Every person I spoke with on this topic told how some directors are holding back the process. They're uncomfortable with computers, they don't like email, they distrust the web . . . and another attempt to wire the board bogs down in a clumsy, costly mix of new electrons and old paper.

Although overnight change just doesn't happen in the boardroom, you may want to consider making comfort with technology a first item in board recruitment. Very soon, a director who won't surf the Web will prove as impractical as one who won't use the telephone. How are benchmark boards using technology to supercharge their governance?

- Before its acquisition by Hewlett-Packard, Compaq was leading its directors into the tech age by putting all the board's info mailings on an encrypted CD-ROM. All board members were issued a Compaq laptop with a software suite that includes a reader for the CD. Sherry Walker, a former legal assistant to Compaq's vice president for compliance, found directors enthusiastic about the ease and speed of CD board books, but concerns about security stalled a planned move to send board info online or to wall off a special board-only web site. "We keep hoping to find a process that allows us to move files onto a secure server," Walker said, "so directors can get in via the Internet past our firewall." Also, some board members still preferred hard copies of info. "All directors don't use the technology." Note: And this was at a *computer* maker!

- At one of the world's foremost data-processing companies, the corporate secretary tells me that her office is currently working on a confidential "intranet web site created for the directors." The site will be "loaded with as much info as the directors might want to see," including financials, agendas, news, and strategic info. Security is the paramount concern. "We're in the business of security, so we're designing it very carefully." Still, she expects that the board won't go 100 percent electronic any time soon. "Some of the directors are technical, some not. . . . I think there will always be a need for board mailings."

- One of America's biggest flooring makers is also a key innovator when it comes to board info technology. The corporate legal counsel tells me that they have "a beta site up for directors, where we put up minutes, reference materials, the charter, bylaws, items from the directors manual, and telephone contacts." The board web site also serves as an intranet with secure email service between directors. "Through this site, directors can have a conversation among themselves, or if, say, the chair of the governance committee wants to send a message only to committee members, he can."

- The previous company tried an e-board web site strategy that's so intriguing it deserves its own bullet point. "We're going through our outside legal counsel . . . they host it. They've already tackled all the security issues, so 90 percent of those headaches are lifted." Such a strategy could offer several bonuses: Law firms have already invested heavily to keep their sites safe, the board creates its own electronic presence away from management, and there may be some evidentiary/discovery benefits in housing your e-board site with counsel.

- The downsides to the e-board? Most tie into the human factor. "You can build in security," notes the corporate counsel, "but some weaknesses relate to the people who have access." Boards already have a problem with members who leave confidential papers behind in airplanes or hotels rooms, and e-board books add to the risk. Government laptops stuffed with top-secret files going astray have become an ongoing Washington embarrassment. Also, as all the cases noted previously show, directors are still sluggish in making good use of current info technology. And if you have techno-Luddites in your boardroom, how good a job can they do at keeping your company up-to-date?

In-service training is now vital to serving on any board of directors, as directors are forced to get up-to-speed on governance changes and prepare for the future. Deloitte & Touche can help out with a new series of online education programs at their Deloitte Learning web site (deloitte-learning.com). Sessions of value to directors include a capital markets overview, complex financial instruments, executive pay, and essentials of the SEC. Best of all is the price—free.

Of course, getting better organized in the boardroom assumes that you're able to get everyone *to* the boardroom on time. Arranging travel for board meetings is a very high stakes game, with the company's ultimate VIPs often jetting in from around the country. Given the security and terrorism scares of the past year and a half, though, your directors may spend as much time being patted down as they do deliberating. Every corporate travel manager or corporate secretary shares horror stories of board travel itineraries gone disastrously wrong, but a few steps can increase your odds for a boardroom full of happy travelers:

- Paperwork trumps everything. Draw up checklists for every step from when directors board a plane at their distant city to when they touch down there again on return. "We try to make a paper trail so everything is documented," advises Vanessa Merchant, who arranges board and corporate meetings for Capital Travel in Minnesota. Know who the contact person is at each step: travel bureau, airline, airport transport, or hotel. "Make a contact on the inside, stay in touch with them, and always make nice—it works to your advantage."

- Know everything you can about your directors. "We put together a registration that includes name, email, fax, food needs, allergies, and preferences, and put this into a database for each traveler," says Merchant. Your corporate secretary's office would find this director file enormously helpful. As an added feature, include all director pager and cell phone numbers, plus full contact info for the board member's own staff.

- International companies, or those moving board meetings around to different countries, face further headaches. "Make sure directors have documentation to travel abroad, and for every step of their trip," Merchant emphasizes. Maybe you got the director from her home to your board meeting just fine, but if the next step of her trip (to Botswana) falls apart, guess who gets the blame? "We sent a group of directors to Spain, but it turned out four of them needed visas, so we had to send them back."

- Rolf Shellenberger, senior travel planner for top business travel firm Runzheimer, notes that one of the least considered links in the director's itinerary (and one of the most commonly fumbled) is airport transport. "The director can just jump into a taxi, but that can get expensive" (and adds to director hassles). He suggests a "meet and greet" approach, where a driver picks up the director at the airport. Little is more reassuring to a harried business traveler than to see someone holding a sign with his or her name at the airport. This approach helps on the return route too and may be even more needed, as foul-ups seem to happen more often on the trip home.

  Shellenberger notes that major cities often have "destination management" companies that send a traveling concierge to the airport to hand deliver the VIP to the driver and keep track of every step of the process. For a member of the board, this could be well worth the modest added cost. "People should anticipate every movement," Shellenberger adds.

- As directors become more a strategic part of the company, more firms are upgrading their travel options. New Runzheimer figures show that 34 percent of corporate travel managers now give board members special travel privileges (first-class air, lodging upgrades, and full-size rental cars), up from 23 percent in 1992.

Beefing Up Your Boardroom Talent

The Parson Group came in at number one in *Inc.* magazine's 2000 list of best small companies, and Parson chief executive and founder Dan Weinfurter gave much of the credit to an excellent board of directors. The Chicago-based financial consulting firm was America's fastest-growing private company that year, with an eye-popping annual revenue growth of 27,992 percent.

So how does a firm that doesn't even require a board of directors not only recruit one with superstar talent (including past Kmart chair Don Perkins and former Zenith chairman Jerry Pearlman), but also leverage that talent to spur fantastic growth? Much credit goes to Chicago-area venture capitalists (VCs) J. Jeffrey Louis and Samuel Chapman, who provided Parson's first-tier funding and helped craft a strong governance program from the start. "We laid out the experience we sought [in directors] and worked the personal relationships of the VCs," Weinfurter tells me. Both he and his VC backers considered shaping a strong startup board as "a huge event. It allowed us to attract clients who wouldn't associate with any firm that seemed fly-by-night, and also provided a lot of contacts."

How does a startup sell corporate heavyweights on joining its board? "The pitch is that they'll have a different ability to contribute than they would at a company with 200,000 employees. It boils down to personal satisfaction." The Parson Group also helps keep the time commitment manageable for such busy achievers, with board meetings held quarterly for half a day, not counting committees. Board pay is wholly in company equity, and although the company is still private, the board has the power to sack the CEO.

Suppose you're not as well connected to big-league board talent. How do you lure such names to your board? Weinfurter says *any* group of business people can discover surprising talent if they just comb their extended network. "If you're cold calling for director talent, use the people you do know. I just joined the advisory board of a tech firm after I got a call from a neighbor." Classmates (a current Parson director knew one of the VCs from Harvard Business School), civic groups, trade associations, and even family connections are a few other unconventional board resources you should tap.

Building a board from the start for excellence is the ideal, but how often do you get the ideal in business? What if you could start fresh with a major company—*plus* the added advantage of knowing what you did wrong the first time around?

That's the quick take on Washington-based software firm LapLink. Founder and chair Mark Eppley turned over the CEO reins to a proven manager from Compaq in 1996, but tough new competition and development costs led to a run of red ink. By late 1998, LapLink was near bankruptcy, and Eppley returned to the CEO position.

Among his turnaround moves, says Eppley, a high priority was reshaping the board. "We were looking for specific talents for each board position," says Eppley, "so the current board is very strong. Looked at historically, this is the first fully functional, effective board we've had." The board maintains a far tighter emphasis on the diversity of background and hands-on experience in business building, initial public offerings (IPOs), and technology marketing.

Though LapLink's market sector and turnaround needs are unique (as is every board situation, for that matter), their boardroom reboot "shopping list" could offer some good hints for any board recruiting plan:

- LapLink was getting outflanked in sales, so a director "with [a] strong background in sales" within the software industry was needed, according to Eppley. A former vice president of sales and support for Microsoft, Rich MacIntosh, filled this boardroom gap, bringing retailing background to the mix as well.

- "Consumer marketing and entrepreneurial skill" would prove helpful to a company trying to reinvigorate itself in the market. Tim Choate, founder and chairman of FreeShop International, which he'd recently taken public, filled the bill. Better still, he provided the board with a deep background in online retailing.

- A pick "outside the computer industry, but with strong general business background" was Louis Kapcsandy, chair of Baugh Enterprises, one of the region's largest construction companies. Originally from Hungary, Eppley says Kapcsandy "has an amazing background," and offers the board big-picture business insights. Other board members bring targeted background in finance and venture capital.

In sum, says Eppley, the board mix is "well seasoned, likes a challenge, and [is] very strong." The original board Eppley had helped assemble for the firm, back in the 1980s, "was typical of any venture startup, associates or partners of investors in the company." Eppley now "absolutely" wishes he'd set up the original board along the lines of this new and improved model (a good suggestion to all entrepreneurs out there). "You want to have the strongest board you can get."

The search for good directors to serve on a board has become tougher and tougher, a toss-up between opposing trends. New rules on director skills and independence, tighter search criteria, and greater job demands on top managers have prompted more "help wanted" signs in the boardroom.

John Johnson, who heads the board search practice for TMP Worldwide (the folks who run the Monster.com job search site), sees firsthand how these trends are hitting the search for board talent. New rules for financial talent to serve on U.S. board audit committees are rewriting the wish list for director searches. "We've seen a number of companies scurrying to find directors who came up through the finance ranks," says Johnson, "someone who comes from the Big Six [audit firms] or is a CFO.

"Companies tell us that they want someone experienced in driving new technologies," he continues. Here e-commerce is the key area, which would require someone with board experience at a company savvy with new technology, but not necessarily the 25-year-old techno-geek who was a lucky IPO millionaire.

Turndowns of board offers by top board talent are a serious problem that's growing worse. "More candidates are just telling us they don't have time to talk, that they can't sit on another board," says Johnson. Beyond the raw time issue, CEOs and other prize catches are becoming choosier about their board slots as well. "CEOs are prizing their time more," Johnson remarks, "and are more likely to ask what this board seat can do for their own company." This means more selling on why a candidate should consider *your* company.

Naming foreign directors to the boards of U.S. companies remains mostly talk rather than action, observes Johnson. "Everyone likes the idea, but then you get into the practicality issues. If you have six meetings a year, and that foreign CEO doesn't have some other reason for being in the United States, he'll either be doing a lot of teleconferencing or missing meetings altogether." Also, although European companies today are much more likely to name pan-European members to their boards, this trend actually makes it tougher for U.S.-based boards to snare these talents. "If I'm a European CEO looking at board offers, it's a hell of a lot easier to serve on a board based in Stockholm or Paris than one that makes me fly to New York."

So what are the most in-demand talents for the boardroom? For the near future, the hot candidates are as follows:

- Financial skills. No surprise here, and number one skill on every board shopping list. Sarbanes-Oxley and the SEC demands for financial literacy on audit committees are fueling the boardroom demand for "former partners at Big Five accounting firms," according to Susan Shultz, head of SSA Executive Search. "Former and current CFOs are also getting lots more attention, as well as CEOs who came up through the finance side."

- "There's continued interest in technology expertise on the board," notes Roger Kenny, founder and managing partner of the Boardroom Consultants firm in New York. "A wide spectrum of positions can absorb this technology expertise, and a lot of companies are getting more involved. Boards may go as far as to add consulting people with this background."

- More boards are now willing to look beyond the standard "active CEO" job description in their search for talent. Charles King of the Nordeman Grimm search firm in New York observes that "a lot of top people's plates are full now, and I spend a fair amount of time looking for up-and-comers. They may not be on the company's radar, but they generally have more time available than a CEO, they have intellectual curiosity, and they're more willing to make a board commitment."

- Titles, top profit and loss business experience, and a strong success history continue to be important, but Roger Kenny sees a growing demand that board candidates have a *specific* boardroom talent to contribute. "Boards are much more cognizant now that good businesspeople don't necessarily make good directors. They want someone with previous board experience, so we can check out how well they handled themselves in the boardroom."

Better boards will demand better committee members as a first priority. What new standards will we see now in setting best practices for audit committee membership?

- "I think the current financial literacy requirements are defined in terms so basic that they're a joke," says David Tate, a corporate attorney based in San Francisco. "Essentially, you have to be able to read financial statements. You shouldn't even be in

BONUS NOTE

Roger Kenny also sees boards making "more requests for a non-executive chair. There is a sense that there is now a separate job there, beyond the CEO/chairman duties, and that boards now need an independent leader who can help manage the board."

business if you can't do that." Up-to-date knowledge on the specifics of audit and complex financial instruments is the new coin of the realm.

- Independence standards for committee members have shot upward almost overnight. A year ago, no one gave a thought to minor interlocks and consulting arrangements such as those found at Enron. Now, charitable donations, consulting ties, family relationships, and past employment are all banned and make front-page news if found. If *your* audit panel members' other ties to the company made the headlines, would they pass the "smell test" for disinterest and independence?

- Most board audit panels still tap their members only for the expertise that they bring in from the outside. Why not make continuing education an audit committee requirement? Most audit firms would be glad to arrange regular in-service update programs for committee members. "It's important not to just be good at accounting, but to think like an auditor," says Larry Rittenberg, an accounting pro on the faculty at the University of Wisconsin.

- Rotation, tenure, and term limits will be coming audit committee concerns. The fact that Robert K. Jaedicke, retired dean of Stanford's graduate business school, headed Enron's audit panel, looks great at first glance. But Jaedicke held the role since 1985, making his ability to look at Enron financials with fresh, objective eyes questionable. Although it's already difficult to recruit top audit talent to serve on the committee, not letting these savants hang on for years might also be required.

As we demand more of our corporate boards, the search for top-caliber directors has become a priority. But who *don't* you want on your board? The following are some candidates who, at first glance, might seem okay, but bring hidden liabilities:

- **The Staffer** This is someone who lacks proven line responsibility. "You want someone who has proven capability on how to run an organization, who's able to take a strategic rather than tactical view," counsels Kelly Kincannon, head of major search firm Kincannon & Reed. "This is someone who's been a success somewhere, who isn't limited in perspective." But this doesn't need to mean a CEO-only club.

BONUS NOTE

Better audit committee members require better committee meetings too. Frank Borelli, former chair of Financial Executives International, counsels, "The [audit] committee chair should always be the one who sets the meeting agenda — not the CFO or the audit firm."

- **The Generalist** Board oversight is more technical and deep today, so some directors need to know the nuts and bolts. "Directors may bring a specific skill set that you need," says Kincannon. "In one of our current searches, the board wants someone with a strong science background to vet the technology that came before them."

- **The Oaf** "You don't want someone who doesn't have good personal skills, who can't ask good questions or assimilate information well," asserts Kincannon. This seems obvious, but spotting the person who can't fit into the unique world of the boardroom can be tricky in advance. Seek out background clues from people who have worked with the board candidate both in a day-to-day business setting and in a more collegial environment. Does the candidate contribute? Does he or she rub people the wrong way?

- **The Albatross** Maybe the candidate has a major corporate failure on his or her resume, a bankruptcy, or a company that faced serious legal issues. "There could be negative perceptions," says Kincannon. "Look closely at anyone who's been with a major failure." Don't make this an automatic blackball, though. Look also at the context and the candidate's role with the company. In Silicon Valley, for instance, brushes with failure are almost a rite of passage, and a candidate who's successfully steered a company through tough times has gained valuable insights.

Although this demand for talent is shaking up boardrooms everywhere, it's a life-and-death matter for startups trying to succeed in the new century's sluggish economy. A young startup company may have a great idea, market potential, or hot technology, but that's just not enough anymore. A strong success buzz on the firm (which can be self-fulfilling) often depends on who you know.

Silicon Valley tech firms can gain an enormous boost if a name lead investor or venture firm is connected with it, bringing credibility and contacts. But wise board recruitment can also give a startup the winner's sheen —if you add a "golden director." Ed Merino, president of Office of the Chairman board recruiters and consultants in California, says that "a marquee name in the boardroom can be tremendously important, like gaining a name lead investor."

But recruiting such a big-name believer isn't easy for the striving startup, especially given how the major venture firms have pulled up the drawbridge since the big chill of 2000. How can you do the mutual selling needed to land a golden director for your boardroom?

- Work your extended network, and consider recruiting help. "Go to a recruiter with a golden Rolodex," says Merino. "They can assess both your company and potential board talent, and suggest people who could really benefit socially and financially." Tapping such third-party "matchmakers" extends your reach, and adds a verification buffer that can make both you and the potential boardroom star more comfortable. Don't be afraid to aim high; shoot for a director who'll bring a "wow" from investors, clients, and job prospects.

- Any golden director will require some selling on your prospects. "This director will ask, 'Why do you want me? Why should I join this board?'" Merino cautions. "They want to add value, but will have to believe that they really can." A star talent for your boardroom will want to be more than a name on your letterhead. "They help you solve problems, and their network becomes your network."

- Don't add someone who's mercenary, but realize that "people do what they perceive to be in their own self-interest," notes Merino. "These talents don't come cheap and like to be compensated." Equity for director pay can make this practical for the young firm; it increases this director's buy-in and actually adds to their endorsement value with other investors (especially given how valueless many tech stocks became).

- A golden director can help lead you to platinum directors. "As an example out here [in Silicon Valley], Buy.com founder Scott

Blum initially made connections with [former Pepsi CEO] Donald Kendall, who happens to be John Scully's father-in-law. That got Scully involved as a director [in July 1998], and it snowballed from there."

Q: Our company is a major presence in our community, but we recently settled a discrimination suit that brought local attention to our diversity efforts—or lack of them. We have an essentially white, male board of directors at present and realize that we need to add some fresh faces, but we know few area candidates, and major national board names likely won't have time for us. Any ideas?

A: Pressure to add women and people of color in the boardroom is filtering down from the Fortune 500 level, but this only adds to the problem of finding qualified candidates. When board diversity first became an issue 20 years ago, boards and recruiters started tapping a fairly narrow circle of eminent women and minorities, who have since become "boarded up" (that's why Carla Hills and Vernon Jordan seem to pop up on every other Fortune 500 board).

To refresh the diversity of your board, you'll need to refresh your thinking. "There's a great deal of networking involved," counsels Charles King, a board search expert as well as a specialist in diversity board searches. "Women and minorities now have a variety of business groups and organizations, and they're willing to be helpful."

Your current outside board members likely know someone in their own or another company who is a contender. Even those "name" women and minority directors who may be out of your reach "know some excellent candidates who aren't," suggests King. "They're often mentoring good people in their own organizations, and you can tap these relationships if you're willing to take a step or two down. Every top minority director could be a source for two or three other candidates."

Indeed, for success in adding talented women and minorities to your board, it's vital to look outside the narrow circle of CEOs and top names. "You'd be surprised at the number of presidents and COOs of multibillion-dollar corporate divisions who don't get public recognition," says King. "These people are doing an outstanding job and have full P&L responsibility, but they're not CEOs, and don't get tapped for boards."

Q: Our software company is growing fast and looking toward an IPO next year. However, our product competes with some really big, well-established firms, so we need both to build credibility in the market and keep posted on the latest in our industry. I want to establish an advisory board that includes some major names in our sector, but how can you lure board talent like that when you're still a little guy like us?

A: Building an advisory board of heavyweight mentors is smart, but you're right, gaining their notice won't be easy. Well-connected senior managers from name companies, top partners in venture firms, and successful entrepreneurs are in great demand for both corporate and advisory board seats.

The first, most obvious lure involves dollar signs, or at least options on future stock. A *BoardroomINSIDER* subscriber who works extensively in board recruiting observes that "the monetary consideration, the upside potential, has to be their first consideration."

But this pro also notes that "the strategic nature and position of the company are important too. Is this a launch that will make my name and help my resume?" In short, if you can really make your pitch to venture sources and managerial talent, you should also be able to make a strong pitch to board candidates. If not, maybe the company idea itself needs some rethinking.

You can use other monetary levers to lure advisory board talent, however, and some are not only more effective than others, but can cost less and leave everyone happier. An entrepreneur in Florida recently told me of his success in drawing very high-income execs to serve on the advisory board of his construction company through the smart use of charitable donations. These board members receive only a modest expense check, but a sizable donation (which could be in stock) is made in their name to a favorite charity. This has proven a highly powerful tool for attracting A-list board members who would yawn at the same amount going into their own bank accounts.

Finally, seeking talent for an advisory board may actually be easier now. Corporate board talent is overstretched, in turmoil due to new independence and market demands, and scared over new board liabilities. Service on an advisory board avoids these headaches and might even prove a welcome respite.

And Once You Find Good Directors, Train 'Em up Right

Orienting new directors is a must-have first step in board effectiveness. However, the guidance on orientation as a *process* has been lacking. Bringing a board newbie up to speed requires more than just dumping a basket of "to read" material on his or her desk. A personal contact between the new director and key staffers is more crucial today, so a curriculum plan and schedule for these contacts are also needed.

Barry Ashton, chair of the Calgary Co-Op Association in Canada, is a member of numerous boards, and heads his own management consulting firm. Ashton has developed a neat, 1-day orientation program for the new director that should fit smoothly into any corporation:

8:45 a.m.	Welcome and agenda review
8:45—10:15	Corporate overview (company history, legal framework, and business structure)
10:15—10:30	Break
10:30—11:00	Corporate plan overview
11:00—11:30	Review of mission, vision, and values; strategic direction; structure; distribution; products and services
11:30—12:00	Corporate finance overview
12:00—1:30	Lunch with board chair and senior management
1:30—2:30	Role of the director (governance model, liabilities, board policy manual, and info sources)
2:30—3:00	Corporate affairs overview
3:00—3:30	Board functions (work plan and meeting schedule, evaluations, individual evaluations, board training and development, chair and CEO evaluation, corporate secretary evaluation)
3:30—3:45	Board and shareholder communication and services
3:45—4:00	Wrap-up and follow-up questions

That takes care of the schedule, but what sort of info should be part of your orientation package? It's useful to see what best-practice boards put into something as basic (yet essential) as a new director's company introduction package. A spokesman in the corporate secretary's office at mining titan Phelps Dodge gave me a peek at their new director corporate fact book. The index includes:

- The company's mission statement
- Corporate and governance essentials (statement of incorporation, company history, state incorporation laws, date of the annual meeting, the number of directors on the board, an outline of Phelps Dodge's capital structure, and a fiscal year calendar)
- A copy of the corporate bylaws
- A directory of the current board members
- Board committees and their membership
- A directory of company officers and top executives
- The board's meeting schedule for the next year
- Copies of the latest Phelps Dodge annual report, 10K and quarterly proxy filings
- The corporate code of ethics
- Director membership criteria
- Director compensation and benefits info (compensation, the stock ownership plan, retirement and deferred compensation policy, director's insurance, SEC insider trading regulations, share purchase rights, and charitable contribution and dividend reinvestment policies)

Breaking in new members of your board, as well as keeping current members up to speed, is an expanding and difficult job for any corporation. Now imagine that your company is made up of very large, very diverse units (beverages, movie studios, record companies, and theme parks) and, to top things off, is split between two countries. Seagrams, Limited, in Canada faced just such a governance challenge, but met it head on with an excellent board-training program.

"When a new director joins, we have them meet with key personnel," says a staff member in Seagrams' corporate secretary office. "This includes the CFO, treasurer, controller, tax people, internal and external audit, and business unit heads. The director has a one-on-one session with each of them." Meetings with the business unit heads often take place in the field, at Seagrams' various divisions such as the Universal entertainment facilities. "We make sure that they are exposed to the major areas of the corporation."

The Seagrams board program is complicated by the unique binational split between the conglomerate's U.S. and Canadian identities. "We have both the U.S. and Canadian people counsel directors," says the staff member, "but a lot of the governance aspects are relatively blurred between the two." The result is a director knowledge system that is both intense *and* uniquely suited to the company's needs.

How to Save Time, Money, and Sanity in the Boardroom

Think Y2K was scary? Forget that. Corporate America—and indeed all of global business—faces a subtle but more serious threat that will make those clocks clicking over to midnight at the end of the last century seem like a mere distraction. Without our noticing it, the nineteenth-century model of corporate governance is breaking down at the start of the twenty-first.

Even when they're working at 110 percent, the contradictions, dangers, and demands directors face on a board have become a serious threat. The time, effort, and oversight required of boards seem to be doubling every few months, just as the top executives who make up our pool of directors must focus far more on their day jobs. Although the public isn't inclined to feel sorry for the elite who serve in our boardrooms (especially after hearing their excuses for the recent corporate scandals), the impact of a slow governance meltdown on our economy would hit everyone. For the moment, forget adding more laws, more responsibilities, and more training. What directors need right now are more hours in the day. Here are a few ways to find them.

Executive assistants (EAs) have saved the bacon of many top executives by helping them stay organized, on schedule, and on message. Since the people who serve as corporate directors have often reached a professional level requiring a smart EA for success, it pays to ask how effective EAs make their bosses successful in the boardroom. Kitzi Tanner, a vice president at executive assistant search firm EASearch.com, talked with some of her sharpest clients and brought back these tips.

One EA's boss is with a large venture firm and serves on 10 boards, which could be a logistical nightmare. But his EA eases the load by "keeping an Excel spreadsheet with all the boards, schedules, contact info, email, and phone numbers," says Tanner. This spreadsheet is then rolled into a master schedule both for this VC partner and the firm's other partners.

Knowing who's who at the companies where her boss is a director is vital says the EA (and especially assistants for the CEO and other directors). But one key tidbit often overlooked is the company attorney's name and all contact information (including the EA). Then, if legal papers, signatures, or transactions require quick attention (and they usually do), everybody's EA can get on the phone or fax and quickly network the business through.

As you can imagine, trying to set a long-term board schedule for a busy director like the previous VC (who also serves with lots of *other* busy directors) could be a nightmare. But by interfacing with the EAs for all these other board members (and the company secretaries), a board schedule for the next year can be smoothly set.

Committee chairs have their own administrative burdens that too often are not met. "Many of these chairs are just not well organized," says Tanner. She counsels the EAs she works with to get together with the corporate secretary at the firms whose boards their bosses serve on. She encourages them to make sure committee books are fully prepped, the director is well organized for the committee meeting, "and that they get there on time."

Finally, remember that good EAs can prove invaluable in previewing the director's board book before the meeting. One EA goes over the package to highlight key presentation material, flag items needing signatures, and query unclear items. She thus streamlines a condensed Cliff Note's version of what too often is an oversized lump of undigested data.

What if you're an active executive who also serves on boards, but lacks available EA talent? Learn to compartmentalize your board roles for greater efficiency. Serving as a good director today means being able to multitask, to give 100 percent attention to one board in the morning and 100 percent to another in the afternoon. How do you stay organized?

- As much as possible, try to keep similar roles on different boards. Serving on the audit committee of each, for example, lets you build targeted finance skills and simplify your board cross-training headaches. For some folks, though, the opposite approach may work: Serving with audit on one board and compensation on another could help keep the jobs straight. Find out which works best for you.

- Put technology to work. Your palm organizer should be stuffed with contact info for every board's company, giving you a full directory for each. Also, serving on a board gives you the influence to push the board's administrator (typically the corporate secretary) toward using technology in ways that cut director burdens. Board info mailings on a CD, combined with an ultralight laptop, let you review a full meetings' worth of material on the flight in without a bulging briefcase of paper.

- Use multiple board seats as a way to pick the best from each boardroom. Board procedures differ greatly from company to company. As I've noted, this ad hoc approach is one of the great weaknesses of the corporate board. But you can boost board professionalism by swiping good ideas from Board A and suggesting them at Board B. If one board uses a particularly time-efficient agenda, pitch this program in other boardrooms as a timesaver. Both you and the other directors benefit.

- Encourage smart scheduling. A single director has limited power when it comes to laying out meeting schedules, but do what you can to avoid flying from Company A's meetings on Wednesday to Company B's board session on Thursday. A schedule that allows at least a few days' recovery time keeps you from burning out and overlapping your governance oversight.

Nancy Sylvester, an Illinois-based parliamentarian and business consultant, gave me some excellent timesavers you can put to work right inside the boardroom:

- Board members have their meeting agendas to tell them topics, but Sylvester suggests also adding "a code to each item to show action required." For example, an asterisk for items requiring a vote, a star for presentations, and so on, with a key to the codes at the bottom. You might even try adding typical time allotments based on experience. For example, an * means a vote that typically goes 15 to 20 minutes. This helps everyone know how much time an item should take and keeps the meeting running smoothly. Better still, as Sylvester notes, "this makes it the whole board's responsibility to keep the meeting moving along, not just the chair."

- Here's one problem a seasoned parliamentarian sees too often, along with a solution. "People might know the general terms of a motion, but after a few minutes they forget the exact wording," says Sylvester. Give all board members and staff multicopy NCR carbonless notepads to jot down the exact wording when the motion is made, and then make sure copies go to the board chair and secretary (at least). This should cut down on later "I voted for *what?*" protests. If your boardroom is wired for video displays, just pop the wording up onscreen or try a low-tech flip pad. Through any of these methods, "the exact wording is right there in front of everyone," according to Sylvester.

- In most cases, the basics of motions to be approved in the board meeting are known in advance. So why not "send out the text of the motions by email before the board meeting," suggests Sylvester. Directors will be able to review the suggested wording, make any changes they'd like to see, and email the revision back to the company secretary or the board chair. Then, when the motion comes up on the agenda in the actual meeting, "debating and passing the motion can take 5 minutes instead of 2 hours."

- Board meeting packets vary in fatness, density, and timeliness, but all of them tend to be a one-way medium. Info goes to the directors, but director responses or questions don't happen until the actual meeting. Sylvester asks, why not "include a sheet that asks board members to fax back questions for staff on any agenda items?" This could be a general query back to the corporate secretary, who then routes the question internally, or might even include specific fax numbers for the relevant staffers. The staff could then answer back, but it's more likely the queries would prompt the staffers to have research ready at the board meeting itself, saving time and hassle. "The information we got back from directors was wonderful, and if two or three members of a six- or seven-member board all ask the same question, that's a sign that you need to get your act together."

- Try to build a total board sense of responsibility for meetings and for keeping the discussion on task and productive. "Directors don't come to the chair's meeting or the company's meeting," Sylvester says. "They should see it as *our* meeting."

It seems like such a simple question, but solid answers are almost impossible to find. How much time per month should a director devote to board duties? The 2002 Korn/Ferry study of directors at the top 1,000 U.S. corporations finds an average of 15.3 hours monthly, but this is only the centerpoint of a wide variation scale. Barry Ashton (mentioned previously in the chapter) chairs the board of the Calgary Co-Operative Association, Limited, and their bylaws recommend a time commitment more than *double* the previous figure: 300 to 400 hours yearly per board member.

Do you have an accurate measure of how much time your own board members commit to boardwork per month or per year? Although few boards do this, gaining such a benchmark could be enormously useful in making your board more effective. Here are some ideas for setting your governance time budget:

- Be sure to include *everything*. Outside directors should spend at least 1 hour on boardwork outside the boardroom for every hour actually spent in board and committee meetings (and usually more). Company info review, research, calls to management and other board members, time to and from meetings, the annual meeting, chats with company execs, networking and contacts on the company's behalf—you'll be surprised at how many extra minutes sneak onto the director's timecard.

- Start with some sampling. Convincing all your directors to keep track of their time usage would be great data, if you could get it, but you'll have better luck asking just two or three sample outside directors to log their time. See who's most supportive of the idea, and try for a variety in board duties (the audit committee chair will doubtless clock in more time than someone who's just one member of the nominations committee). Avoid inside, employee directors, for now; breaking out their board time from management duties will be difficult.

- Put someone in charge as timekeeper. Typically, this would fall to the corporate secretary's office. However, you could expedite the process by printing up some timesheets with the previous headings or investigating timekeeping software.

- Helpful hint: If you have any lawyers on your board, try starting with them as a timekeeping guinea pig. Lawyers are pros at keeping track of billable hours and can put this expertise to use for your board research.

As you can see, corporate staff is vital to any effort to squeeze more governance into less time. Directors today have too much to do and too little time to do it, so the staffer who kills director time wastefully is committing governance murder (and possibly career suicide). Here are a few excellent, staff-targeted efficiency tips from some of corporate America's top governance thinkers and executive assistants:

- The board's duties are well known, and yearly corporate events that they touch on (annual meetings, fiscal year ends, and key corporate filings) are set years ahead. Why, then, do many boards still set their meeting dates from meeting to meeting? This makes your board too uncertain and clumsy for busy top execs. "The company should provide a schedule of meetings 12 and preferably 18 months out," counsels Reggie Babcock, president of Corporate Governance Consulting Services.

- This has been mentioned previously, but the point can't be overstated: View the board meeting as an overall menu of board and committee meetings to be mixed and scheduled in the most efficient, compact manner possible. A 1-day (or preferably 2-day) schedule can proceed as a seamless whole through the effective juggling of committee meetings that flow directly into approvals by the full board, plant tours, and vital chat time over dinner.

- Even the most efficient board schedule will bring some downtime for directors, though. Help your busy outside directors stay productive if they have a couple hours to kill. "Make sure directors have some office space of their own available so they can drop in to do work or get Internet access," suggests Babcock. Designating a staffer to give them office or clerical support for the day can help these execs meet their own time needs. "Don't ever let a director feel he's wasting 3 hours between meetings."

Financials, Frauds, and Fumbles: Why "Audit Committee" Is an Oxymoron

Perhaps the most probed boardroom materials and procedures of all time are those used by Enron, particularly the board's audit committee. And how many boards can point to a U.S. Senate subcommittee investigation and report named in their honor? "The Role of the Board of Directors in Enron's Collapse," published by the Senate's Permanent Subcommittee on Investigations in July 2002, is telling on how much the audit committee of a major corporation doesn't know about dollars and sense—and mishandles what it does know. The senators found that two Enron directors in the dock "declined to characterize Enron's accounting as high risk or aggressive. Director and Comdisco Corporation chairman Norman P. Blake characterized Enron as engaged in 'leading edge,' not 'aggressive' accounting." Lord John Wakeham, meanwhile, was comfortable with Enron's accounting principles and was "shocked" in 2001 when Arthur Andersen began to backtrack on its earlier approvals.[1]

Of course, such denial of the audit outrages that directors swallowed deserves some sympathy due to the sheer volume and complexity of deals dumped onto Enron's audit committee. The Senate report marvels at the "long list of related entities disclosed in Enron's 10-K filings . . . which were approved and signed by Enron board members." Almost 3,000 of these distinct business entities were included, 600 of them crowded into the same postal box in the Cayman Islands. Directors were to review, analyze, and approve the financial and fiduciary soundness for each of these mini-Enrons, yet "no board member who signed the 10-K filings expressed an

---

[1]"The Role of the Board of Directors in Enron's Collapse," Report of the Permanent Subcommittee on Investigations of the Committee on Governmental Affairs, United States Senate, July 2002.

objection to or concern about Enron's thousands of related entities or the complex transactions in which they were involved."[2]

As noted earlier, boards typically receive poor, indigestible, and off-target information on the company. However, special damnation is deserved for the quality of financial information the board sees. In no other area is the part-time, amateur status of the corporate board more obvious than in the quantity and complexity of financials directors must digest. The staggering intricacy of Enron's outside entities and their accounting differ only in degree (and, we hope, honesty) from the financials at most large corporations. The distracted outside executives who make up a typical corporate board can offer at most several hours per month to plumbing financial covenants, audit treatments, and legal opinions—oh, and by the way, sign this. In no other aspect of corporate governance is there, in the words of Ralph Waldo Emerson, such a "worthlessness of amateurs to cope with practitioners." The fact that it took months after the Enron case broke before any criminal indictments were filed hints at this mismatch. Even with full-time staff attention and subpoena powers, the feds were still boggled by the intricate financial web woven at Enron. Would a harried audit committee member trying to absorb a briefcase-busting financial report on a flight to his meeting stand any chance?

Maybe, but only if we recast the role of the board (and specifically the audit committee) in coping with financial information. Over the past year, the Securities and Exchange Commission (SEC) and stock exchanges have laid out tough new rules for board audit committees, but most focus on membership and compelling the committee to swear in blood to its oversight. Even though these are all vital, such mandates miss the point of how boards actually work. More important is redefining audit's job and the material it reviews—not *who* does the job (or how many oaths they sign), but *how* the job is done.

These new demands require your audit committee to change and change fast. Start with a few big issues:

- Strong communication channels from the board to staffers are vital. Every corporate scandal seems to have had a whistle-blower somewhere in the organization trying to alert top management to impending doom. Yet contacting a board member with this warning is still too often a breach of protocol. It's time for directors to build open backchannels to staff that offer

[2]Ibid.

free communication, updates, and warnings. (Building these backchannels will be covered in a later chapter.)

- Boards must audit staff pressures and values along with just the numbers. If everyone from the CEO down faces huge pressure to show constant earnings growth, hit targets, or avoid charges to the balance sheet, then the entire reporting structure will distort itself to support these goals. Even if the numbers the CFO gives you seem acceptable, the board must now also know if a gun is pointing at his or her head.

Follow these big issues with the vital little issues that mean so much. Audit committees must start by hammering out a strong charter and job descriptions, but treat these not as an end in themselves, but rather as a game plan for the committee's agendas and functions. What are the handful of vital "desert island" things our committee *must* do, and what are the specific figures we must see to do them well? Are there measures that will give us quick, regular updates in addition to larger, more detailed quarterly reports? Just who decided what information the audit committee needs—the committee itself or the chief financial officer (CFO)?

Finally, do members of your committee have the needed "financial literacy" to make such decisions? In January 2003, the SEC fleshed out the new Sarbanes-Oxley requirements by requiring companies to publish the financial expertise vitae of audit committee members. Will your committee members' savvy stand up to this public spotlight?

The new SEC and stock exchange rules put the audit committee in the driver's seat. But reforms are worthless unless your committee members have a good road map—and know how to drive.

Running a Better Audit Committee

Former U.S. secretary of commerce and head of the Audit Committee at Dow Chemical and other major boards, Barbara Hackman Franklin is the one person you go to in order to find out how the last year's convulsive change is shifting our boardroom audit standards. Her observations?

- "When it comes to materiality and disclosure, I'm sensing a shift. One is on items that are more of a liability overhang, like the asbestos issue . . . those liabilities need to be disclosed. Also, there seems to be a shift in definitions. The old standard of materiality was a matter affecting more than 3 or 5 percent of net worth, but now we need to also look at whether something could cause damage to the company's reputation, no matter its size."

- "When I chair an audit committee, it's important to keep the channels of communication [with staffers] as open as possible. You do it by having committee meetings that are not too formal, with lots of candor, and also by talking *between* meetings. I try to talk regularly with the controller and the CFO, so when an issue does arise, it's not a big deal. Communications are *so* important to this committee."

- Although finance and audit expertise on the audit committee are vital, Hackman doesn't want the trend to go overboard. "You need a mix. I like to have an operations person as well as someone from academia on the committee. They can ask the dumb questions that aren't really so dumb."

- "Another key to audit committee effectiveness is a closed executive session, with no note takers present. If the chair of the committee wants someone to know what happens, I can tell them."

- "The audit committee has to control its own agenda. I like to get our staff people gathered around a table before the year starts, review our company risks, and then ask which [risks] come under the committee's bailiwick. Then we write everything down, and it goes to the committee, and then to the CEO to see how he feels about it. Usually, he likes what he sees. Then we shape the agenda from that."

- Greater audit oversight comes at a price, though. "Meetings are taking longer; that's for sure. We've been having four meetings a year, but if they get any longer, we may have to rethink the whole schedule, not just of the audit committee, but of the board as a whole."

- An audit pro's take on what happened at Enron: "This is the equivalent of 9/11 for the corporate world. These are not stupid people, but something at Enron just didn't work."

The Accounting Industry Reform Act of 2002 (the Sarbanes-Oxley law, among friends) was the U.S. government's first (if hasty) reaction to the year's corporate scandals. It's impossible to discuss shaping up your audit committee without reviewing the specific changes this law will impose on it. Here are the key items directors need to know:

- All members of the audit committee must now be independent from management (though the independence measures are not as strict as they could have been). Audit committees will now be a lot busier, with direct responsibility for selecting, paying, and monitoring the work of the outside auditor. The committee also must sort out disagreements between the auditor and management. (More on the auditor aspects will be covered later.)

- The audit committee also gains responsibility for setting up an internal whistleblower system for employees to report accounting and audit concerns. (The committee will also serve as the ultimate destination for these happy tidings.)

- Stock trading and reporting windows for insiders have tightened sharply, and that includes board members. The old rules gave insiders up to a month to report trades to the SEC; now it's *the day after the transaction*. Senior officers and directors must also now fit their trades into the same trading blackout periods imposed on their pension funds. (Check with your corporate secretary to make sure that your trade processing and notification system is up to this new turbo-charged mandate.)

- The do's and don'ts of making corporate loans to a CEO have been much debated after the Tyco board granted heavy benisons to CEO Dennis Kozlowski, but the new Accounting Reform Act makes the matter much simpler: Just don't. Such loans are now banned in most circumstances (and the ban applies to members of your board too). But stay tuned for loopholes and workarounds in this policy.

- Early drafts of the law required the board's chair to swear to the accuracy of financials, as CEOs now must already do, even if the chair is an independent outsider. Since this means no one in his or her right mind would thus want to serve as a separate chairman, the clause has been dropped. Also, the SEC itself can now ban someone from serving as a director for securities violations or "demonstrated unfitness." Previously, only a court ruling could do this.

Since the main boardroom focus of the new Accounting Reform Act is on the audit committee, let's take a closer look at how its provisions will affect the way you do committee business. For some insights, I checked in with David Tate, a California-based triple-threat CPA, attorney, and savvy audit committee observer. The main audit points of the new law are as follows:

- Expect to spend a *lot* more face time with the company auditor. The auditor must now report to the committee on audit treatments used, alternatives, and why the auditor chose treatment A over B. "Material written communications" between the auditor and management must also now be CC:ed to the committee. Tate suggests that your committee be more active in this discussion and "inquire about alternative [audit] practices even if those have not been discussed with management." In sum, auditor relations are now firmly in the hands of the audit committee.

- Many consulting services are forbidden for the audit firm that performs the corporation's quarterly and annual audits. The firm can handle tax consulting if the audit committee approves in advance. Some other consulting can likewise be okayed by the committee, but only in limited circumstances (and I wouldn't want to be a member of any board that later has to defend bending this rule).

- Very soon your audit committees will require at least one member who is a "financial expert." (The law defines this person as having education and experience as an accountant, auditor, CFO, and comptroller, with knowledge of Generally Accepted Accounting Principles [GAAP], experience with comparable financial and auditing statements and internal controls, and knowledge of audit committee functions.) At the moment, you can still get by with an explanation if you do not have this expertise. Do you want to go on record as saying that your audit committee lacks the needed know-how? I didn't think so.

- As noted, all members of the audit committee must now be provably "independent." This means no consulting, advisory, or other compensation from the company, and no affiliation with the firm or a subsidiary.

For updates on audit changes of the Accounting Reform Act, see David Tate's web site at http://users.rcn.com/tateatty. You can use Google to locate many good online summaries of the law's overall provisions, but one that focuses on the specific governance impact can be found at the Weil Gotshal Manges law firm's web site (www.weil.com).

The effective audit committee begins with an effective audit committee charter. The Sarbanes-Oxley law and the SEC and stock exchange listing requirements almost overnight transformed charters from being a smart board idea to being a vital necessity.

James Bean, CPA, is a first vice president with California Federal Bank. He recently helped another major bank's audit committee with a complete overhaul of its charter. "The old charter was very small and outdated, totaling maybe two paragraphs," Bean says. The new charter covers several pages of everything an audit committee needs to know and do, and it is such a best-practice job that the American Institute of Certified Public Accountant's (AICPA) *Journal of Accountancy* dedicated an article to it. The following are Bean's first-hand tips for creating an effective audit committee charter:

- Support for a strong charter must come from the top. "The impetus comes from the chair of the audit committee," Bean explains, "but if the chair isn't leading the process, the director of internal audit should look at the current charter, make recommendations, and take charge of the process."

- Your audit charter now has to meet some tough scrutiny, so benchmark the best. Get a thorough briefing from internal staff on the new audit reform laws and regs, but Bean also recommends that you "research publications on the topic, talk to your audit committee members, contact industry professional groups, and get in touch with other firms in your industry" (their internal audit staff may be surprisingly openhanded on sharing). The AICPA offers good audit charter blueprints, but a smart first stop would be your outside accountant. The major audit firms have all produced excellent guides for drafting your charter (most for free).

- The drafting process for a new charter will vary. The pen may be put to paper by the chair of the audit committee, but the director of internal audit will likely have an even more specific audit background and be in a better position to devote time to the process. If the staff writes the proof charter, "the committee chair should then review it to make comments as a first step," says Bean. After following this route in preparing his bank charter, Bean says it "went to the CEO to see if the responsibilities outlined are appropriate." Then it's on to the full audit committee for comment and approval, and finally to the full board.

- The committee needs to review financial statements before press releases go out. I've seen cases where they didn't review statements until after the numbers were released. That means the committee is just a rubber stamp. The committee needs to review and update the charter annually, and when they do, they should make a self-evaluation survey. This should be part of the charter itself.

Even if you already have a charter for your committee, chances are it doesn't meet the latest demands for spelling out accountabilities, procedures, and verifications. For state-of-the-art takes on what your audit committee's charter must include, check out these links:

- The New York Stock Exchange offers a great boilerplate audit committee charter that meets its new listing mandates at www.nyse.com/content/publications/NT0000AE66.html.

- Jim Kaplan's AuditNet site provides valuable sample charter language at www.auditnet.org/docs/ac_charter.htm (by the way, the AuditNet site offers a lot of other valuable audit goodies).

- The Institute of Internal Auditors is also on the case, with a good sample charter at www.Theiia.org/ecm/iiapro.cfm?doc_id=1796.

- David Tate (cited above) offers an excellent boilerplate audit committee charter guide at http://users.rcn.com/tateatty/audit_committees.htm.

- George Johnson, who heads his own accounting firm in Detroit, chairs the audit committee for local community bank TCF Financial. Banks have long had tougher audit standards than other corporations, and Johnson helped TCF's audit committee craft a benchmark committee charter for oversight and meeting agendas. You'll find it at the *BoardroomINSIDER* web site, www.boardroominsider.com/guidelines.htm.

- To see how a corporate governance leader uses the audit charter in practice, stop by the Pfizer Co. web site to see their committee's charter online at www.pfizer.com/are/mn_investors_corporate_charters.cfm.

The key elements to be addressed in any audit committee charter are as follows:

- Recommend the outside audit firm to be used by the company.
- Review the company's annual and quarterly financial statements before release.
- Review with the outside audit firm what issues and financials the committee needs to discuss with the outside auditor (crucial with the recent audit rule changes).
- Review regularly the committee's own charter, and recommend needed changes to the full board.
- Receive an annual statement from the audit firm on all relationships it might have with the company to ensure independence.

The next step is to actually *use* your charter and the new reforms to improve the way your audit committee functions. "I would probably contact company counsel first, the CFO, and maybe the outside accounting firm," suggests David Tate. Tate, who works extensively with audit committees, finds that many are flying blind when it comes to building the new audit demands into how their committee functions. "I still see considerable variation, and I don't think there's a lot of information out there yet."

Remember that even the best audit charter won't address the mechanics of how the committee actually functions. "Most committees just put into the charter whatever the lawyers tell them to," Tate says. "[N]o charter goes into anything like sufficient detail."

In revamping your committee's agendas, pay the most attention to timelines, warns Leland Graul, national SEC director for BDO Seidman. "With the audit committee and the auditors more involved now, there are real pressures to get through all the documents in time for filing deadlines," Graul says. "Some simply can't get things done in time. I see more companies prepping their statements until the forty-fourth day of a 45-day filing period." With higher pressures on internal audit and the CFO, the committee must ratchet up its own productivity to not be a bottleneck.

Though BDO Seidman sees no real change in audit committee schedules yet, Graul suspects they will have to change. "We still see the pattern of quarterly meetings, but from my perspective, there needs to be an increase, to five or even six meetings a year. Committees must now say that they were there when the audit was planned and met with management before earnings numbers were released." Graul notes that the typical committee member works about 50 hours per year, but that an internal poll of his firm's partners suggests that "audit committee members really need to put in 100 or even 120 hours per year, more than double."

Dan Doheny, head of the KPMG Audit Committee Institute, says a new KPMG survey finds that the average number of committee meetings is up to 4.3 yearly from 3.9, and at those meetings "they're doing more work." Also, audit committee meetings are "increasingly timed to key events like earnings releases, so they'll be more timely." Better leave some free time on your calendar for 2003.

Of course, board audit committees wouldn't have proved so hapless at so many companies if they didn't have a few fundamental problems. Some of these problems are hidden in plain sight, yet committee members simply ignore them. Fred Golden, a seasoned governance consultant, has launched a new firm called Verification Specialists that concentrates on advising boards, and he shares several of the most common chronic audit committee ailments:

- **The Too Late, Too Little Syndrome** "Many audit committees, especially at smaller and midcap firms, have not been looking at their audit issues enough," says Golden. "They meet once a quarter, possibly talking with the auditor and the CFO in the same phone call." As noted previously, the audit committee time commitment is trending up. Audit committees won't be able to meet as often as the reformers would like, but the heavier use of online and teleconference updates, plus more frequent checks on key financial measures can improve your committee's immediacy.

- **Thinking Inside the Box Syndrome** "Committees have not been considering alternative accounting treatments enough," says Golden. Make more effort to ask the auditor, "are there other ways this can be shown, and are we account-

ing for it in the best long-term way?" Compensation, depreciation, and amortization are key areas where fresh accounting
ideas bear looking into.

- **The Hobbled Committee Syndrome**   The new accounting reforms confirm that the audit committee must be the outside auditor's boss in practice as well as in theory, but real change
will doubtless lag. Further, Golden believes that, for audit committees to be effective, even this change is not enough. "The
committee needs to be responsible both for external *and* internal audit. Both should report directly to the audit committee."

- **The Audit Amateur Syndrome**   Sorry if anyone is
insulted, but Golden (and many other observers) finds audit
committees simply lack the internal and outside expertise to
handle their job, and the new reforms won't cure this ill. "A
CFO on the committee isn't enough. Every member should
have a purpose. Also, you need continuing education for the
directors on changes in law and accounting treatments." Plus,
"the committee should pay outside consultants. It's probably a
lot cheaper than trying to do everything yourselves."

- **The "Whose Job Is It Anyway?" Syndrome**   This has
become an epidemic problem with new expansion in board
duties. When setting up your audit committee's charter/guide-
lines, ask the company internal audit staff and outside auditor
to go over them and mark up changes and updates they
suggest.

- **The Blurry Business Risk and Performance Factor
Syndrome**   Failure to identify key risks demanding committee review is a growing problem, audit pros tell me. With the
committee having to sign off on ever more certifications and
assurances, a basic review of the financials is no longer adequate. Once again, ask audit staff what new benchmarks the
committee needs to see, and put in some agenda time reviewing the adequacy of your info flow.

- **The Anguished Agenda Syndrome**   Does your audit
meeting agenda reflect the actual time needed for each item?
Are your meetings crowded for time (meaning too much work
for the time available)? Perhaps worse, is your committee able

to quickly breeze through its agenda (which could mean a shallow, perfunctory review)?

- **The One-Sided Dialogue Syndrome**   How much real face-to-face time and familiarity do you have with internal audit and finance staff? Can you have informal chats with them, or is discussion handled like diplomatic communication? Do you have full-name and contact info for audit staffers logged into your PDA? Also, are most of your committee contacts funneled through company management? If auditors or risk managers had concerns on a finding or exposure, how openly, quickly, and fully would they be likely to tell your committee chair?

- **The Yesterday's News Syndrome**   How does your committee get its news? Is there an internal company structure to supply this intelligence?

- **The Committee versus Board Syndrome**   With audit committee work more technical and central to the governance role, communication between the committee and the full board must be effective. Who handles committee minutes? Are your full board's chair and the audit committee chair in agreement on the committee's mandate? Don't just make audit the board's dumping ground for new duties.

The U.S. Institute of Internal Auditors is a rich resource for audit committee info and advice (stop by their web site at www.theiia.org for a full shopping list). Their checklist below is titled "What can audit committees do to establish open-door reporting?" but it's really an excellent 12-point best-practice summary for the committee itself:

- Ensure an adequately staffed, professional internal audit function.

- Review and approve the internal auditing charter (as opposed to the committee's own charter).

- Concur on the appointment or removal of the chief audit executive.

- Exercise an active oversight of the internal audit function.

- Regularly review the independence and objectivity of internal audit.

- Review and preapprove audit plans and budgets.

- Evaluate audit results.

- Assess how well audit plans were executed, and question deviations or gaps.

- Review past audits to determine whether management has taken effective corrective action on any shortfalls.

- Request any special audit projects.

- Build in confidential discussion between the internal auditor and the committee.

- Recommend external quality reviews of the company's internal audit process.

Although a strong audit committee charter is important, how do you translate it into effective oversight on a meeting-by-meeting basis? George Johnson of TCF Financial (mentioned previously) shares a sample agenda used by his audit committee. This well-thought-out timetable wrings maximum value from a $2^1/2$-hour committee meeting. Although some elements are specialized for the banking sector, most items will fit well into your own audit committee agenda:

- Call to order by the audit committee chairman.

- Presentations by outside regulators—if necessary (15 minutes).

  At one or two meetings per year, banking regulators present the results of their examinations to the audit committee. The regulators speak at the start of the meeting and leave when they are done presenting.

- Approve minutes from the prior audit committee meeting (5 minutes).

- Report on significant accounting matters by the controller (15 minutes).

- Report on asset quality and the results of loan reviews by the executive vice president in charge of asset quality (30 minutes).

- Report on corporate compliance activities, including internal compliance audits (15 minutes).

  This report is given by the vice president in charge of compliance.

- Report on TCF's information security program by the chief information officer (15 minutes).

- Internal audit report by the general auditor and key audit managers (15 minutes).

  This includes a report on significant internal audit findings since the last meeting, as well as discussion and approval of changes to the annual audit plan for dollars and manpower. Internal audit staffing changes are also reported.

- Discussion by the audit manager of the results of the internal quarterly risk assessment done by senior managers for each area of the company (10 minutes).

- Report by the audit director on the filing of the most recent form 10-Q report (previously reviewed with CFO, audit chair, and independent auditors before filing) (5 minutes).

- Report by the partner from TCF's independent auditor concerning reports they have issued since the last meeting as well as the progress made in conducting their annual audit (10 minutes).

- Executive session by the members of the audit committee without members of TCF management present. As appropriate, the members of the audit committee may request the external auditors and internal auditors to stay for the executive session to respond to questions (15 minutes).

Interim meetings are held with the audit chair and the general auditor at least twice a quarter. As you can see, the whole agenda includes time allotments for each item (typically 5 to 15 minutes), and Johnson is careful to stick to these time limits.

Speaking of audit committee agendas, here are four suggestions for items you'll want to include in your committee's timetable:

- **SEC Section Fair Disclosure (FD) Update** Richard M. Steinberg, U.S. corporate governance leader for Price-WaterhouseCoopers, says, "I'm not sure committees are looking at policies and controls on material before it's disclosed, such as who should be speaking to analysts." Steinberg suggests that the CEO's office or the person in charge of external communications should prepare a report to the committee on FD compliance.

- **Risk Management Update** "The audit committee should ensure that management has a broad-based risk management architecture and an ongoing risk identification process," says Steinberg. This report is best given by a chief risk officer, the vice president in charge of risk management, or the chief operating officer (COO). Note this is less an update on current risks facing the company than a check on company structures for spotting these risks.

- **Independence Check for the Outside Auditor** Committees are now required to annually review the independence of the outside auditor. "The auditor submits a letter to the committee on services provided the company," says Mark Terrell, partner in charge of KPMG's Audit Committee Institute. This requires more than just a "rubber stamp certification," warns Terrell. The 2000 Public Oversight Board report on audit effectiveness (the O'Malley report) set out 10 items that audit committees should evaluate in judging whether nonaudit services impair auditor independence. These measures are even more useful now; be sure to ask your company audit staff about them.

- **Quality of Earnings** "I'm seeing more audit committee discussion on this," says Larry Rittenberg, accounting professor at the University of Wisconsin. "It's something the SEC is pushing, trying to focus the committee on asking auditors for details of how and when earnings are recognized." Rittenberg points out that a number of companies (such as Lucent) have taken recent stock hits after allegations of booking revenues too early.

Better (and Smarter) Audit Committee Members

New demands that your audit committee members be more independent are of little value unless they also possess finance savvy. Although the SEC mandates on financial literacy for audit members remain a bit open ended, the stock exchange rules are a bit more specific, especially those of the NASDAQ.

No doubt many firms need to tighten up qualifications for their audit members (too often it serves as the training ground for new directors). But as some governance experts (such as noted academic and board member Charles Elson) are pointing out, tougher standards will likely be hammered out in future court cases. This means a strike suit lawyer will grill the audit committee chair of some failed company and demand that he or she proves personal financial literacy.

Since you don't want to be cited as the court case showing what financial literacy on the board *isn't*, here are some tips for bringing your audit committee up to speed:

- William Allen, former head of the Delaware Chancery Court, expects that "at some point the liability lawyers will try to make something out of this." He foresees "development of more formal courses for committee members who may want a review." In the end, there "won't be liability for those who attend some course and show effort . . . this should be more aspirational."

- Michael Fitzpatrick, a partner with the Phelen Reid law firm, urges the boards of listed companies to check not only the new laws, but also the specifics of their stock exchange when it comes to audit qualification. "[Audit literacy] means professional experience, and at least one member must have past financial employment."

- Consider a "tiger team" of pros within the audit committee or board as a whole that can look "specifically at finance, the use of capital, and return to shareholders," suggests Denny Beran, assistant director of audit at J.C. Penney. This variation on the standard finance committee could give your audit function a nucleus of expertise that should lift and support the rest of the committee.

- Ongoing financial education for your audit committee members will soon become standard. "Eighteen percent of the audit committees we surveyed are looking at continuing education programs," says Scott Reed, senior manager of KPMG's Audit Committee Institute. "Committees are seeking more info from their outside auditors, and asking members to attend in-house and external training." Since director time is precious, outside training programs need to be brief, focused, and productive.

- Not only are educational programs popping up at business schools and audit firms to fill the financial literacy gap, but boards are also looking at new committee members to meet this need. Leland Graul, national SEC director for BDO Seidman, suggests a fresh talent source: "Some [audit] firms are making their retired partners available to serve as audit committee members." In most cases, this wouldn't impair the director's independence, but double-check with company counsel first to make sure.

So has your audit committee (and particularly your committee chair) caught up with what it needs to know? To help you find out, Financial Executives International (FEI) offers a handy online fnancial literacy test that quizzes your audit committee directors on some essential concepts and standards. You can find the FEI Financial Literacy Test at www.fei.org/download/finlitQuiz.pdf. The 24-question quiz will take you about 15 to 30 minutes (and no cheating with outside aids). For a warm-up, here are a few samples to review your audit know-how (answers follow):

1. What is the purpose of private meetings between the audit committee and the auditors, both external and internal?

   A. Facilitate private evaluation of the CFO.

   B. Allow the auditors to express concerns to the committee without management present.

   C. Allow the audit committee to press the external auditors for lower fees.

   D. Reinforce the independence of the committee to the management team.

2. Cash flow per share is defined by GAAP as:

   A. Net income plus depreciation divided by shares outstanding.

   B. Cash flow from operations on the cash flow statement divided by shares outstanding.

   C. The change in cash in the balance sheet divided by the shares outstanding.

   D. No GAAP definition exists. Analysts/companies devise one to suit their own purposes.

3. Illegitimate earnings management practices include:

   A. Overaccruing restructuring costs in one period and reversing those charges into income in future periods.

B. Building up various liability accounts (by accruing more expenses) in good quarters and decreasing them in bad quarters.

C. Recording revenue before the products or services have been delivered.

D. Postponing recognition of revenue into future quarters even though the firm has completed its earnings cycle.

E. All of the above.

ANSWERS: 1. B 2. D (No common measure of cash flow per share exists) 3. E (All of the above, and all are being targeted by the SEC.)

All right, maybe your test results left some of your audit committee members a bit sheepish. Time for some audit triage—are membership changes needed around here? And what can you do to boost the skills of both your current audit directors and new members quickly? Martin Zelbow, who has served as an interim CFO for 21 companies in recent years, has looked closely at what audit committee members need to know, and who no longer makes the cut.

"If you haven't previously been the CEO or CFO of a public company, you have no business serving on an audit committee today," says Zelbow. "Academic background in finance doesn't count. You need to not only know what constitutes GAAP, but have first-hand knowledge of how companies operate and how accounting decisions are made in the real world."

Realize that, even if you recruit a director with prize financial experience, it will still take some time before he or she can deliver real value to the audit committee. "New members have a steep learning curve, with a lengthy process of coming up to speed," Zelbow explains. "I've been CFO of 21 companies, and it still takes me at least 3 months, full time." Given the amount of time any outside director can dedicate to your financials, assume at least a year.

Speaking of time issues, be frank with new recruits to the audit committee on the time commitment required. "Committee members will need at least a half-day every month on top of any meetings," says Zelbow, and the time demands of those meetings have climbed sharply too, especially telephone chats. The committee chair should put in another 2 to 3 hours a month in talks with the CFO, the chief accounting officer, and anyone else who can offer value.

Zelbow has put together a handy menu of items that should go to every audit committee member, especially new recruits. This includes:

- The audit committee charter and committee minutes
- Management letters and any comment letters from the outside auditors
- The current engagement letter with the outside public accounting firm
- Internal correspondence regarding accounting policies and any related correspondence from the outside auditors
- A copy of the company's accounting policy manual and corporate policy statements
- Two years of SEC filings and 5 years of annual reports
- The current budget
- A comprehensive description of the company's capital structure, covenants, and amortization schedule
- A list of major accounting estimates and accruals
- An organization chart of the accounting and financial departments and resumés of senior financial executives
- A list of banking relationships
- Relevant reports and comment letters from regularity authorities
- A summary of significant legal matters
- Major contracts
- Internal audit reports
- Security analyst reports
- Insurance binders
- A summary of employee benefit plans
- A description of any currency and interest rate hedging activities
- A description of risk management practices

When recruiting fresh blood for the boardroom, any number of trends and countertrends are at work, but directors and headhunters all agree on one hot source: people who are CFOs of major firms. "There has been an extraordinary increase in demand for sitting CFOs to chair audit committees," Mike Nieset, top board recruiter with Christian and Timbers, tells me. The new regulations make strong finance knowledge on audit a must, but the herd instinct in board recruiting means that the CFOs of name companies are becoming "boarded up" even faster than company CEOs.

If you want to lure a top CFO to your board, you'll need salesmanship and innovation. Here are a few ideas:

- Expect real due diligence of your financials before these prospects say yes. "They want to meet with the current audit committee chair and the external auditor," says Nieset. "If they're not seeing a level of strength in the business plan that makes them feel comfortable, expect a turndown." And if they don't like what they see of your financials, what does that say about your current audit competence?

- Synergies between your company and the CFO's firm will help. "If it's a business related to your primary job, you can bring added insights," says Robert Ryan, CFO at Medtronic Inc. and a member of several outside audit committees. "If it's a complementary industry, it supplements your job."

- You might think that these busy, in-demand board candidates would want to board up on lightweight audit challenges, but not so. "It's not so much what your company does as what you are," notes Mike Nieset. "A really terrific CFO candidate will consider a board primarily based on what they see as their ability to contribute. Everyone has big day jobs, but people will throttle up for a challenge that satisfies their intellectual curiosity." Globalization, mergers, and technology are a few of the fields that can whet a prospect's appetite.

- Your own CFO can help attract CFOs to the board. Bring your CFO into the search process by tapping into his or her CFO networks and professional groups. At the least, any CFO board candidates will want to talk with your CFO as part of due diligence, and a good rapport here can be crucial to luring the candidate. A CFO will know what sort of questions to ask another CFO and can tell immediately if the answers don't sound right.

- Don't pigeonhole a CFO board candidate to exclusive audit committee duties. The ability to stretch out in some other areas of board work beyond the green eyeshade stuff could be attractive to a candidate. "One reason senior finance people are a hot board ticket is because they have a broad view today," notes Robert Ryan. "We're really pushing finance to be more like general management."

Starting Fresh (and Right) with Your Audit Firm

After your board's audit committee gives itself a talking to, it's time to take a fresh look at your outside audit firm, how well it's performing, how independent it is, and where its loyalties lie:

- Start out by closely reviewing your letter of engagement with the auditor. Scott Fargason, a certified internal auditor, attorney, and faculty member at Louisiana State University, says, "Look at the details of the deliverables they offer, not just when they'll submit the main reports, but interim reports too." Review their complete contract with your company and the guidelines they'll be following.

- How long has the same audit firm partner been in charge for your company? Switching partners within the firm every few years is less disruptive than changing firms, yet can still bring a fresh perspective. Also, it's standard procedure to have a reviewing partner back at the firm who oversees the auditor's work. Rotate this reviewer as well to improve independence. The Sarbanes-Oxley law requires rotating the lead auditor every 5 years anyway.

- If finding a new auditor seems wise, putting the committee in charge of the whole engagement process not only ensures independence from management, but it also sends a message to the auditors on who their boss is.

- When reviewing either your current or a new audit firm, Leland Graul of BDO Seidman suggests that you "ask the auditor what their litigation history is and what controversial positions they've taken with the SEC." If the firm (and particularly the office you work with) has a reputation for pushing the envelope, they'll bring that attitude (and rep among SEC staff) to your account.

- Expect your auditor to give more in the way of presentations and discussion, not just to your committee but to the board as a whole. "Look for *much* more detailed presentations on what happened in the previous year, particularly on past adjustments," says Graul. It's harder for an auditor to quibble in a meeting room than in a paper report.

- When it comes to putting auditors on display, it's fairly common for your audit partner to show up at the annual meeting and nod mildly when introduced. But governance pro Carl Hagburg, editor of newsletter *Shareholder Services Optimizer*, says that post-Enron, the auditor him- or herself may face some tough queries from the shareholders on hand. "People rarely asked questions of the auditor, but that will change now," asserts Hagburg. Make sure your auditor will be able to face this public spotlight.

If you can get someone to ask you the right questions, you won't have to worry about the answers you have to give. So what questions should smart audit committee members ask auditors and financial staff to get the real story on the company's situation?

- "What are the vulnerabilities of our financial reporting system?" Note that you're not asking if any flaws exist, but are *assuming* they exist. This gives outside auditors and others a prod to be honest. "Nobody likes to deliver bad news, but if the committee wants to hear it, it must be willing to drag it out," says Mike Young, an audit fraud pro with the law firm of Wilkie Farr & Gallagher.

- "Are the financials we see showing *all* the associated risks?" Once again, do the reports seen by the board really answer the right questions? Will the company be surprised by a disaster the committee never even heard about?

- Here's a good question for outside auditors from Larry Rittenberg. "If you were following the *concepts*, as well as the rules, of GAAP, would anything in these financials be reported differently?" See if this question causes any squirming or hedging.

- "Do we pay our audit firm for any services *other* than auditing?" The issue of audit firms making more for consulting services than for their audits has caught fire as a conflict of interest issue. Walt Disney Company seems to be ahead of the curve here by announcing that it won't contract any consulting work from its audit firms, and vice versa. Further, Sarbanes-Oxley specifically bans certain consulting work by auditors. Still, too many audit committee members have no idea how (or how much) money the audit firm may be making money on the side with the corporation.

- "I don't understand this item—please explain it further." Martin Zelbow urges that committee members should "never hesitate to ask about what they don't understand," especially on complex accounting issues, finance options, or foreign exchange items. "You have certification to ask anything . . . there are no dumb questions."

Shuffling auditors will be much more common in the future, yet changing audit firms is not as simple as switching travel agents. Larger public companies in particular can prompt investors to ask "what's the problem?" when they switch auditors. The dark assumption here is that the auditor wouldn't let the firm get away with some mischief. How does a board sort through these issues when considering an auditor switch?

A first step is for the board to take charge of any change process. "The decision to make an auditor change should be solely at the discretion of the committee, but it's not that way in practice," says Roman Weil, noted finance expert and professor at the University of Chicago. Although all the new reform rules push the actual audit firm engagement into the committee's lap, you'll still need to personally take the reins.

Get beyond the pressures both for and against switching. Ask if changing auditors would meet some *specific* needs of your firm right now. One good reason is "a changed focus of the business, with a need for greater auditor expertise in that area," notes William Shaw, accounting professor at Southern Methodist University. This issue is most serious when a growth company goes beyond an early, narrow focus to diversify into broader areas.

Review the major reasons for switching auditors (or staying put). Yes, a new audit firm may be able to cut the costs, but "if the CFO comes to the board and brags that he's been able to knock the auditing job down by $20,000, the board should be suspicious," counsels Roman Weil. Many variables exist in audit costs, and a cut-rate job may deliver just what you pay for. Another good reason for switching, says William Shaw, is "if the committee suspects the auditor is qualifying his opinions," typically due to management pressure. The problem here is that most audit committees wouldn't suspect the auditor's opinions unless the auditor *tells* them there is reason to be suspect: a fiscal catch-22.

If an auditor change is being seriously proposed, seek a complete estimate of all costs going in. Retraining, sharing data with the new firm, and hammering out common definitions between staff and the auditors add expenses and time that may or may not pay off. "Understand the costs of the change—make sure they don't exceed the benefits," says Shaw.

Finally, seek outside advice on the switch that answers to the board. "There should be a mandatory review of the auditor by an outside advisor, such as another audit firm with no interest, or a retired auditor," says Roman Weil. If you want to make the evaluation an inside job, Weil suggests that you "deputize the CFO to do a study, but at the committee's behest."

Another fallout of such debacles as Enron and Global Crossing is much more interest in how truly independent the firm's outside auditor really is. Although audit committees have usually seen some background on the audit firm's consulting and personnel ties to the company, a board that doesn't know *all* the details is headed for trouble. Certain conflicts have now been banned outright, but does your committee know about any other auditor/corporate ties that might be hidden away?

- Is the outside audit firm performing any of the *inside* audit functions, and if so, how many? Enron was slammed for farming out many of its internal audit tasks to outside auditor Arthur Andersen, but such contracting is not uncommon. In the future, though, such an arrangement, which pretty much lets auditors audit their own work, will be outside the pale.

- Does the audit firm perform any other consulting work for the company? Sure, new regs and formulas are now used to calculate how much consulting work is too much, but be aware that the rules here are shifting overnight. Barbara Hackman Franklin, one of America's most respected audit committee pros, reports that one of her boards had a rule that any consulting expenditure with the audit firm over $500,000 required board approval. In 2001, this limit was considered fairly strict, but at the audit committee's first meeting in 2002, the approval threshold was lowered—to zero.

- Major corporations have long had a revolving door between the outside auditor and inside staff positions, with audit partners easing directly into high-paying jobs with the company. Although this offers nifty career options, it weakens auditor independence. Such moves are limited by SEC rules now, but consider doing a family tree of the backgrounds of your company's own audit staff and your audit firm.

- Here's one overlooked conflict, according to Carol Zacharias, of CNA in New York. "Does the outside audit firm's own retirement plan hold stock in the company?" This sounds like a whole barrel of conflicts, yet it is not uncommon, especially with some young venture firms (the ones who most need an independent eye on their accounts).

No surprise here—the massive new auditing reforms of the past year will make the audit process a lot more expensive for every publicly traded corporation. What can your audit committee do to help ease the price shock while assuring that the job is still done right? The Bond Beebe accounting advisory firm of Bethesda, Maryland, must have been reading your mind, because they've put together an excellent list of ways you can help cut company audit fees. You'll find the full list at the company web site (www.bbcpa.com), but here are some main points to keep in mind:

- Boards must take an active role in planning the audit. The SEC now wants your audit committee and the outside auditor joined at the hip, so use this face time to get a complete list of items the auditor needs for fieldwork. Have these ready and waiting when the auditor arrives, cutting the prep time needed.

- Look into how accounts payable and payroll info are filed at your company. Are there ways it could be set up and organized to make it easier for auditors to access? (Try *asking* the auditors.)

- Most fiscal years keep auditors busiest (and their time most expensive) from January through April. Do you have enough flexibility to move some audit work outside this costly prime-time zone?

- Speaking of schedules, if your company plans a new accounting procedure or software change, try slotting it at the start of the audit year so your auditor won't have to handle two different systems within the same year.

- Draft as many of the basic financial statements, including footnotes, internally before sending them on to the auditor. This will save them preparation time (and expenses).

Putting **Your Committee to Work**

After sorting out the previous issues, your audit committee has to get down to its job, which often involves hard work and hard questions. Let's assume for a moment that management *isn't* trying to work any overt fraud on your board. That still leaves the director with an enormous amount of financial info that needs careful review for good oversight, often more than an already overstretched businessperson can cope with. If you had to cut to the literal bottom line, which financials should you look at first to gain the most insight on the organization's vital signs? Paul Broni, managing director of the Mercury Partners venture capital firm, suggests that the actual numbers are less important than the directions they're heading and their proportions to each other (expenses compared to sales, for example). Check out the following:

- "Start with the income statement. Go over it top to bottom. Look at revenue. Is it increasing quarter to quarter, and is it tracking with what the budget calls for?"

- "Look at expenses. Is anything consuming more than in the past. Are sales increasing faster than revenues? Maybe then the company is growing less efficient."

- "Check the balance sheet to make sure that accounts receivable is not growing faster than sales, and that none are out of date. Look at fixed assets. Are there some that are no longer worth anything, but are still on the books? Also, look at inventory to make sure that it's not building faster than sales."

- "What is the revenue booking policy? Do you book a sale on a verbal commitment, when you get a purchase order, when it's invoiced, or [when it's] installed? If management stuffs the channel, they can make the numbers look good, but it will unwind in the next quarter."

- "Make sure that assets aren't being overvalued. Some people never want to write off aged receivables that are never going to become cash. Directors need to insist that the company own up to these and take a charge."

These checks and balances are crucial to good committee financial oversight, but in the current audit environment, it can't hurt for the committee to do some extra digging. Here are a few financial broom closets worth snooping into for danger signs or red flags:

- If the company and the board lay out policies for major business matters, loud alarm bells should go off if the CEO seeks a waiver. As noted, Enron had a sound board policy against incestuous internal partnerships between the company and managers, but the board was twice willing to blithely vote for variations in the policy. Some corporate governance pros now think that these votes may prove to have been the Enron board's greatest liability danger.

- Outrageous stretch goals for the company and its people were a lauded feature of 1990s management, but the board needs to look closely at such goals and ask what the long-term price will be. "If you see targets that are objectively unobtainable or overly aggressive, executives may face unbearable pressure to meet them," notes Mike Young of Wilkie Farr & Gallagher. Staffers might meet the executive pressure by fudging numbers, stuffing delivery channels, or other mischief.

- Don't just accept revenue figures as stated. Dig for dangers in how those revenues are recognized. "Again and again I see pressure to use the wrong accounting principles for recognizing revenue," warns attorney and audit committee counselor David Tate.

- Manual journal entries, especially lots of them late in a quarter, are a big red warning light too many boards ignore. Often, something is being hastily tidied up at the last minute and may well blossom into a full disaster for the next quarter.

Disclaimer statements are a standard part of any company's financial press releases nowadays—the part about "this contains forward-looking statements . . ." blah blah blah. Postscandal, though, more boards and specifically audit committees are getting into the act. In a May 2002 *Business Week* article, Emily Thornton scolded "Audit Committees' Duck and Cover" approach to taking responsibility. AOL/Time Warner, Waste Management, and Hershey were a few of the firms adding new caveats to their audit committee filings, limiting their responsibility for the accuracy of company numbers. Is this just a case of boardroom CYA or does it serve a real business purpose? And how should you construct such caveats?

Qualifying statements "are helpful in making clear what information the board relied on," says Charles Demonico, a partner with the Dickie McCamey & Chilcote law firm. However, Demonico states that "it doesn't take away the board's responsibility to be reasonably informed." Such caveats are more legally weighty when positive rather than negative (stating what the board *is* responsible for, rather than what it *isn't*) and aren't broad hand-washing evasions. "Saying that we as a board aren't responsible for anything else we haven't seen sounds like shirking," says Demonico, and this won't impress either plaintiffs or judges.

Audit committees should take a reality check approach, suggests Karl Groskaufmanis, an attorney with the Washington office of Fried Frank. Post-Enron, there is "a growing public expectation that an audit committee can micromanage financials, but that's disconnected from reality." A group of outside execs with their own full-time jobs, meeting only a few times a year, can do little to spot overt fraud. The summary of your disclaimer should be "we can only act on what we receive." Even then, Groskaufmanis cautions "the greatest value of the statement is to give comfort to the audit committee."

Disclaimers in corporate filings are okay, but are even better in the board's basic documents. "Every board has an audit committee charter, and that's a public document," notes Toby Myerson, a partner at law firm Paul, Weiss, Rifkind, Wharton & Garrison. The charter is to be reviewed yearly, and every 3 years it is attached to the proxy, so use the charter to spell out precisely what the powers (and limits) of the committee are, how it fits in with the company's audit process, and what GAAP standards are being used. This can result in a fuller, better thought-out committee disclaimer, and one that seems less a running away from specific numbers. "If [the charter] shows the committee is starting out properly, the final results are likely not negligent," observes Myerson.

So What Exactly Is the Board Supposed to Do?: Competing (If Not Conflicting) Governance Agendas

One reason why corporate boards fail receives too little notice: The board is an institution in search of a role. Like the British House of Lords, its legal powers and trappings have survived long after its original function has faded. The board's historic legal muscle, when paired with its modern contradictions, limitations, and ineptitude, leads to some truly scary mismatches. Corporate boards are a daffy tool for trying to oversee a twenty-first-century corporation, but that hasn't stopped reformers and regulators from dumping ever-larger mandates into their collective corporate lap. The result is like giving an infant a loaded gun—and then telling Junior to fire it in two different directions at once.

The corporate board is the one entity within a corporation expected to take a disinterested, long-term view of what's best for the company and its shareholders, and to maintain the sacredness of accounting rules. It is also supposed to pressure management to keep the current stock price up—and tends to look the other way on accounting tricks needed to achieve that goal. It is the ultimate fiduciary for the interests of shareholders, the true owners of the enterprise. It has the legal power (and increasingly a social duty) to consider the company's *stakeholders*—employees, communities, and suppliers. The board is responsible for retaining top talent by crafting competitive pay packages, and it is also responsible when that pay package is called an obscene giveaway. In younger or pre-IPO companies, directors represent specific investors, founders, or venture firms whose interests may well conflict with those of the company overall.

One of the most frustrating of these competing agendas is what I call the "mentor versus monitor" board conflict. At young companies, the board's role is very hands-on and results oriented. Directors are expected to tap their networks heavily to help raise funding, lure talent, and make connections, as well as to actively mentor the often overwhelmed founders. As a director, I'm expected to serve as an effective advisor and booster of the company (a job talented people love).

At the top corporate level, though, boards fill more of a monitoring role. They review financials, strategy, and management; oversee results; and serve as independent shareholder fiduciaries, acting as enforcer and superego (a job no one could love). Established corporations definitely require the independent, objective oversight of a monitoring board, yet we've seen that the board is a singularly hapless tool for delivering this supervision. This monitor aspect gets most of the attention when we define governance (especially in the wake of our corporate scandals). But the mentoring role is the one that actually puts food on the corporate table for younger companies. To further muddy the waters, the company itself must ultimately outgrow that mentoring board. Does a General Electric or BP *really* need board members out there shaking loose deals and funding? Further, the mentoring board, for all the value it offers, is by definition not an objective monitor of the company and its management. Being hands-on also requires dirtying your hands.

Boards face another corporate schizophrenia, though this one is more positive. Knowing how a company looks from the outside is difficult for those on the inside. However, this objective view can be one of the board's most valuable contributions. Recall that the board's status in the corporation is unique. As the shareholder's proxy, the board is both the ultimate insider *and* the ultimate outsider, with (at least in theory) the company's supreme power. This gives them a special outside perspective on the corporation's public image, investor relations, and market status. Directors spend most of their time in a wider world than company management. At the same time, boards hold the power to make management listen to this perspective, even when it's something a CEO may not want to hear. Directors are thus dual insiders/outsiders in a way that seems more like quantum physics.

In short, we cannot describe the job we have given a modern corporate board without using such terms as *paradox, conflict, contradiction*, and *oxymoron*. As the role of the board has become more vital, ever more competing forces tug at the directors for attention—too often in opposing directions. Or as Yogi Berra once observed, with perfect governance insight, "When you come to a fork in the road, take it."

Sorting out the Contradictions

The boardroom is not what you'd consider a psychologically healthy place. Uncertainty over roles and powers, chilling legal dangers, and the impossibility of admitting that you just don't know something create an environment that's not exactly conducive to big group hugs. "There's a propensity to be very cautious and conformist," notes Dr. Steven Berglas, psychologist and a columnist for *Inc.* magazine. What are some of the most common psychodramas he sees in the boardroom and how do we cope?

- In companies with charismatic founders, the board can become too dependent on its leader. "We have this magic thinking about the founder," Berglas says. "Without him on the throne, the realm will crumble." Directors can respond by ignoring unpleasant boardroom realities. "Directors can be totally in denial, with unspoken agreement that they won't talk about their CEO being depressed, or ill, or getting divorced." Boards need at least one member willing to speak the unspeakable and have faith in the rest of their management team. "Good managers and a charismatic founder are not heavily correlated."

- The boardroom climate is a good one for silently nodding your head, and fair for offering observations, but a poor environment for asking questions. "Asking questions is something board directors don't see as their role," observes Berglas. "They think they're here to opine, and that it aids consensus building." Yet in truth this not only creates a board full of dilettantes, but also weakens any value that directors may contribute. "Why do boards feel they have to hire an outsider to ask pointed questions, but won't let one of their own members do it?"

- What's the nearest psychological model to the boardroom? Berglas, who's observed many boards over the years, nominates juries. "They have a lot of commonalties. There are voting blocks, strong differences, and egos. Decisions are more emotional rather than rational, despite what directors tell you. A board isn't set up to function like a jury, but then neither is a jury. Consider how wildly irrational the dynamics of this meeting are. It's like the movie *12 Angry Men*."

Outside directors on your board who were considered wholly independent just last year may no longer be. The definition of director independence has shot upward overnight. You might dismiss some of the
following new tests with "but everybody does that!" Whether everybody
will be doing it *next* year, though, is another matter. Are you as independent as you thought? Ask yourself these questions:

- Is a director also consulting? Historically (and now famously at
  Enron, Tyco, ImClone, etc.), management has paid board
  members for their consulting expertise beyond boardroom
  input. Now, you'll need to ask yourself, what is the provable
  strategic value of this director's consulting work? How do consulting fees compare to the standard director fees? (Modest
  board income with fat consulting fees flunk the smell test.) Is
  the board member really the best source for this consulting?
  How does this work go beyond the value you'd already expect
  from a board member?

- Are there third-party connections? AIG CEO Maurice
  Greenberg also heads his own holding company, and six other
  AIG directors serve on its board. FreeportMcMoran and the
  separate McMoran Exploration jointly own a third services
  firm, one that paid members of their boards $1.7 million in
  consulting fees. These two- or three-degree separation ties
  will come to light as disclosure standards tighten.

- Are there any obscure business-to-business connections?
  Outside directors employed by far-flung enterprises who serve
  on the boards of major corporations may discover that they
  have some distant (yet substantial) relationship. For example, is
  one of your subsidiaries a vendor to one of *their* subsidiaries?
  This is also an issue in smaller communities and tight venture
  environments, where everyone invests in everyone else.

- What about charitable connections? Giving by the corporation
  to a director's pet cause has long been seen as both a standard
  board perk and a source of overall do-gooding. Contributions
  to director charities at Enron and Tyco, however, have put this
  practice under a spotlight. As noted earlier, Tyco director Frank
  E. Walsh in December 2002 pleaded guilty to failing to tell the
  company's board about $20 million he received as a finder's fee
  for helping to arrange a Tyco acquisition. However, Walsh

himself only received $10 million—the other half was a charitable donation to the Community Foundation of New Jersey.

Q: I'm a venture firm partner and serve on the boards of several of our startups. As you can imagine, these companies have strategic similarities, and in some cases they overlap in markets, key personnel needs, and potential customers. This brings up a problem that I never hear much about. How does a director on several boards build internal "Chinese walls" between what he knows as a director of this board and as a director of that board? Where do you draw the line between being able to keep a fiduciary secret and failing to exploit a strategic opportunity?

A: Directors often face this quandary, and for every black and white rule (don't push the board at Company A to buy your Company B), there are a dozen gray areas. (You know that a valued tech talent is looking to leave her current firm, and both Companies A and B urgently need her skills. Who do you tell?)

"There are three issues to keep in mind," observes Hal Shear, president of the Research Investment Advisors venture firm in Boston and a director on four boards. The first is disclosure. "Begin by pointing out to the CEO and management team that you have a potential for conflicts." As a second rule, Shear advises the CEO to speak with his own team to make them aware that the director, while having a fiduciary duty to the company, also has a duty to the venture firm and its partners. And finally, Shear lets his fellow venture capital (VC) partners back at the firm know that "good governance should not require asking a director to do things that could create a conflict." In short, make clear to all involved that you recognize your duties to them, but are willing to make decisions based on what's right.

None of this tells you what to do in a particular situation, but the issues involved in what to share from board to board are so many and so vague that every answer you'll need must be a custom fit. That's why strong, open disclosure to your fellow directors and management is such a vital tool. In effect, it builds some guardrails around your behavior, relieving you of some of the burden. "Assume that every gray area has the potential to end up in *The Wall Street Journal*," counsels Shear. "A good CEO won't try to put a director in a bind like that." Even if the CEO of Company A wants you to share some juicy dish on Company B? Yes, says Shear. "Ask the CEO if that's really the way he wants you to conduct governance, and point out that it can work the other way as well."

Q: I'm a venture investor who serves as an outside director on the board of an established tech company. I'm also an investor and director with another firm, one that has a technology that could be of value to the first company. I want to develop a deal between the two, but I'm uncertain where the ethical boundaries lie, especially now, with the new laws and crackdowns. How can we handle this deal while staying on the safe side?

A: Despite all the change in the air, directors can still avoid conflicts by using tried-and-true boardroom tools. "The rules are the same, but they're applied with much more vigor," says Jeff Kaplan, a partner with Arkin Kaplan & Cohen in New York. For starters, he advises that you "disclose, disclose, disclose." Make sure that any possible conflicts are brought to the board, that they are noted in the minutes, and that your abstention from votes or discussion is spelled out.

For added backup, consider an independent review of the transaction. An independent review committee of the board, made up of outside directors with no interest in the transaction, has always been a good idea, but today would be smart for almost any transaction that touches a board member. The committee can review the deal, its value, and its fairness; report back to the whole board; or even give a go-ahead itself, if so empowered. Hiring an outside consultant, attorney, or investment banker to appraise the deal is also effective and adds to impartiality.

In either case, the decision process must be scrupulously honest and unbiased, and be defensible as such should an unhappy shareholder object. If you would personally benefit from the deal, this backup is even more vital. However, that you would benefit is not necessarily a reason to drop the deal, even in the current climate. It only has to be fair and reasonable in a business sense to pass muster.

And if the committee or outsider should give a thumbs down on the deal? Don't try to press on regardless. You'll be lawsuit bait.

How Directors Can Help (without Being Part of the Problem)

Q: I'm a partner at an area venture capital firm, and I'm about to join my first board with a startup technology company we've invested in. Although I know I'm here to watch out for my firm's interests, I also want to help mentor the company founders. Any advice on how I can most effectively combine these roles?

A: As a board member with a young venture company, you're in an ideal position to mentor the founders through early growth. Indeed, you can add more value as a mentor from the boardroom than in almost any other position. For some specific tips, I asked Christine Comaford of Artemis Ventures in Sausalito, California. Artemis is a hot area tech venture fund (and recently merged with the Novus fund), and Comaford is famed as a savvy mentor with heavy boardroom experience.

"A good board member really has to dive into the company and be ready to pull in all of their contacts to help with finance, marketing, design, whatever is needed," Comaford says. "Be ready to grab your Palm Pilot.

"How much personal help you can offer the founders depends on the level of trust they have. The majority of our CEOs call us first before they make a presentation to the [full] board. They can run radical ideas by me first, and I can say I don't quite like this, or try it this way, and then they won't get their heads torn off in the board meeting."

"It's really smart for CEOs and directors to schedule regular calls, particularly with the most influential board members. At the earliest stage, we talk with the CEO at least once a week, sometimes daily. When they get to the series B [funding] stage, and sales are taking off, we might move to every other week. Many CEOs overlook this investor relations commitment within their own boardroom."

P.S. Artemis Ventures' web site has some excellent tips on how young companies can build effective corporate and advisory boards. Check out "How to Build Effective Management Teams" at www.artemisventures.com/docs/teams.doc.

Here's a common problem for young, growing companies. The founder/entrepreneur, who may be used to calling all the shots, suddenly must learn to work with a board of directors and often has serious problems in being "broken to harness." If you're a CEO who's struggling with those first board blues, how do you (and your board members) cope?

Your background as both a boss and employee is a major factor in how you cope with a whole boardroom full of bosses, says Steven Robbins, head of consultants VentureCoach.com. "How do you like your subordinates to deal with you? What does it mean to you to be a boss? Have you successfully been able to manage your bosses in the past?" Robbins asks. "If the entrepreneur hasn't been accountable to a boss in the past, it's going to be difficult to learn now."

Robbins urges that you realize the board isn't just there to judge, but to contribute. "See them as a resource . . . hold the *board* accountable for helping you run the business and for providing oversight." This not only helps level the relationship, but it forces the board to add more value.

Another way to keep the ball in your board's court (and benefit everyone) is to make sure of "what criteria they use to judge your success," Robbins says. "If it's something simple, like share price, push for some richer criteria," including company culture, profit measures, or specific milestones. "Try to take the lead in determining what they account for."

Determine whether your problem is with the board as a whole or some of its members. "The founders I work with who have a board problem tend to have issues with the board as a group," notes Robbins. "But some of the members are there just because they want a board seat, and don't contribute much." He recalls an entrepreneur who accepted a venture firm's junior associate on the board as part of the funding package. Unfortunately, Junior "just doesn't have the perspective, so the founder spends a lot of time on board education." Moral of the story: Don't just accept board members if they can't contribute.

Boardsmanship tactics could also be a problem for the novice board chair, warns Randall Walti, head of Oaktree Consulting in California and a seasoned startup counselor. "Never come to the board with an issue that you haven't presold to them individually," Walti asserts, "and be sure to keep them informed."

Younger companies often must face some tricky issues that seem to pop up sooner or later, and a good board structure can be a huge help in dealing with them. Hal Shear of Research Investment Advisors has gained years of experience with boards from the inside and has seen how most of these common flashpoints are handled. "All companies have stages and challenges," Shear notes, and he sees the following as the most typical board-room challenges:

- **Use (and Abuse) of Name Directors**   The top three or four investors are typically on the board in the beginning and "add credibility in the marketplace and in recruiting talent. This early credibility is tremendously important. When it comes to sales or drawing a senior manager, they can really open up doors."

  It can be tricky here, though, to draw the line between a director actively making sales calls (going too far) or at the other extreme serving as "just a name on the letterhead" (not going far enough). "It's unrealistic to assume that Henry Kissinger would have much active involvement, but if a director's just a name, people see through that."

- **Making Full Use of the Board**   Young companies in particular have a long learning curve when it comes to best using the board, the founders either expecting miracles from their Rolodexes (see previous info) or fretting that the board will boot them out (see the following). But Shear finds a board can be a highly versatile tool that smart boards put to innovative use, such as helping the company come to grips with strategic and cultural change. "I remember one example where an early venture investor had a conversation with the founder, and the board was also involved," Shear relates. "A year later, the VC took some actions that meant the exact context of that discussion needed to be remembered. The directors were able to supply that context. Without them, there would have been nothing between the founder and the VC."

- **Outgrowing Your Early Board Members**   The young company goes through great changes up to the IPO stage, but "the IPO is not the bright line mark for change," Shear observes. "That happens earlier, when [the company] reaches 50, 100 employees. The company starts moving in different circles and needs new board talent. If you are a director with a tech background and the initial technology push is over, your value is not as high."

  At this point in company growth, it's valuable to have director evaluation in place, less as a tool to judge whether directors are pulling their weight than to decide what new talents you need. "Directors need individualized job descriptions. This is usually done in two stages: first, a shopping list of specific people, and second, a list of general board talent."

- **Self-Dealing**   Board members are only human, and there will be times when their interests conflict with those of the company. Shear recalls a case when "a venture capital director on the board of a young company recruited the company's head of sales away to another venture." A strong policy against self-dealing written into your governance guidelines, as well as a thorough disclosure regimen, can help fend off such instances of your directors versus your company.

- **The Nervous Founder**   Speaking of your company, Shear sees a common problem among founders and entrepreneurs in dealing with a board. "The more naïve founders worry about what control they'll be giving up to a board. At its simplest, there is no control other than performance. If you perform, you control. If you don't, you don't."

Q: I know it can be difficult for CEOs and boards to deal with chairmen/founders who have problems in letting go. But what about the other side of the story? I'm a founder who brought in a CEO, and we all agree that he's doing a good job. But I still find my fingers itching to get involved in day-to-day issues. How do founders kick the habit?

A: For starters, the founder and the board need to turn the chairman's role into a real job. One reason that board chair positions separate from the CEO have never caught on in the United States is because there has never been much of a full-time role there. So perhaps the chair and board can "develop a formal job description for the chairman," suggests Dennis Ross of Marsh's Boardworks consulting venture. Aside from the basic boardroom duties, this would "spell out whatever mentoring role is to be played, as well as other distinct chair responsibilities" (outside contacts, investor relations, fund raising, recruitment, and consulting). Too often the role of chair is treated as an impressive afterthought. No wonder they itch to get back in charge.

Or, as a founder, maybe you should work at doing what you do so well—starting up new ventures. Take charge of launching new subsidiaries or joint ventures of the company, or integrating acquisitions. Such "intrapreneurial" ventures can offer an enormous opportunity for the company, and let a savvy founder do what he does best.

Those Inside Director Blues

Partly a member of the CEO's team, partly a director with fiduciary duties, the inside (or executive) director on the board is increasingly in a tough spot. New reform laws and stock exchange regulations demand ever more independence in the boardroom (and fewer employee directors). Meanwhile, the inside directors who remain are too often viewed (even by the CEO) as a safe board vote for management.

Leonard Hadley is retired chairman and CEO of appliance maker Maytag (and even returned for a brief stint as interim chairman). He currently serves on a number of other major company boards (John Deere and Snap-On). Here he offers several good insights on dealing with those inside director blues:

- "To me, the problems faced by the inside director today argue against the position. You don't really need inside directors other than the CEO, except maybe the CEO in waiting. It relates to how good the board is overall. It's critical to use board seats well, and you don't want too many of them going inside."

- However, *effective* use of the inside director is a marker of both a good board and a good CEO. "Deere and Snap-On each have only one insider today," Hadley says. "But both CEOs are mature and confident, and willing to defer to the insider from time to time. If the two disagree, the CEO may preface the discussion with a comment that he and Joe or whoever disagree on this, but this actually gives the insider the ability to feel comfortable [stating his views]. On some boards, this relationship makes directors uncomfortable, but in others it works fine. It depends on the tone set by the CEO and whether he feels secure."

- If your company's execs don't belong on your board, how about letting them serve on the boards of other firms? "It's a very individual situation," Hadley cautions. "[S]ometimes this may serve an excellent purpose, especially if the company offers the employee the ability to carry back some value for our own company. But in other situations I've said, 'No, don't do it.' There's no rule of thumb for allowing your employees to join other boards. You just have to choose carefully."

- As noted, tighter rules on independence are not only edging insiders off boards, but also outside directors who may have some ties to the company, however vague. Hadley sees this as a mixed blessing. "There are cases where you don't want to kick people off boards, but you have to wonder if some people are conflicted. In some cases, I've received a board report from someone with a tie to the company, and I've had to wonder . . . due to a conflict, did this report have the teeth it should have?"

Q: I'm COO of our corporation, and the CEO has suggested that I join our board. A couple of our other top execs are members of the board, so this move may or not end up as a succession sign. However, I'm uncertain about my role as an inside employee board member, working with the outside directors, my relationship to the CEO (who's also chair), and so on. Any tips?

A: Although most execs see a board seat as the ultimate "in" club, the real governance responsibilities "in some ways make it a no-win position," says top management consultant Deb Cornwall. The CEO will define how you fit into the boardroom. CEOs who strongly manage or even dominate their boards "are inclined to instruct the inside directors on what they can and can't say," observes Cornwall. If the company hits a bad patch, it can be difficult to give this CEO bad news in your executive capacity — and fatal to do so in the boardroom.

Not only can the CEO assume you're a safe vote, but you'll know far more about what's really happening at the company than any of the outside directors. That could leave you biting your tongue in a board meeting when there's a tidbit the CEO wants to keep private. Plus, the outsiders *know* that you know these things, and they may try to pump you for insights that could leave you in trouble.

If results really start slipping and some tricky boardroom politics are at work, you could even be approached about an end-run coup against the CEO.

This all sounds scary, and is, but it's likely any exec who's reached your level has the political skills and boss sensitivity to navigate such a minefield. Be sure to sit down with the CEO at the start to pin down his views on your board loyalties. Listen both to what he says and to what he doesn't say (if the message is "I made you and I can break you," you probably won't be hanging out there for long anyway). Speaking of career prospects, serving as an inside director greatly increases your board value at other firms (assuming the CEO agrees), and it also gives you a leg up with recruiters filling other top exec positions. "It gives you important CEO qualities, seeing how a board works," says Cornwall. "It's an important part of your career repertoire."

Q: I'm CFO at our company and also serve as an inside director on our board, but lately this has become an honor I could live without. The problem is a major new strategic move our chairman/CEO is driving. I don't want to go into details, but I see a potential disaster for the company if we take this approach. I've tried making my case to the CEO on this, but he's adamant, and it's clear that he doesn't like the idea of internal opposition. Our board meets next week, and the new strategy is a key agenda item. As a director, I have a fiduciary duty to oppose this move and vote against it. But as CFO, I know who I work for. How do inside directors deal with these quandaries?

A: This is the biggest problem facing executive directors, and there won't be any easy answers. Leonard Hadley (mentioned previously) faced just such a dilemma when he was heir apparent at Maytag. He sees your attempts to make a case with the CEO in advance as a wise first move.

"Any insider works for the CEO," says Hadley. "He's the boss, and the place to disagree is in the boss's office, not the boardroom." Put some more time in with the CEO to "personally spell out things," he adds. "[T]he value of any good staff member is to have different points of view, and the fact that it might become a board issue doesn't change that."

If the preboard plea fails, you still have a few options, though not great ones. I've heard of outside directors in this dilemma deciding that the night before the board meeting was a handy time to come down with a serious case of the flu. Coming to the board meeting and abstaining on the vote, though, "is not really an option," notes Hadley. "About the only legitimate reason to abstain is when an issue involves you personally."

A more political, though dangerous, choice is for you to discreetly get on the phone with outside members of the board who might share these concerns. Present your views, along with why you can't present them in the board meeting. These directors can then run with your arguments in the boardroom and may bring much more clout to the process.

Of course, "you do this at your own peril," notes Hadley, who dealt with a similar situation in his Maytag days by laying it on the line at the board meeting. "I had a case where I spoke my mind at the boss's displeasure. I was concerned about being unemployed, and it was painful, but I felt I had to do it." Bear in mind that Hadley later ended up as chair of the company, despite taking his risky stand.

What Shareholders? Private and Family Company Boards

Although lots of legal sticks and carrots define the duties of the director at a public corporation, when we're talking about *private* corporations, the roles and responsibilities get murkier. Although many of the legal forms remain the same, others are not, and the boardroom's politics may be far different.

If you serve as a director on a private company board, how are your duties different? How is the private firm board a different animal? On the downside:

- The private firm board can still get away with some of the clubby aspects that are becoming taboo at most public companies. "Members may be very well qualified, but they're still basically buddies," observes Stephen Fowler, head of the online board search service Boardseat.com. "Country club" private boards are also a complaint of Jim Casparie, CEO of Angel Strategies in Newport Beach, California. "A lot of these boards in private or family firms are simply an extension of the primary owners or the management team," Casparie says.

- The private company board can be more of a class system than the public corporate board. "The company may have different classes of owners," says Fowler, based on seniority, funding structure, or majority/minority splits. "Now although directors have a duty to all investors, on the private board you're really there to represent a particular class of ownership."

- Private board members may have fewer oversight tools. "Public companies have very distinct reporting requirements," says Fowler. But on the private company board, "numbers are more from management accountants, so there is less of an independent pass on them." This oversight problem extends to other info sources as well, with private companies facing less scrutiny from outside analysts.

However, positive differences can also be noted between serving on a private board and that of a public company. The strengths of a private company board include:

- **Greater Membership Variety and Flexibility** Bluntly put, it's simpler to get rid of private board members who aren't pulling their weight and easier to add new members when the company seeks a new strategy. "Your role on a board that's 6 months away from going public is completely different from one that just got its first round of financing," notes Jim Casparie.

- **Able to Take a Chance** Private board members are responsible to fewer constituencies, and this can give them greater freedom. "I think a strength of private boards is that they can be more speculative," says Howard Morgan, head of the Arca Group venture consultants and member of many private boards. "Directors can be more speculative in their thinking, without having to be so mindful of all those shareholders."

- **More Hands–on Governance** "I think private company boards provide more attention to detail," adds Morgan. "Private company owners are looking for specific advice from their directors, such as on technical matters, while on a public board that's more unusual."

Board decision making is tricky enough, but when the board includes a strong family ownership bloc and the CEO is an outsider pushing unpopular ideas . . . Well, Ford's Jac Nassar was booted by Motown's Ford Family in 2001, and Carly Fiorina stirred an investor relations nightmare trying to pitch Hewlett-Packard's Compaq takeover to Hewlett family board members. Wise CEOs know that family affairs must be handled carefully, especially if family representatives are still on the board. What boardroom lessons can CEOs learn to keep themselves and relatives from ending up on opposite sides of the table?

- The CEO cannot take the family for granted. The CEO who takes over at a firm with a continuing family presence is typically savvy enough to consider this bloc on the way in. But with time, CEOs too often "stop their concerns about communication," notes Don Jonovic, head of the Family Business Management Center in Cincinnati. "They feel that the board hired them because they know what to do, so why not just go ahead and do it?" Such attitudes are encouraged by the quiet way family ownership often flexes its powers, not making its views known until the CEO has already pushed too far with an unpopular idea. If the family legacy (or worse, endowment) seems threatened, the CEO suddenly finds his sleepy boardroom has become a tiger's den. Still, too many CEOs believe they are exceptions to this rule (as at least one CEO per decade has at Ford).

- The CEO misreads the family. As noted, family ownership blocs, trusts, and family board members can be subtle in expressing their views on CEO strategy. Worse, though, these views will often seem contradictory, competing, and uncertain (in short, a typical boardroom, but with a shared gene pool). Intrafamily squabbles and politics can leave the CEO stranded in an unmarked minefield of agendas.

To survive, learn who the one or two family opinion leaders are, get close, and don't let go. "It's the same as dealing with your major customers and your biggest investors," says Jonovic. "If someone is head of a foundation or a trustee with the family trust, you spend more time with them." Also, don't assume that you have converted family reps or board members because you have silenced them. At H-P, Walter Hewlett claimed that he initially approved the Compaq takeover despite misgivings because of management pressures. The folks with their names on the building have the privilege of changing their minds.

- Strategic goals may have been unclear going in. "There can be a mismatch between goals and objectives," observes Jonovic. "The CEO, the board, and family members may agree that the company needs to grow or increase the stock price, but actually getting there may take the CEO into areas the family finds sensitive." Particularly if a new CEO comes in with some bargaining power, he should strike agreements on a strategy with the board that both sides can live with.

- One aspect of dealing with the family company is crucial but often ignored: The CEO must "make sure that his management team is behind him," says Jonovic. Lieutenants who are disgruntled or dissatisfied with your strategy and family board members who have their doubts about you will seek each other out like opposing poles of a magnet, and "subterranean communications can undermine you." Remember, no CEO boardroom coup succeeds without inside help from upper managers.

- How did Carly Fiorina get so blindsided by family opposition to her Compaq deal? Jonovic opines that "she probably overidentified herself with the strategy and failed to ask the board what they really needed before launching the deal. That left her with little wiggle room."

Q: I'm an outside board member with a mid-sized, family firm. I'm close to the family members, but as an outsider I can also sympathize with the nonfamily managers here. Several rising talents can be found among these managers, but the family is tight knit, and the executives seem a bit frustrated in dealing with them. Succession, strategy, and reinvestment issues are a few of the splits between the family and the outside managers. I see both sides of the matter, but, as a director in the middle, how can (or should) I serve as a go-between?

A: The hard truth is that family/manager go-betweens tend to get crushed. However, if real management talent is allowed to slip away, no one wins in the end.

Start with a look at what you shouldn't do. "Don't triangulate," says Paul Karofsky, head of the Northeastern University Center for Family Business. "Don't talk to one side and then relay messages to the other." A better approach is for you to facilitate and to urge (or even nudge) both sides into expressing their concerns directly to each other. One way to help this is to serve as a boardroom advocate for solid performance evaluation. "Objectify career tracking and compensation issues . . . often emotion rules these in the family firm."

As another "don't," remember that you may be just as inclined to favoritism as anyone else in this scene. "I saw one situation where a nonfamily board member was instrumental in recruiting an outside president," recalls Karofsky. "After a few years, though, the president's performance was slipping, but the director was so closely allied with the guy that he lost his objectivity and saw himself as the president's advocate on the board." This delayed ousting the president, and when the family finally had to fire him, the director lost his seat on the board as well. Moral of the story: Objective performance measures are crucial, even if they work against you.

Advisory Boards: A Governance Workaround

Given the contradictions, dangers, and turmoil facing the corporate board concept, it can help to find alternative workarounds that lift some of the burden. One such tool is the advisory board. These informal panels offer the insight and judgment of a corporate board, but without the liability dangers and legal responsibility. These multifunction groups are growing particularly popular at family-held companies, where a "guidance but not governance" role is well suited to dealing with family owners. Jack Veale, president of Connecticut consulting firm Part-Time CFO and a regional National Association of Corporate Directors head, has helped shape a number of advisory boards for family firms and observes that:

- "Family firms, and especially the founders, seek a group of mentors. They usually want people they already trust: the CPA, the lawyer, and their good friends." Although independence is usually the benchmark for any board, Veale sees honest "cronyism" as both a hallmark and strength of the family advisory board. "Don't dismiss the element of trust . . . in the family dynamic, the advisory board is all about trust. You want someone who can guide your children." Still, this means picking *talent* that you trust, "not just golfing buddies."

- Try the family advisory board *after* you sort out your intrafamily battles. "[Advisory boards] aren't effective with the highest level of family issues; those have to be solved first," Veale says. "They're not family psychiatrists; it's your job to get the relatives to stop fighting over who threw ice cream at whom at age six." Or for that matter, which son has been more loyal and deserves the top slot. Use the family advisory board to advise on *business* matters.

- What sort of business matters? "How to buy other companies, mergers, financing, launching new products, or entering new markets," Veale answers. The board can also advise on trickier issues, such as ownership structure and succession. Although trusted advisors, the panel should be willing to challenge the CEO. At one of Veale's advisory boards, two managing brothers were pulling the company in different strategic directions. "We challenged the brothers as to what the direction of the company should be and helped facilitate an agreement."

- As to board mechanics, "the size of the advisory board is not large," says Veale, "3 to 5 members, though some are as large as 10." If the founder has 10 friends who are savvy in business, he's probably already got company matters well in hand. The advisory boards are typically paid by the meeting, from $700 to $2,000, and meetings are usually quarterly, running a half-day, with some going to a full day. The family CEO chairs the advisory board meeting. Other family members can attend in an ex-officio status, but it's wise for the CEO to include some private time with the board.

That last point should not go without further explanation. As advisory boards have grown as a governance tool, one of the most common questions has been how (and how much) do you pay these board members?

A rough rule of thumb is to pay advisory board members about as much as you do your corporate directors, or perhaps a bit less. Susan Stautberg, head of the Partner.com advisory board service in New York, sees payments ranging from "about $25,000 per year at a big bank to $1,000 per meeting and stock options at young firms." The average seems to be $1,000 to $4,000 per meeting, plus expenses, with meetings an average of four times yearly.

Still, when it comes to advisory board members, you get what you pay for, says Ed Merino, president of Office of the Chairman in California. At the tech firms Merino works with, though, hard advice is often paid with that softest of currencies, stock options. "A lot of times they don't have the cash to get world-class talent. At some techs, advisory board members get up to $3/4$ of 1 percent of equity." Options for these directors tend to have a long tail of time for exercise: 3, 5, even 10 years if the directors want. Advisory board members will have even less direct impact on share price than corporate board members, so "it may take years to create value."

Most advisory board members are paid on a per-meeting basis, but Merino supports paying advisory directors more like corporate directors, with retainers, especially if you pay with equity, which "takes the place of a meeting fee." There's logic behind this idea. The faster pace of business today means that convening an advisory board meeting every few months could be too little too late. Advisory directors now are more often "on call or on the phone," says Merino, so a retainer makes more sense.

In a recent consulting assignment with a technology company working toward its IPO, I discussed adding an advisory board in addition to the standard board of directors. An advisory board is a terrific tool for giving a young company a window outward to trends in the industry, plus sources of talent, capital, and joint ventures.

But we also cooked up an added what-if twist that I thought I'd share. In order to best tap these insights in real time, how about requiring that each advisor prepare a brief monthly (or even biweekly) memo of intelligence the company can use? Between their regular meetings, put this talent to work as your correspondents on their particular expertise. What does the rest of the industry think of your company? What hot talent is ripe for

BONUS NOTE

Advisory board members are the first people you should look to when seeking to hire a consultant. They already have the knowledge of your company and its needs, and a consulting assignment puts a member to work on a short-term dedicated basis.

recruiting? What venture source is interested in what you just happen to be developing? What are the up-to-the-minute trends and opportunities? The corporate board chair could review these updates for immediate gems, but the advisory board can also boil the collected dispatches down for a general perspective report at their face-to-face meetings.

Here's one final advisory board thought starter. Richard "Chip" Morse, a partner in the Massachusetts law firm Morse, Barnes-Brown, Pendleton, serves on the boards of lots of regional tech startups and offers a way *advisory* boards can make life easier for the CEO in dealing with their *corporate* boards.

"A lot of these CEOs are young and inexperienced in running a company, and don't know how to prepare for and manage board meetings," says Morse. "They can use a meeting of their advisory board shortly before the corporate board meeting as a training ground to practice their presentations and try out notions so they don't appear stupid before the people who sign their paycheck."

The day I spoke with him, Morse had just come from such an advisory board meeting. A week before the corporate board met, the CEO got together with the advisory crew for a run-through, complete with "a draft agenda and CEO's report to the board." The advisors were able to spot a few holes in the CEO's presentation, which are now fixed. "I think giving your presentation a tryout before going to the formal board is a terrific idea," concludes Morse.

Investors versus Creditors: Your Biggest Board Conflict

The tech and dot-com massacre of the past few years, combined with our economic slowdown, has seen many companies go from swimming in capital to wondering who to lay off first. For some corporate boards, this brings the hard choices and soul searching of bankruptcy. Bankruptcy is a major trauma for everyone involved in a business, but for the board the demands are particularly harsh. You may end up viewing laid-off workers as the lucky ones. How do you as a director survive the dangers of bankruptcy?

- Realize that your legal duties will change. Boards have a well-established fiduciary duty to shareholders, but when the company goes bankrupt (indeed, *before* it goes bankrupt), your legal duty "shifts to include creditors," notes Myron Sheinfeld, an attorney with the Houston law firm of Sheinfeld Maley & Kay and an expert on board duties.

119

"Once a company enters the vicinity of bankruptcy, you gain a new legal duty to see that nothing is done that could be unfair to creditors. Also, all board actions must treat the creditors equally." No preference can be given to easing the shock for certain vendors or classes of creditors. But when do directors of the troubled company face this new mandate? That's the tricky part. It varies by the state, type of business, financial situation, and creditor structure.

It gets worse if what's left of the company is under a legal shadow. By the end of 2002, bankrupt WorldCom was being run by a squabbling board, two different judges, a court-appointed monitor, a creditor's committee, new CEO John Sidgmore, and Chairman Bert Roberts. "It's almost easier to figure out who *isn't* in charge," quipped *The Wall Street Journal*.[1]

- Boards flirting with bankruptcy should seek good guidance early. "The board needs to talk with counsel, auditors, and outside experts immediately," counsels Sheinfeld. "Be willing to hire outside expertise." The company may need to pinch every penny, but legal second-guessing is far more likely if you fail to spend a few strategic dollars on seeking sound outside counsel.

- The board also needs to stay in close, constant contact with management. "Ask management lots of questions," advises Sheinfeld. "What are they doing to develop business plans to keep the company solvent? What is the current status of tax payments, receivables, payables, collections, and cash? Where are we on payroll, insurance coverage, and any lawsuits? The CEO has to be able to answer this to the satisfaction of the board."

- Prepare to put your life on hold. "Assume you're going to be completely immersed no matter how things work out. Spend a lot of time on the phone with management and other board members." Also, bankruptcy is the moment when you as a director must put your Rolodex to work for the company. Sheinfeld notes that, "If I'm a director, I'm going to be work-

[1]"Who Runs WorldCom?" *The Wall Street Journal*, 16 October 2002.

ing my contacts and keeping intimately involved." This can mean getting on the phone with banks, creditors, suppliers— anyone who can make a difference.

- A strong paper trail is crucial for the board. The bankruptcy or workout period spawns endless legal dangers for directors, so "create a very careful record of what you've actually done," counsels Richard Swanson of the New York law firm Thelen Reid. "Take careful notes, show how you evaluated and picked alternatives, and keep good agendas and minutes." Even your busy, quick telephone conferences should be documented to keep the paper trail solid.

- Finally, smart directors avoid the temptation to bail out. Legally, a director may actually be in *more* danger if he or she quits while the bankruptcy battle is under way. "The director can't just walk away with impunity," says Sheinfeld. "The best protection for the directors is to go into bankruptcy with the board intact."

Your board is a crucial part of any company turnaround effort, but is its membership really up to the task? Ronald Posner, cofounder of San Francisco turnaround firm NetCatalyst, specializes in boardroom changes needed to sort out the dot-com meltdown, where a whole industry is in turnaround mode. His advice on beefing up boards to take on a turnaround is insightful and to the point:

- "Most boards don't like dealing with negatives," says Posner. "They prefer positives, and typically don't include turnaround people. At the point of going public, they always assume things will go well, but those board members struggle in a turn- around." That leaves your board little choice but to lose some upside talent and add some savvy cleanup people. Football teams have dedicated offense and defense squads for a good reason.

- Okay, so what specific talent will your board need for a turn- around? "You'll want an ex-CEO who has dealt with a turn- around, and someone from the financial community who has also dealt with it," Posner explains. "You'll be needing different money-raising talent now." Those who have been there will also know another aspect of turnaround governance. "Assume going into a turnaround that the board will have to work hard, really digging in." Don't plan on vacationing for a while. "I've gone in assuming it will take 6 months, and it ends up taking 3 years."

- Knowing the talent your board will need isn't the same as being able to recruit it. "There are added financial and legal liabilities, so that makes it harder to attract talent. Obviously, you'll have to work to convince them that the company has a future, and offer compensation that's attractive." Since lack of cash is probably the reason a turnaround is needed, be generous with equity.

- Structure the board to drive the turnaround. "I've found that one of the board members should be elected to head a turnaround task force," Posner says. "Otherwise, the board just doesn't act. Maybe this person is the board chair or some other director willing to take action." Forming a dedicated board task force to power your turnaround offers the advantages of speed and specialization, without having to drag a full board through every step of the process.

The Howard Hughes Syndrome: Directors Are Cut off from Staff, Shareholders, and Major Decisions

T he last years of industrialist, billionaire, and eccentric Howard Hughes found him a bizarre figure that still continues to fascinate American culture. Retreating from his industrial and financial empire, Hughes closeted himself in the master bedroom of his luxurious Las Vegas hotel suite, seeking shelter from a world teeming with germs and social change. He kept in contact with his massive business holdings solely through a handful of trusted staffers, and even the staffers were required to disinfect themselves and any papers brought into his presence. The bedroom was kept dark, except for three televisions glaring constantly, piping their filtered worldview into Hughes' corporate clean room. Hughes allowed his hair and nails to grow to ghoulish lengths, and would lay naked in his bed for days at a time, isolated from a world over which he nevertheless continued to exert enormous power.

Well, maybe this metaphor is a bit of a reach for corporate directors. After all, they do have their day jobs at the top of the business world (and tend to be fastidious about their nails, too). Yet the feeling that outside board members are amazingly out of touch with the corporation for which they bear ultimate legal responsibility is hard to deny and is a key weakness of their governance.

It would certainly help if the corporation had staff dedicated to board operations. Unfortunately, such a luxury remains very rare. Despite the heavy new demands it faces, board information, logistics, and operations are still treated as afterthoughts, usually by an already overworked corporate secretary's office. Even if it should gain a few notches in importance, though, the board will still lack a permanent staff presence of its own. Though the board of directors is a constant legal entity, it only has a real, corporeal existence for a few hours every other month. The rest of the time, no one within the company follows up on its priorities, represents its views, or keeps it informed—except for the CEO. As keeper of the board's info pipeline, the chief executive wields basic veto power over what information and voices get through to the boardroom. Though this censorship is far from absolute, it is still a truism that the board sees the corporation through the CEO's eyes.

Below the level of that chief executive, board relations with staff tend to be brief and regimented. The idea of directors building their own informal networks with finance, audit, investor relations (IR), legal, marketing, production, or research is considered unseemly. Hardly anyone came out of the Enron disaster looking good, but one person within the Enron staff gained some whistleblower cachet. Enron VP Sherron Watkins famously sent an August 2001 memo up the company pipeline warning that the company's valuation and accounting scams could "implode in a wave of scandals." Lesser known is that a few days later Watkins relayed a similar SOS to a partner at Enron's audit firm Arthur Andersen.

But guess who *didn't* hear anything from Watkins? As far as we know, no one on Enron's audit committee heard a peep about her concerns until the company was already in meltdown. Don't blame Watkins—most board audit committees do little or nothing to build backchannel info pipelines to company staffers. But this don't-ask-don't-tell model is changing fast. *Time* magazine featured Watkins on its cover, along with two other whistleblowers as "Persons of the Year" for 2002. Indeed, one of the other whistleblowers featured, WorldCom's Cynthia Cooper, has an even stronger employee/board linkage. Her report to the WorldCom board uncovered the massive accounting fraud that pushed the firm into bankruptcy.[1]

Perhaps the most insurrectionary aspects of the Sarbanes-Oxley law are its mandated whistleblower structure for audit irregularities and board-reporting requirements for corporate counsel. Smart boards will view these not as troublesome false alarms, but as golden info opportunities.

This narrowing of the info arteries may be most apparent when it comes to the views of shareholders. On paper, the shareholders elect the board, which then hires management to fulfill investor interests. In reality, this fiduciary triangle is turned on its side. The CEO keeps worried about

[1]"The Whistleblowers," *Time*, 30 December, 2002, cover story.

investors and analysts, and on occasion tells the board a tidbit or two that supports his or her agenda. The only nexus between board members and the shareholders they serve is a name on a proxy ballot and a quick wave from the front row at the annual meeting.

But shareholders are increasingly making their views known in the boardroom, whether the board is ready or not. As of January 2003, the Investor Responsibility Research Center (IRRC) tallied 546 governance related proxy proposals, more than in all of 2002, fueled largely by the flowering of corporate scandals. The biggest increase among these proposals was corporate governance issues (director independence, ending staggered boards, poison pills, and auditor independence). In 2002, a proposal for greater board independence at EMC Corporation drew 22.5 percent shareholder support (and this against management opposition), a remarkable level for such a technical issue.[2] When investors suddenly give a damn about how independent their directors are, those directors need to start building bridges.

When added together, such info blockages keep the board in the dark on some of the biggest decisions it must make. Mergers, acquisitions, strategic moves, investments, and joint ventures have traditionally *not* been causes for boardroom debate. Rather, they featured some brief head nodding over a management presentation and then a quick, perfunctory (and unanimous) yes vote. Among the corporate scandals, this acquiescence resulted in corporate directors under oath in courtrooms and congressional hearings, swearing to God that yes, they were indeed out of the loop and signed off on things that later proved disastrous. Even Howard Hughes wouldn't have debased himself like that.

Building Board Backchannels to Staff

In the good old days (and they're still not so old at a lot of companies), all communication between the board members and company staff was funneled through the CEO's office. The board saw only company reports and projections that had been processed by The Boss.

Times are changing, though, and more boards are insisting that they have direct access to such offices as the CFO, corporate counsel, investor relations, auditors, and whomever else they please. But change brings uncertainty. Just what *are* the new rules of etiquette for contacts between directors and managers?

[2]IRRC press release, "IRRC Tally Shows Record Support for Shareholder Proposals in 2002," 14 June, 2002.

"We're seeing more written policies on boards communicating with staff," observes Carter McNamara, chief at Authenticity Consulting. Laying out a formal policy, discussed by both directors and the CEO, makes clear that the board's ability to reach out for information is important, but also compels thought on the logistics involved.

No boards today will accept a written policy summed up as "no contact," but the next stage of discussion involves the role, if any, the CEO's office will maintain in the process. Sometimes a policy will "suggest that the board notify the CEO that they want to contact a staff member," notes McNamara. But if directors need to ask permission before proceeding, how much power do they really have? A compromise might be a general notification to the CEO's office concurrent with the contact. Or, as part of its policy setting on the issue, the board and chief executive might outline a list of titles and offices that directors can contact whenever they wish, with people deeper down in the company reserved for a "notification" basis.

A problem with some board contacts is that directors frankly don't know who to get in touch with for what infobit, leading to frustration all around. At Agilent Corporation, corporate secretary Craig Nordlund tells me that "each board committee has a staff contact, so if anyone on the committee wants information, they can go right to that staffer." The audit committee, for example, uses the internal audit or controller's office, and the compensation committee uses the head of human resources or executive comp. Directors can also use the corporate secretary's office as a liaison if "they want to arrange a site visit or go to a research lab."

Setting a good policy on board/staff contact can pay off by demanding good faith on both sides. The CEO must accept that directors today can talk to "his people" on their own without palace intrigues being the result. Directors, meanwhile, must realize that they can gum up the works by being indiscreet, clumsy, or intrusive. Talking about a reasonable policy is the first step in making it work.

As the Enron case shows, it's no longer safe to have an out-of-the-loop audit committee, lacking the human intelligence so prized by spy agencies for insight on what's really going on. But how does your audit committee (and the board as a whole) build its audit and finance networks?

- "If the system is corrupted, there will be some well-meaning people desperate for it to be discovered," says Mike Young of Wilkie Farr & Gallagher. He calls for the audit committee to build into its charter unrestricted access to information and people at all levels of the company. "They need the liberty to walk down the hallway and pluck info from anyone."

- The committee can build stronger relationships going in with key staff by being active in their hiring. "The CFO should be interviewed by the audit committee chair during recruitment," observes Martin Zelbow, the seasoned interim CFO we talked with in the "Reason #7" chapter. "This lays out a foundation for continual dialogue . . . the CFO must feel free to call the committee chair directly."

- Building communications on the way *out* can help, too. When key members of the corporate finance and audit staff leave the company, consider seeking a confidential exit report from them to the chair of the audit committee or even scheduling an informal exit interview. If someone is leaving because he or she believes the company's financials are being shaded, you'd like to know about it.

- Building good communications with your audit staff can also benefit by keeping management in the loop or at least within earshot. "I would say to the chief audit executive, *in front of the CEO*, that I want him or her to look in depth at any complex transactions, particularly things like partnership, and report back to the audit committee in executive session—without the CEO present," suggests James Roth, president of the Audittrends consulting firm.

- Perhaps best of all, build informal relations between the audit committee and staffers to get a fix on the rewards, pressures, and ethics these staffers live with daily. Your board should know if execs are being rewarded for taking the high road or if they gain the biggest spiffs for pushing accounting and ethical rules to the limit.

Q: The corporate frauds have our board spooked, especially when we hear how the directors seemed so badly misled until it was too late. I'd like us to institute some sort of effective backchannel (or whistleblower) communication program between the board and executives to ensure that people feel free to come to the board with a misconduct issue. But we also don't want to micromanage from the boardroom, or build a paranoid spy culture. Any ideas?

A: Let's take a closer look at how such whistleblower circuits work and how they can include the board. "The crux of any system is that it has to be safe and easy to use," says Peter Lilienthal, founder of Intouch Management Communications Systems, Inc., in Minneapolis, who encourages a telephone-based system. What if every staffer in your audit, corporate counsel, finance, and compliance departments received the personal telephone numbers and email addresses of all board members, along with a memo encouraging employees to call with confidential concerns? Sounds subversive, anarchic, and maybe even dangerous—but effective.

It may be better to start with a broad employee attitude survey to gauge frontline views of company ethics, attitudes, and values, says Peter Stark, president of Peter Barron Stark Consulting. "You can look at the data and actually see the problems," Stark asserts. He suspects that a confidential survey at Enron would have showed an ethical disaster waiting to happen. He also suggests that directors must be the ones who reach out to employees by sitting in on various management committees with executives. Managers just won't put their careers on the line to contact board members unless they're on a first-name basis.

Still, we know that the board can't be everywhere. But the board (and particularly the audit committee) can help keep the numbers honest by assuring that strong, effective, omnipresent financial internal controls are in place. What sort of things should you be watching?

- Look closely at off-balance sheet debt, suggests audit educator and consultant Robert Jensen. "Where is it? What is the current value?" he asks. Know what assets are offsetting this debt and what sort of controls are keeping an eye on it.

- Take a *very* close look at controls over speculative investments. "Especially derivatives," Jensen says. "A lot of top managers are tempted to speculate on these, so you'll need strong controls."

- When it comes to the company's audit results, what is "material" and needs to be disclosed, and what does not? The answer has changed sharply over the past year, and the audit committee should be shown how the company's internal definitions of materiality have evolved to keep up with new rules and regs.

The board's relationship with corporate counsel has tended to be distant and formal, with counsel drifting in and out of board meetings and offering an occasional opinion. But recent reform legislation and stock exchange rules will push your board and counsel into a much tighter relationship. Compliance demands, sorting out the new laws, and reshaping board membership and structure will call for more legal input into your governance. Is your board on a first-name basis with counsel, and do you know what questions to ask? Consider the following factors in shaping your board's new relationship with counsel:

- Your board and committees are now expected to meet a lot more without the CEO around, and also in closed-door executive sessions with key officers, such as the head of internal audit. Maybe you should add some designated board-on-one time for corporate counsel as well. David Sirignano, an attorney with the Morgan Lewis firm in Washington, suggests adding a private counsel briefing to each board meeting. "If you create a venue, then you're forced to talk. Substance follows procedure."

- Consider evaluating your board's relationship with the corporation counsel's office. Are board relations a line item in the counsel's evaluation? More importantly, are relations from your side built into your *board's* self-evaluation process (outreach needs to begin from the boardroom)? Measure items like the amount of discussion the board shares with the counsel, how well the board has been informed and upgraded to meet governance reforms, and the role the counsel's office plays in preparing the board book.

- One minor idea could have a major impact. "The board chair, or the chair of the audit committee, and counsel should share personal phone numbers," says Sirignano. Try extending this to cell and pager numbers, as well as email addresses. Aside from the anytime-anyplace dialogue potential, this sends a message to both sides that the lines are open.

- Building bridges to the current counsel is good, but getting the board involved in selecting the next counsel could be even better. When hiring a new counsel, management should at least keep appraised of the selection process, and Sirignano says it may even be appropriate to bring some board members into the interview process.

Boardroom isolation can be a problem for succession issues as well. With CEO turnover increasing, more companies look outside the firm to find new candidates. The board is missing an opportunity to build good communications if directors don't tap their personal contacts to aid in the searches. The hands-on, active directors of younger companies in particular often know someone who could be an ideal interim or full-time CEO candidate. How can your board best recruit from this personal network of talent (while avoiding potential problems)?

- Networking, yes, but freelancing, no. The CEO search should still be channeled through "a search committee of the board—that's an absolute requirement," says Tom Sherwin, president of recruiters CEO Resources. "You can't have everyone running off to find their own guy. The venture guys will say you've got to have someone with a big finance background, and sales and marketing directors will push someone with a sales background." If directors with a hot contact are on the committee or must present their name to it, you add a layer of professionalism to the search. Even those with a pet candidate will be more comfortable with the process and less likely to view the prospect's rejection as a personal affront.

- About that CEO search committee: Select two or three directors with the most connections as members, but make sure the group still answers to the whole board. "The committee can introduce the CEO to the rest of the board and act as liaison," says Sherwin. "Otherwise, every member of the board may want to interview the candidate, and that becomes a time-consuming three-ring circus." Worse, it convinces the CEO prospect that the board is disorganized and intrusive—a bunch no one wants to work for.

- Build a sound CEO job description. "By writing a job description, you make sure there's agreement on what your candidate looks like," Sherwin emphasizes. Although you want board members working their Rolodexes for talent, preagreement on the skills and background sought will lessen disputes and misfits. Also, it's a must if you decide to deal with a recruiting firm.

- When directors use their connections to find talent, watch out for poaching problems. If you are a director on the boards of Company A and Company B, and approach a talent at B to take over the top slot at A, then your personal fiduciary duties become an issue. In such cases, the director should "at least discuss the issue first with the CEO of Company B," suggests Sherwin.

A vital aspect of board contact building among staff is the CEO succession process. Here an active board can play an important role—helping to keep a prize second-in-command from jumping ship for a top slot elsewhere. At biotech giant Amgen, COO Kevin Sharer served as #2 behind CEO Gordon Binder since 1992, despite the siren song of CEO offers from other firms. Amgen's strong, active board was a key part of keeping Sharer over the long haul.

Board member Steve Lazarus, a general partner with Arch Venture, notes that "The board can be extremely helpful in these situations. Individual board members have a strong duty of care to establish relations with the successor, and if possible keep him on board." This means that "all communications don't pass through the current CEO; that becomes the eye of a needle."

Building relations with the successor can mean a delicate balancing act between the current and future CEOs. "The CEO is almost by definition in an ambivalent situation," says Lazarus. "He has a clear duty to get a successor in place, but not to be a lame duck. The board should try to have discussions with both of them present, as well as its own discussions without them."

Close personal time with the successor candidate can also help the board ensure that it really wants this candidate after all. Don't assume someone will grow after he or she takes the CEO's seat. "I don't believe you should turn the CEO slot over to an apprentice," Lazarus remarks. "If the person isn't ready, then the board isn't carrying out its duty." In one famous fumble, the board of Coca-Cola in late 1999 squeezed out new CEO Douglas Ivester, despite his careful grooming by predecessor Roberto Goizueta and initial high expectations. In retrospect, Lazarus "can't believe that Ivester went bad all of a sudden. The board was not as intimately aware of Ivester as it should have been." In sum, close relations between the board and #2 will help you keep the best—and weed out the rest.

Q: So far, the CEO succession process at my company has gone well. The current chief executive gave our board a good plan with an inside candidate he's been developing for several years. This front runner is the CEO's protégé and has built up an excellent record. But I have some nagging doubts about his maturity and leadership skills. How can I (or should I) address this with the other board members, who all seem pretty well sold on the candidate?

A: Despite your current CEO's endorsement, if a new CEO isn't up to scratch, it's the board that hasn't been doing its job. "The issue isn't the individual, but the process," says Deborah Cornwall, president of the Corlund Group consultants. This means that if you're having second thoughts, start with the board committee responsible. "Take the chairman of the committee aside to discuss your concerns and have it viewed objectively," Cornwall suggests. Raising concerns about the process at this stage may seem like locking the barn door after the horse is stolen, but the stakes of a leadership failure are so high that you must be willing to act.

Obviously, though, you're in a tricky political situation, so your concerns must be raised discreetly, or doubts about the candidate could prove self-fulfilling. "One option is professional coaching," suggests Deedee Meyers, head of the DDJ Meyers firm in Arizona. She recently consulted with a company "that selected an internal CEO candidate. Though I thought she may not have the maturity needed, I told them I'd go along with the idea if we hired a professional coach." The new CEO seems to be progressing under this tutelage.

The CEO coaching route could be the answer for your problem. It can be approved by the board as a minor detail in the ongoing transition without casting doubt on the new CEO. But a coach brings a trained eye to the candidate's real potential, can help him or her shape up in a hurry, and gives some insurance to your transition process.

How Do You Look to Shareholders?

"No comment" just isn't a viable investor relations policy for most companies nowadays. Investors (not to mention the Securities and Exchange Commission [SEC] and regulators) all want to know more (and more accurate) info about your corporation, its results, and its prospects—and they want to know it now.

With the stakes for good disclosure policy rising, your board should take a close look at how up-to-date and accurate company disclosure policies are. "The company should have a disclosure policy in place, and it needs to be updated and reviewed regularly," notes Warren Grienenberger, a partner with the Chapman & Cutler law firm in Chicago. Though the board has ultimate responsibility on disclosure policy, "actual disclosure is handled by the hired hands, counsel, and accountants," says Grienenberger. So how does the board keep tabs on this crucial policy?

- Decide who will serve as your disclosure pipeline. "Normally, it's corporate counsel who follows developments in disclosure law," says Grienenberger, but auditors, compliance, and investor relations staff should also be keeping tabs on changes to their turf. It may be wise to designate counsel as your disclosure "conduit," the person who collects intelligence from the other offices and interprets changes in disclosure policy.

- How often should the board be brought up-to-speed on these changes? "I suggest that most boards have in-house counsel provide a report once a year on company compliance proce- dures," suggests Herbert Wander, a partner with Katten Muchin Zavis in Chicago. "That way the board can spot any weaknesses and ask what's being done to improve them." For such a Q&A session, it might be wise to have the CFO, outside auditors, and the corporate secretary involved too. Given the tsunami of reforms that have hit in the past year, you might consider a disclosure update as a part of every board meeting for awhile.

- The fact that boards need to get the whole gang together for a thorough disclosure review shows one of the biggest weak- nesses in its oversight: knowing who does what. "The board should ask not only who prepares the financial reports, but who reviews them, and how many people review them," notes Wander. "Who writes the press releases? How many people review them?" SEC and regulatory filings, as well as IR mate- rials, could also benefit from a board looking into the chain of command.

- Keep your board up-to-date on hot disclosure issues. For example, "the SEC is really getting serious on selective disclo- sure," says Wander. "Another issue is the concept of materiality in disclosures. This has been greatly enhanced [by the SEC]. The board needs to ask management how it's reacting to these changes, and whether or not we're in compliance."

- What's the coming issue in disclosure? "More companies are coming out with prerelease alerts, both positive and negative, on whether they'll make earnings estimates," Wander notes.

"Whether the company does this or not, the board should be aware of policy and have discussed the pros and cons at the boardroom level."

Q: I serve on a board that has a good working relationship with the CEO, but the recent corporate scandals have made me realize something disturbing. Almost everything we on the board learn about the company—its financials, market position, regulations, and so on—comes through the CEO's office. I trust our CEO, but are there other data we as directors should be seeing for more of a shareholder's eye view of the firm?

A: One area where the board can set its own destiny today is in information about the company. The Houlihan Lokey investment firm in New York helps craft board info packages of the sort investment bankers review on firms. Bob Hotz, a senior manager, suggests that you seek more info on "competitors, such as their financial performance, key ratios, how costs compare, and their depreciation policies . . . [I]f your company differs, why?"

Also, as a research analyst, Hotz not surprisingly suggests that your board dig into what analysts are saying about your firm, but don't stop with just a couple of positives. "There might be 15 analysts who are positive, but one out there will have a different twist," Hotz says. Other tips: Make sure that info comes monthly, rather than wait for a bundle just before board meetings, and look closely at revenue trends for both your company and competitors.

In August 2000, the SEC approved Regulation Fair Disclosure (FD) as a tool to compel greater corporate disclosure to investors and to eliminate early "whisper" estimates going to favored analysts. Although the pros (and cons) of Regulation FD have filtered throughout your corporation by now, be aware that it also has a specific impact on the board, so keep the following points in mind:

- Remember that the disclosure rules apply not only to company top managers, but also directors. "Originally, the rule named 'directors,' but that was revised to 'senior officers,'" notes Sean P. Prosser, a senior associate in the San Diego office of law firm Brobeck Phleger & Harrison. "However, the SEC already *defines* 'senior officers' to include directors." Thus, the potential cost to the company of your idle chat about the next quarter just shot up.

- Sure, most companies don't include board members in IR presentations, but that's not your only window of liability. "Directors may have ties to a lot of communities, like venture capital, mergers and acquisitions, or financing sources," says Prosser. "When they do, they're still speaking for the company, and if anyone is likely to trade on or publish what's said, there can be trouble."

- "The board needs to be advised on what the company's plans are for complying with FD, and be sure that it won't be violated," notes Prosser. "The board shouldn't have to ask," agrees William Quinlan, a partner with the law firm of McDermot, Will & Emery. "Counsel should be making sure they're briefed on FD, what it means, what the exposures are, how the company is protecting itself, and whether policies have been reviewed." In short, if management doesn't raise the issue to the board, the board must raise it to management.

- The board should insist on a formal, comprehensive company disclosure policy and make it stick. "Think seriously about trying to curb communications," says Quinlan. "Put a program in place that covers who is authorized to deal with analysts. Conventional wisdom tells you that this was a good idea anyway, but FD makes it vital." Speaking of policies, take a second look at your insider trading rules too. These border on disclosure policy and will also be affected.

- Accept that your company and your board members must change some basic behaviors for Regulation FD compliance, even if it proves painful. "Younger companies jump into communicating with both feet; preaching is good business," notes Quinlan. "These companies need to communicate heavily with investors and analysts, but now they may need to pull back, and this can hurt them."

First, let's assume that the board of directors definitely needs to know how shareholders see the company. Secondly, let's accept that the Internet has become the most broad-based, democratic tool for company communication. Therefore, the board has a strong duty to review the company's web presence to ensure its value as an investor relations tool. But the board's Internet IR role demands more depth than just saying "dump the popup ads." How do you bring a unique board perspective to the way your company presents itself on the web?

- Ron Gruner, founder of Shareholder.com, suggests that you begin by putting yourself in the shoes of your target holders. "Are we providing an appropriate mechanism for our shareholders to give governance insight?" This pushes you beyond asking how much info is provided to ask how effectively shareholders are able to interact with you online.

- Ask your IR people if they're researched how online technology can better serve your info audiences. A survey by *IR Magazine* found that 82 percent of investors and analysts want you to email target info to them, and 95 percent of individual investors used the Internet to research stocks (and half of these used the company web site as a primary tool). Does your company's IR give it to them electronically the way they want it? Does your IR staff know whether your target investors do most of their online research at home or at the office? Do they know what percentage of these investors has broadband access? Those still stuck with a dial-up connections ain't gonna love your cute video and audio tricks.

- Is IR keeping up with the latest digital media? How about PDA and pager info delivery?

- Try asking some innovative questions on how the company could use online technology for better, faster (and cheaper) governance. "Electronic proxy voting is well suited to the net," suggests Gruner. "If you could replace paper ballots, you could reduce the cost by a factor of 5 or even 10. If it currently costs 50 cents per shareholder, you could cut the cost to a nickel."

- Want to see a state-of-the-art corporate web site from an IR point of view? Visit British Petroleum's BP.com site, especially for its in-depth corporate governance info (www.bp.com/company_overview/corp_gov/index.asp).

An annual meeting is the one day of the year when shareholders actually get to see the people who represent them in the boardroom. Unfortunately, most companies will make poor use of their boards of directors. At a time when shareholders are feeling edgy, may have tough questions, and need to be assured that the "lights are on in the boardroom," smart corporations will grab this opportunity to make their board part of a smart investor relations strategy. How?

Carl T. Hagburg, president of a New Jersey shareholder relations firm, has attended 300 annual meetings over the years and finds that "best practice is to have the directors up there on the dais, facing the audience." This way the company "sends a strong message that the directors are there in force, and that you're proud of them—they're literally facing the audience." You're not necessarily leaving the directors open for questions (though they might be), but it is a great sign of governance full disclosure. At the least, put your board members in the front row, introduce them, and have them stand and give the group a wave.

As noted, expecting board members to answer shareholder questions is not the norm, but with the past year's corporate convulsions, norms are shifting. "Committee chairs, at least, should now expect to speak," says Hagburg. This remains a bit edgy, but "especially with the new audit committee rules, the committee chair needs to be prepared for questions." Executive pay and options are also hot issues now, so your compensation committee chair may also come in for some grilling.

However, the annual meeting proper isn't the only board IR opportunity here, notes Hagburg. "Directors can be made available at the meet-and-greet session with shareholders." Especially if a contentious proxy issue is expected, your directors can "spend a half-hour before the meeting mingling and shaking hands to defuse tensions."

Be prepared for a potential director downside at your annual meeting, however. In recent years, activists attacking companies on hot social or environmental issues have carried their battles to other corporations whose boards the target firm's directors or top execs may serve. "For years, unions who were trying to organize the Albertson's firm were pursuing its directors at their own companies' annual meetings," Hagburg explains. Put some research into any such spillovers that your directors may bring from other firms or that your top execs may face from outside boards they serve. You may have an activist lightning rod hidden away in the front row (and a potential embarrassment sitting at the board table).

And what sort of questions will those shareholders be asking? Start out by assuming that your corporate governance *will* be of interest to those shareholders. As noted earlier, governance-related proxy proposals are booming. Carol Bowie, governance chief at the IRRC, closely tracks the issue and sees a "substantial increase" in proxy votes on governance topics. "This was not a huge issue, until recently," she says. Audit committee independence seems to be the biggest proxy beef. But what sort of questions can your board expect from the floor (questions for which you'd better have answers)?

- How are outside directors defined as "independent" on this board? Is there an independent nominating committee that comes up with board candidates, or does management lead the process?

- What is the attendance record for each board member?

- Has our audit committee come into compliance with independence and skill guidelines from the Sarbanes-Oxley law, SEC, and major stock exchanges? How does the board evaluate the oversight and skill of the audit committee members?

- What is this board doing to ensure that another Enron situation won't happen here?

- Has the audit committee been fully responsible for engaging the outside audit firm?

- How often does the committee or its chairman meet with the audit firm partner in charge? Does it ever meet with the auditor without any company management present?

- Does the company have any consulting arrangements with the outside audit firm, and has the board reviewed all of these and approved them?

- Do any of the outside directors have other business arrangements with the company or members of management, such as consulting fees or cross-ownership?

Annual meeting season is often a time of busy schedules, big expenses, and big headaches for the corporation. Despite a growing movement to make the annual meeting less of a costly extravaganza, the program is still a time and expense sinkhole for staff. Carl Hagburg, the IR pro quoted earlier, offers some moneysavers the board should ask IR about:

- Use that expensive annual report you've printed up. It can take months to produce and cost up to $10 a copy, so squeeze every dime of marketing value from it that you can. Since you always end up with more copies than you need, have sales put them to work as leave behinds with key customers, info packages for employee prospects, or IR tools for retail brokers and investors.

For that matter, the board should use this opportunity to ask why so many pricey surplus copies of the annual report were printed last year—and cut back.

- Put your proxy card to work for some low-cost, high-value market research. Investors have proven very responsive to questionnaires enclosed with proxy materials, and the mailing costs have already been factored into the proxy mailing.

- Put your Non-Objecting Beneficial Owners (NOBO) file, the list of street-name holders, to work. Combine it with your file of registered holders, and you'll likely find a lot of overlap between holders and households that will allow you to cut costly duplicate mailings.

Q: I've been approached about joining the board of a fast-growing company, but I don't know a great deal about the firm or its people. What's a good place to start when researching a company?

A: It's amazing how many people join a board of directors when the only information they have on the company comes from the company itself. A solid background check on the firm, its industry, officers, competitors, and prospects in order to keep you from marrying in haste is crucial. But even after you join a board, some directors complain that they're not getting the info they really need on the company, and in some cases suspect management of hiding data or even misleading the board. In either case, the ability to pull off some smart boardroom sleuthing is vital.

"It's less sleuthing than intelligence—good solid analysis of data," says Leonard Fuld, president of Fuld & Company, a competitive intelligence firm. "Do a cost analysis, with cost drivers, for major products. What items on the P&L statement are the key ones? If you're a PC maker, for instance, parts inventory could make or break you, so what does storage, inventory, and the cost of parts add up to?" (By the way, if you know too little about the company's industry to judge these key products or services, you don't belong on the board anyway.)

But good sleuthing requires shoe leather as well. "Take a walka-round at the facility to see if the place is hopping," Fuld recommends. With a manufacturing company, get to know folks like shop foremen, shippers, and purchasing managers. "They hear things 9 to 12 months before anyone else."

Bob Chalfin, head of his own business gumshoe shop, would push this research wider still. "I'd speak to the salespeople within the company, customers, and suppliers too," Chalfin says. "That's part of your role as a director."

If you're looking at the prospects of a startup company, much of the bricks and mortar snooping isn't possible. In those cases, substitute research on the people themselves, with some deep background on the major officers, founders, directors, and venture sources to see what sort of buzz exists.

Big Decisions and Big Jobs for the Board

A fidgety economy has slowed the tide of mergers and acquisitions, and it is making more and more of the last decade's brilliant deals look less than brilliant. Good postmerger integration can't salvage a dumb deal, but poor integration can sink the best fit. How can your board build in a strong merger oversight and integration system, and what are the most common deal-sinkers to avoid?

Although any smart board will review the merger or acquisition agreement closely, also insist on knowing about any side deals that didn't make it into the main document. Robert Gilbreath, president of merger software firm Forward Thinking in Atlanta, notes that management, in negotiating deals, often includes informal codicils to keep everyone happy. "They may agree that we'll give your side the VP of sales slot if we get the vice president of manufacturing, for example," Gilbreath states. Division, plants, or markets might be some of the other chess pieces involved. The problem arises when the board doesn't know about these side deals and later either finds their hands tied or that someone on the losing side is unhappy about a reneged pledge. "The board needs to insist to management going in that they know about *all* side deals as part of the due diligence process," says Gilbreath.

Most mergers require some layoffs, and these may be of interest to the board. "Redundancies typically don't come to the board level, but retention of top talent definitely does," counsels Gilbreath. "You may find out that the departure of one key person will lead to three-quarters of the department leaving." Boards should insist on a postmerger plan that addresses this issue, particularly the effect of these "keystone" managers jumping ship.

Another postmerger human factor involves balancing pay scales. "A major issue is when you have positions at the two companies that were roughly comparable, but one was fairly high paid, and the other low," warns Robert Sahl, a partner with WMS management consultants. The board should, at least through the integration, be more involved in the CEO's management pay-setting plans than usual. Make sure that the new unified pay system "positions you where you want to be in the marketplace and to know what it will cost to get there," according to Sahl. He advises that the board seeks a pay-setting scheme that combines job measurement and market pricing rather than solely one or the other.

A final concern is more premerger than postmerger, but it shows the board's increasing role in deals. Gilbreath finds that "boards are growing more strict on the format and quality of information they see, and demanding better due diligence. They're more willing to say 'wait a minute' nowadays."

Although boards have long shown a weakness for waving through hot deals cooked up by management, economic slowdown and global uncertainty have changed the rules for vetting mergers and acquisitions. What should directors look at in reviewing merger deals now?

"I think directors are looking at the same things as before in acquisitions, but the values have come down," says Morton Pierce, chair of the merger practice at Dewey Ballantine in New York. "There's more a sense of pessimism now." Pierce sees boards looking at deals more defensively today and not as a way to expand or leap into a hot new market, but rather as a consolidation or retrenchment tool.

These forces are also stratifying deals by the condition of the company, says Pierce. For healthy firms, deals still tend to be weighed with the upside measures of growth and are a buyer's market, while companies that "are teetering on the brink are more likely to be forced into a deal for survival," according to Pierce. This merger trend is good or bad depending on whether you're the pursuer or the prey.

Short-term measures of the upside and downside of deals are now far more crucial, says Roger Rogowski, principal of Columbia Financial Advisors in Seattle. "When looking at proposals, boards now have to ask what it will do to immediate earnings." Also, all-stock deals have lost their luster. "There may be more desire for cash versus stock," notes Rogowski.

The demise of pooling as a merger accounting tactic and low interest rates are factors shifting this balance.

So has the past year given boards a tougher view of the deals management brings to the table? "By and large, no" says Pierce. "If the opportunity comes along, it will still be pursued, but I think that boards have shown a growing skepticism over the past few years." Most boards already realize that they now must take a tougher look at mergers and acquisitions.

If your board needs to take this tougher look before approving merger and acquisition deals, what questions should you be asking (and what closets should you be peeking into) before it's too late?

- "Due diligence is an ongoing problem," observes Roger Rogowski. "It's been sloppy in many cases, and companies don't get good information on risk." Overzealous estimates of costs saved or revenues enhanced should also be closely challenged.

- Rogowski suggests a good board question for the company's due diligence team: "Give me the five greatest downside risks of this transaction, both between announcement and close, and after the close."

- Then follow up with, "how will you protect against those risks in both time periods?"

- Focus on the *specific* liabilities of the company you're marrying into, advises Rogowski. "In oil, it's the environment; in services, it's retention of repeat customers; in manufacturing, warranties and product liability. Each business can surprise you." The further outside your company's areas of expertise you roam for mergers, the greater the risk of being blindsided.

- The biggest board failure in reviewing mergers, says Robert Apgood, president of Canterbury Group consultants, is valuation. "They don't know what price they should really pay, they don't get a sound value for the company, and they don't know why they really want to buy it."

- Mark Sirower, a noted academic thinker on merger issues and now a consultant with the Boston Group, finds boards too eager to avoid losing a deal even as the price inflates. "Set a firm price and stick to it," he advises. "Are you willing to walk away?" Sirower warns of a last-man-standing mentality that pushes companies to make deals just to keep from being left behind in the rush of consolidation. "This leads to a lot of wacky mergers." Be willing to say no; there will always be more opportunities.

No doubt the oversight that directors offer *inside* the boardroom is invaluable, but it's the networking and contacts they can deliver from *outside* that can really build the company. Particularly at younger firms, you'll want directors to serve as matchmakers and advocates on the outside. But how to do this most effectively? Sarah Gerdes is CEO of Business Marketing Group, a "business matchmaking" firm in Kirkland, Washington, next door to (and closely tapped into) Microsoft. What does this digital-age *Hello Dolly* suggest for putting your directors to work on helping make deals?

- "First, of course, is investment," Gerdes remarks. "Often, management looks to the board for its contacts in the venture world and to identify the best course to seek funding. As the company gets larger, though, potential acquisitions are usually foremost."

- "A second area is recruiting, particularly executive staff. The directors should have lots of experience and a deep network in this area to find outstanding personnel, but this role for the board is often underutilized."

- "The third area [for board networking] is with customers. By the time someone reaches a board position, they should have lots of experience in closing sales, making strategic contacts, and helping provide counsel to marketing." Gerdes sees nothing wrong with putting your directors in a hands-on role in making sales contacts, or even helping to close a crucial deal.

- Number four on the board's matchmaking list is partnerships. "Building these can accelerate your time to market, add innovation, and also help with acquisitions," states Gerdes.

Gerdes says that boards shouldn't hesitate to borrow a tool from the nonprofit board and lay out overt productivity numbers for each director to deliver. "The fundraising requirements of nonprofit or foundation boards are a great model," asserts Gerdes. "Directors may be required to invest in the firm or to bring in so many millions in capital, or initiate so many part-nership contacts, or introduce management to, say, five potential new sales leads. This needs to be thought out and discussed in advance, but could be written into the director's compensation agreement as a factor in setting either cash or equity."

"Does Anyone Know Why We're Here?": Poor Board Meetings and Logistics

ffective tools to help boards use time more wisely and shape more effective agendas, committees, and membership remain rare commodities. Attention to these ho-hum practicalities of boardsmanship may be the single most overlooked tool in improving the quality of corporate governance.

For at least 50 years, our growing collection of college MBA programs has worked to shape the common language and concepts of business management. Despite some grumbling about MBAs versus The Real World, this trend has added universality and professionalism to how our corporations are run. When it comes to the *governance* of those corporations, however, board members are still stuck at the level of anecdotes, old wives' tales, and informal (and often ineffective) networking. This means that we can hardly scold any board for meetings and agendas that are poor because we're only beginning to define board mechanisms that *aren't* poor.

How many directors should an ideal board have? How often should it meet? What is the most effective meeting and committee structure? Can we arrange agendas to offer more and better governance in less time? In my first book, *21ˢᵗ Century Corporate Board* (1996), I observed that board education is like sex education. The continuing demand for this where-do-babies-come-from level of governance info suggests that things are little improved.

Every board (and every board member) has a different answer to these questions and assumes that theirs is the best, but they still remain dissatisfied with the results. No one teaches you how to be a corporate director; you learn on the job, at shareholder expense. The disastrous governance oversights of the Corporate Scandal Class of '02 show us just how expensive this can be.

Perhaps more disturbing, though, is the fact that most of the board logistics and meeting structures at the scandal companies were at least as good as the rest of corporate America's. In 2000, *Chief Executive* magazine named Enron to its list of America's five best boards, and in October 2001, a noted governance publication interviewed Tyco CEO Dennis Kozlowski on his best-practice board tips for new CEOs. (The latter publication was none other than my own *BoardroomINSIDER*, so I reserve a generous serving of crow for myself.)

The corporate scandals and their attendant reform demands mean that the days of amateur board meetings have passed. Boards and their committees now have so much to do, in such detail, that better meetings are a necessity just to stay mediocre. If any board hopes to improve, then learning best practices, rationalizing board and committee work, and not wasting time and effort are essential.

Start with Better Board Meetings

The time and effort demanded by serving on a corporate board has steadily increased, so any ideas that will help you do a better job of governance with less effort are worth their weight in gold. This chapter offers some boardroom timesavers, tips, and advice from people who have discovered ways to provide better boardroom oversight with less.

Elaine Biech, head of the EBB Associates time management consulting firm in Virginia, also serves on several boards and brings her process-improvement eye into the boardroom. Her advice?

- "Board members can become bombarded with information, so I learn to skim over material first for highlights," Biech says. "Learn what's most important for the company and look for that before you dive in. If they hand you a 3-inch-thick binder, it's important to figure out the top three to five issues."

- "It's especially important to read the past board meeting minutes," Biech recommends. This is a great time-saving boardroom tip in itself. Meeting minutes are almost an ideal info summary. Further, reviewing them just before the current meeting is a great way to bring yourself up-to-speed on governance matters as the board left them, allowing you to better pick up where you left off.

- Personal technology definitely has its place in the boardroom. "I bring my laptop right into the meeting to take notes," says Biech. Directors have a bit more latitude in this than other executives may, and if the board is distributing director info electronically, so much the better. Also, Biech recommends that you "keep top board info on your Palm Pilot." The ability to easily store huge amounts of data with such quick, easy access means that smart directors can (and should) keep names, titles, phone numbers, and email for more company contacts.

- Committees are the hot zone for getting things done on boards today. We've discussed how useful advisory boards can be, but Karen VanderLinde, a partner at Pricewaterhouse- Coopers in Virginia, sees great success in a hybrid group, a board "task force." "The board may need to do something at the strategic level, for a new initiative or brainstorming," VanderLinde states. "A limited task force can handle this well."

  The group is chartered by the board and includes members of the board, but it can also tap outside experts, management, and former board members. The task force has a "lifetime of a few months and typically holds half a dozen meetings, a dozen tops," according to VanderLinde, with a lot of its work done over the phone or online. VanderLinde says that the task force has a mandate to deliver solid, strategic bullet points and should have its own chairman, either elected by the group or (preferably) appointed by the board.

What's the most basic definition of the board chair's job? To run the board meetings. But this essential part of the chair's role can bring many pitfalls for board leadership, as well as opportunities to assert and use that leadership most effectively. How does the effective board chair manage the board meeting?

- Consider this as a reason for separating the roles of CEO and board chair. Notice how an executive attains the job of chief executive after a long, strenuous process of proving him- or herself the very best. The role of chairman, however, is usually a title given to the CEO as a final coronation. Distinct talent as a board chair, however, need not be one of the CEO's strong

147

points. "I was never in favor of combining the positions, unless the CEO is not only good, but can run a meeting," observes Ron Zall, head of the Corporate Directors' Institute in Denver.

- Allow freedom of ideas, but maintain discipline on the flow of the meeting. "It's bad leadership to put up with unpreparedness or someone repeating an idea over and over," notes Zall. "A strong chairman knows how to run the meeting to keep everyone focused on the issues, without discussion wandering off in every different direction."

- The meeting agenda is more than just a list on a sheet of paper. "Announce the ground rules on what's to be discussed at the beginning of the meeting. Get the issues out at the beginning too." Although the agenda lets you check off what *must* be covered, this up-front discussion allows the chair to lay out a major unifying theme for the meeting.

- Finally, the chair should lead the meeting by keeping it focused and productive. "Keep the distractions out," counsels Zall. "Make sure they pay attention to what's going on, not getting to the airport or getting their messages" (and ask directors to turn off their cell phones). Also, "get the important things on the agenda early," Zall emphasizes. "For most of us, attention span fades over a board meeting, and the earlier you bring up a major issue, the more attentive they'll be." As part of this, plan wisely for items after the lunch break. A long slide presentation from a staffer who sounds like Ben Stein will likely bring a few snores from around the table.

This leads to another point that is crucial in making your board meetings more effective: Keep things snappy. "Presentations to the board need to be concise and informative," notes Robert Bassett, assistant secretary and counsel at Praxair, Inc. "I frequently give advice on the level of detail our presenters offer so they don't repeat," he says. "[A] lot of our people are tempted to add details of pricing and so on that the board doesn't want."

Staff (typically the corporate secretary/counsel's office) can make a board meeting run much more smoothly with some advance dress rehearsal. "We have a preboard conference with internal management where we run through the agenda and think through the time it will take," says Bassett. The chairman and senior officers attend Praxair's preboard run-through, as do any presenters, staffers, or division heads who will be involved in the agenda. "Often we can whittle down the time involved quite a bit."

Mixing things up in your boardroom can actually make the meeting *more* productive. "More often than not, people sit at the same places all the time," observes board and management consultant John Shulansky. "But if you move them around a bit, you can engender a new community." Directors will strike new sparks with their new neighbors, and the board can actually stir up a fresh chemistry. "Put directors' names on their meeting folders, and put them at new seat locations. Or put the check with their meeting fees at the new spots—*that* gets their attention."

Try turning the typical agenda model upside down too, suggests Shulansky. "Put the most difficult items first. If these critical issues are held off to the end, the board members' attention may be waning. You can address them with greater diligence early in the meeting." Basics, like a chair's report or the approval of the last meeting's minutes, can then be delayed to the end. And if it looks like you'll run out of time for these? "This is a good time to use a consent agenda," Shulansky advises. More on this topic will be offered later.

Staff involvement in board and governance issues usually focuses on the excellent nuts-and-bolts board administrative work by corporate secretaries' offices. But a completely different model for using governance staff is proving its value at many major companies. At Pfizer Corporation, Terry Gallagher is emeritus vice president of corporate governance. In the 1990s, he helped make Pfizer a world leader in corporate governance.

Pfizer's governance issues "are those that deal with investors," Gallagher tells me, focusing on investor relations, particularly in meeting with the investment managers of big funds to pitch the company's governance standards. Pfizer's Corporate Governance office also handles many of the major legal and filing aspects related to governance, such as proxy filings, insider trading rules, and dealings with stock exchanges and state incorporation authorities (keeping them very busy for the past year).

This governance/investor relations (IR) setup has proven popular at other companies as well, including Coca-Cola (where Trey Parris long held this governance position), Aetna, and Texaco. "It varies a bit from company to company," says Gallagher. "Some people are using their IR people directly, while others combine the IR function with corporate governance oversight." As corporate governance becomes more of a vital issue, look for more specialization in how the company supports its board, addressing sub-areas like board administration, legalities, and so on.

To help jump-start your governance guideline update process, I've put together a Governance Guidelines page on the *BoardroomINSIDER* web site (www.boardroominsider.com/guidelines.htm) that collects links to a number of major corporations that offer their guidelines on their corporate web pages. Just click the link, and you'll go straight to the latest in governance yardsticks at such firms as Intel, Boeing, Unocal, Dow Jones, and EDS.

As I said, these are major firms, and by giving their governance guidelines such prominence, you can be pretty sure that the standards are state of the art on setting governance principles. You can mine lots of valuable ideas and measures for such board basics as director terms, committee structure and mandates, independence definitions, and board/management power divisions that will prove valuable. Boeing, for example, includes its excellent, detailed audit committee charter on its page (note that the guidelines are buried a bit in their web page). I've linked to the Compaq guideline page (even though it's now a unit of Hewlett-Packard) because Compaq's governance guidelines were particularly concise and informative.

One other thing you'll notice about most guidelines is that they were obviously drafted with corporate counsel looking over the board's shoulder. Many sticky items such as splitting the roles of CEO and chair, retirement age, and a board seat for an emeritus chair are finessed with terms like "shall be decided by the board as seems in the best interest of the corporation at the time."

Committees: The Next Step in Board Reform

The modern corporate board is a working body, with an emphasis on the word *working*. That means that all the scolding boards now face on oversight, fiduciary duty, and building shareholder value must be translated into the nuts and bolts of boardroom procedure. These ideas need a strong structural *framework* to succeed, and that demands a solid, specialized committee system.

With boardwork more technical, it makes sense to assign more of it to committees able to specialize. The new Securities and Exchange Commission (SEC) regulations on audit committees, for example, lay down such tight rules on member qualification and duties that lax committee activity in itself would be misuse of a company asset. With executive pay packages huge, staggeringly complex, and ever more closely regulated, only a dedicated committee can focus the expertise needed to manage them. In a way, it's like Henry Ford's discovery that he could build a Model T much more efficiently if he broke the process down into a series of specialized steps. It's taken almost a century for corporate boards to learn a similar lesson and realize that they need their committees to provide true professionalism.

But are your committee structures, makeup, and leadership up to the task? Start with a fresh, professional take on what each committee is supposed to do, beginning with the committee charters. Although I offered some targeted information on audit committees earlier, committee chartering should be viewed as an integrated task.

Board pro John Fletcher of Delta Consulting Group, sees charter rewrites focusing on "criteria for membership, composition, self-assessment and evaluation, putting their agenda together, what red flags they should be looking for, and how they get their information." Fletcher adds that "Boards are taking a much more professional attitude about getting the right people and defining their roles." Try this: Take your committee charter descriptions for audit, compensation, nomination, and so on, and ask if they would be detailed enough to fill comparable jobs in corporate staff.

Who actually writes the committee charters? Although the committee itself often drafts these (subject to approval by the full board), it may be wiser to reverse the process. Allowing the entire board to write the charters makes for better coordination of their roles. "I don't think the committee itself should handle its charter," says board structure and pay consultant J. Richard. "These are working committees of the *whole* board, so they shouldn't have autonomy. Everything needs to go back to the full board."

Take a far tougher look at committee assignments and leadership. "It's bad practice just to rotate people from committee to committee," says Ron Zall. Though smaller boards mean there will likely be committee overlap, pulling a savvy finance pro off your audit committee just for the sake of variety doesn't make sense today. Leadership is even more crucial. "A good chair helps to focus and frame issues for the committee, so pick your best," says Zall. "If they're good, your committee will be good. Don't just tell someone that they're chair this year because it's their turn."

With the work of these committees growing so technical and serious, don't demand that committee members do everything themselves. Boards are budgeting extra funds so committees can contract for needed outside consulting help. "Committees are looking for more outside expertise on things like compensation, audit, and legal issues," observes John Fletcher. "Some consultants are starting to work exclusively with boards on these needs." This helps avoid conflicts with what management may want to hear.

It's getting hard to sort out recent U.S. governance reforms (much less how they'll hit your board) without a scorecard, so here's just such a handy scorecard, and online, no less. The McKenna Long Aldrich law firm has published a nifty "Proposed Rules for Nominating/Corporate Governance Committees, Governance Guidelines, and Codes of Ethics" at www.mckennalong.com/attachment.html/articles/693/CorpResp%236.p df. Included are neat summaries of the new NYSE and NASDAQ governance rules, the Business Roundtable's Principles of Corporate Governance, and recommendations from the Council of Institutional Investors. Most helpful is the firm's own list of "Actions Your Can Take Now." I always have a prejudice in favor of any information that answers the board's question of "So *now* what do we do?"

Q: The board of our corporation has a fairly conventional committee structure, with committees making their review and recommendations on their specialties, audit, compensation, and so on. But when their reports come back to our full board for approval, too often members seem to pick the committee findings to death, second-guessing them and rehashing their work. This frustrates many of us and eats up time that could be better used. Any suggestions?

A: The committees of most boards do good work in their fields, but too often the whole board rediscusses their discussions and redecides their decisions, wasting time, spreading confusion, and stirring anger among committee members who see their efforts being wasted. Though this is more common on nonprofit boards, it can be a problem anywhere. How do you ensure an adequate review of committee work without reinventing the wheel?

"If you want something done by a board, clearly spell out its mandate and terms," says Vincent Battistelli, principal at the Governance Group in Vancouver. "Have them do the work, report back with a couple of options, and then don't redo their job." Battistelli says that if the full board can't keep its hands off, it probably lacks respect for the committee, its members, or its leadership, issues that must be addressed through board evaluation.

As for the whole board, "build into your governance policies that, once you assign a task to a group, you won't rehash its calls." And if one or two members of the whole board are constant second-guessers? Battistelli suggests that the chairman offer a little one-on-

one counsel backed up with board-approved time limits. Battistelli provides an example. "Look, Bill, here's what we're gonna do," he begins. "I'll allow you to raise an issue once, but if you try again, I'll cut you off." This limits the amount of damage the board gadfly can do, while still allowing legitimate debate on the committee report.

Stephanie Joseph of the Director's Network consulting firm in New York concurs that the chair must take control here. "That's the chair's job, and if he thinks that the debate is unneeded, the board needs explaining on what its duties are and what to delegate."

Although the United States is mad as hell about corporate chicanery, it's hard to separate this from anger on a closely related populist sore spot: executive pay. Indeed, execs we've seen being led away in handcuffs at Adelphia and WorldCom drew the spotlight less for financial fraud than for looting the company to their own benefit. Even the Sarbanes-Oxley bill touches on CEO pay matters, with clawback provisions for exec bonuses earned through fraudulent numbers. In short, your board's compensation committee will be next to feel the heat on reform.

Assume that if audit now demands at least one member with a solid accounting background, compensation needs a director with strong human resources or executive pay skills. "Boards are woefully put together," says Brent Longnecker, founder of the Resources Connection Group, governance and pay consultants in Texas. "They have namepower, but lack substance. Where are the people with [an] HR or finance background?" Longnecker finds this skill gap strongest on comp where (unlike audit) boards don't even try to recruit a director with pay-setting skills. "The most common qualification for a comp member is that they sit on someone else's comp committee—so what?" Resources Connection checked board bios at the top 200 Fortune firms in 2002 and found exactly *one* comp committee director with an HR background.

Here's a good rule of executive comp for cynics to remember: Whatever corporate reform you impose, it has the effect of boosting CEO pay. Expect your committee to have to juggle the CEO's pay mix to meet the new reform law and other rules, and expect the net trend to be upward. For example, one discussed drawback of CEO results certification is that CEOs will now have to spend more time mucking about in the financials to ensure that everything is on the square. If CEOs must certify their company's numbers (with hefty fines and hard time for misstatements), expect them to make a case that they deserve more money for putting their necks on the line.

Since top executive loans are now largely banned, comp committees may need new tools to tempt and retain talent. "I'm really upset with what they did to [exec] loans," says Longnecker. "They were an excellent form of signing bonus." Boards could offer stock purchase and other loans to attract top execs, and then forgive the loan if they proved successful, or stick to the repayment terms should the exec not work out. Now, new execs can say "forget the loan, give me cash up front," warns Longnecker—and then keep the cash whether they succeed or fail.

Director independence is still a new idea, so it's no wonder that different regulators define it differently. The new reform law, the SEC, and the stock exchanges set a standard for audit committee independence. The IRS, meanwhile, sets a standard for independence on the comp committee, which must be met to retain deductibility of CEO pay. Unfortunately, the two definitions are "radically different," warns Longnecker. "Somewhere down the road, we've got to get the SEC and IRS definitions aligned." So don't assume that an outside director is necessarily considered independent for both committees.

When even the retired pinnacle of 1990s management savvy, GE's Jack Welch, is publicly slammed for his rich retirement package, we know that the old exec pay rules are dead. But what does all this populist ripsnorting over pay and perks have to do with you and your board? *A lot.* Even if no one seems to be looking over your shoulder at your CEO compensation plans, don't assume that change will pass you by. How does your comp committee put the new reforms into practice?

- Start by being familiar with how new SEC and stock exchange rules will *specifically* hit your comp committee. The NYSE now requires listed companies to have a compensation committee of all independent directors, that it have a written charter, and that it be posted on the company's web site (the latter gives you a great online source for charter language). How you'll evaluate CEO performance and factor it into pay must also be spelled out. Even if you're not NYSE listed, assume that this wind of change will soon blow your way.

- Assume that you'll have to be much more careful (and likely stingier) in handling out stock options. Top pay consultant Jim McKinney of the Ross Companies notes that "the era of mega-grants is coming to a close," and your committee must take a much closer look at option accounting issues. "It's almost certain that new grants, either restricted stock or options pursuant to exercise, will include tougher holding periods," says McKinney. The next question on this issue for comp committee debate is, how will you enforce these holding periods?

- With stock more of a headache, assume you'll be increasing the cash portion of your CEO's pay mix. This will be more performance based, as all those stock options were supposed to be, but since these spiffs involve real dollars rather than option funny money, performance measures will be tougher. Also, since cash is involved, the tax consequences for your execs are more immediate and serious.

- Your committee needs to be sure that outside compensation consultants work for *you*, rather than management. Consider building any consultant fees into your board budget and handle the contract yourself to reinforce this.

Board governance committees are a growing trend, but how well do they function, and what is their real job? The quick description of a governance committee defines it as the board body that reviews the effectiveness of board governance standards, procedures, and membership, but the committee is new enough to offer lots of variations. Since it evaluates the board's talent needs, the committee is often an outgrowth of the nominating committee, but with a much-expanded portfolio.

This evolution was seen at the Medtronic corporation, where in the early 1990s the nominating committee "was reconstituted into a governance committee at the same time we put together a set of corporate governance principles," recalls senior legal counsel Carol Malkinson. She notes that laying down these governance principles/guidelines and forming the committee have a chicken-and-egg relationship.

Membership of the committee varies, but is limited to outside, independent board members. At Medtronic, all outside directors (nine) serve on the committee (which meets three times a year). Chairmanship of a governance committee can be a good opportunity to establish a lead director, although most boards don't formally give the committee's chair this title. The lead director remains an informal, subtle concept, but if the committee's chair fills this role, he or she will be better able to serve as a liaison between the CEO and the board overall.

Malkinson finds that the process of establishing a governance committee in itself is a powerful boost to board quality. "This mechanism is built for self-reflection," Malkinson clarifies. "[The] act of coming together and talking about governance leads to rethinking of these points."

Grant Thornton consultants have a good online primer on governance committees at the GT web site (http://204.168.25.87/resources/assurance/change/changee.html). The following is a condensed version of their job description for the committee:

- Select, find, interview, and recommend board candidates.
- Make sure new directors receive the proper training and orientation.
- Approve changes in board size, age limits, tenure, meetings, procedures, and so on.
- Approve board member pay, pay methods, and benefits.
- Appoint committee chairs and membership.
- Review the function and value of committees.
- Coordinate CEO and board evaluations.

The corporate board's nominating committee has always been a bit of an afterthought, meeting maybe once a year to discuss whether anyone knew someone who could take Old Fred's place on the board now that he was retiring (assuming the board even bothered with a nominating committee). But the new, improved nominating committee is turning into a powerful oversight tool for all the new governance demands faced by corporate boards. J. Richard, who discussed committee trends earlier, sees some specific changes in nominations. Among them are the following:

- "Nominations [are] evolving into an overall directors' and governance committee at a lot of corporations," Richard says. "They can then do everything from selecting directors to evaluating them, to setting their pay, to naming committee chairs. Also, they set governance procedures for the board, which has become one of the hottest demands."

- Turning your nominating committee into a governance committee is a natural move. It can dovetail board search, evaluation, and board info programs into a rational process that finds the best, uses them well, and grades the results. At progressive boards, the committee also taps many outside talents, like evaluation consultants and search firms. The latter is important, because this new committee casts a much broader net for board talent. "This committee is open to recommendations from anyone," notes Richard. "They know they have to work with a search firm, and they're not afraid to accept board nominations from investors."

- The logistics of this new committee are tougher, though. First, you should direct your best boardroom talent toward it. "I've found that, on average, 75 percent of outside directors are good, and the other 25 percent are expendable, either sleeping, missing meetings, or out of their depth," says Richard. Your three best outsiders would work well, though work demands may "push membership to four or even five." No "once-a-year stuff" either; this committee meets four times a year, with plenty of telephone time in between.

- Leadership? A natural chair for your new governance committee is the board's lead director, either formal or informal. Having a leader with such gravity also makes it clear how important this committee's job is.

Also over the horizon is a renewed interest in board finance committees. Audit committees, by nature, have two limitations. First, they tend to take a somewhat micro view of the company's financials—not asking the best strategy for the use of assets, but rather whether that use is well controlled. Second, the audit committee has a forensic, after-the-fact perspective. A dumb corporate idea can stumble on for years, as long as its bookkeeping is well managed.

With the rise of highly complex, highly leveraged, and speculative business models (paging Enron, Tyco, WorldCom, etc.), the audit committee's role seems ever more limited. Why not, then, form a committee that specializes in a top-down, strategic view of company finance going in?

Finance committees of the board have been around forever, but seem to be growing in popularity. The 2001 Korn/Ferry board survey found finance committees at 40 percent of major corporations, up from 32 percent in 1995. Finance committees are found at "Dupont, Unilever . . . any company with substantial financial transactions," observes Larry Cunningham, head of the Center for Corporate Governance at Cardozo Law School. "There is some overlap with audit, but a finance committee can keep things from falling through the cracks."

A dedicated board finance committee could focus data and expertise on major capital and financial moves of the company on a prospective basis. Complex initiatives (and especially risky ones) such as Enron's internal partnerships, derivatives, and subsidiary arrangements could be approved based on rules set up by the committee going in, forcing managers to pitch the idea. And if the ideas are just too complex for the finance committee to get a handle on? Then they say no. A good ground rule here is that if management can't explain it, the board shouldn't buy it.

Agenda Lifesavers, Big and Small

So here you have a boardroom full of important, high-net-worth people who can only devote a limited amount of time to contributing to the success of your company. Do you *really* want to waste their time with a clumsy agenda? Here's a roundup of board meeting agenda gems:

- Realize that many agenda items can be condensed. "In most boards, administrative matters are almost a rubber stamp," notes Bob Middlestadt, vice dean and board leader at the Wharton School. These items, such as personnel issues and credit line or expenditure approvals, can be sent in advance with the agenda as a proposed board resolution. At the meeting, they can be approved with a single vote (though if anyone wants to discuss an item, they are free to do so). This works like the consent agenda idea discussed later, but it goes a step further to assemble a bundle of housekeeping approvals in advance.

- Speaking of rubber stamps, in the ideal board meeting, the whole board would have such confidence in the work of its committees that all committee recommendations would be swiftly waved through. In reality, though, the full board too often picks apart committee work, slowing the agenda and prompting mass frustration. Middlestadt encourages committee meetings just before the full board meetings, with a strong open-door policy, allowing interested noncommittee members to arrive early and sit in. "By being there to hear the committee discussion (but not taking part), directors will have less to discuss in the full board meeting," Middlestadt says. Lacking a specific confidentiality issue, keep committee doors open.

- Between the actual board meeting with its agenda and the minutes that go out in the next meeting's info pack, a huge gap can take place. This means that directors forget what was discussed and what they may have committed to until just before the next meeting. Bill Chambers, a business strategist with BFO Consulting, recommends that boards respond with this clever gem: interim minutes. "Have someone at the meeting transcribe minutes as you go, and when you finish the meeting, print off a copy of what just went on," Chambers suggests. These are not the true minutes, but an interim record that directors can take home to remind themselves of business to be done and review for mistakes or omissions.

  Bob Middlestadt also suggests that the CEO prepare a brief memo to directors just a day or two before the board meeting. This is a sort of personal note to the agenda, "one or two pages of bullet points on items in the agenda the CEO would like to discuss, or to add detail or context," according to Middlestadt. Such an "agenda addenda" can speed the meeting by highlighting focus points.

Board agenda planning, as with so many other aspects of business, goes faster if you (1) break it down into a process with distinct steps and (2) reuse common elements. Katherine Combs, vice president and corporate secretary at Excelon Corporation, was 2002 chair of the Corporate Governance Committee of the American Society of Corporate Secretaries. She has built a bulletproof board planning/agenda/minuting system that serves her well at Excelon. Combs starts her board agenda building a year in advance. "The board and committees have charters, and some have calendars, so we start blocking out agendas around the things they say they'll do in their charters," Combs says. "There are approximately four meetings per year. We can look at the charter and say that in July, for example, we suggest that they do this and that.

"Then . . . my staff [and I] try to meet with our board chair on agenda development, and with the committee chairs too. We end up putting together a matrix that shows each board and committee meeting, and looks like a spreadsheet," Combs explains. "This shows at a glance when things

BONUS NOTE

"Don't take a break for lunch," Bob Middlestadt recommends. "This just breaks the rhythm. In most boards I'm on now, if the morning's work goes past lunch, they just bring lunch into the room and continue the work."

are going to be considered." Last-minute items need to be included, of course, but fit smoothly into the matrix format.

But this process doesn't end when the board meeting adjourns. Combs states that by "developing advance materials and scripts for the meetings, we can reuse text so it becomes the meeting's minutes . . . you want to reuse boilerplate when you can." Combs' staff requires only a day for processing the meeting minutes with this system, which also smoothes workflow and eases long-term board work planning.

Boards have also discovered another agenda tool. This tool can cut the time you spend on boilerplate board matters, and sometimes even help eliminate marginal board meetings altogether. On the other hand, some people who know avoid it like the plague, considering it too dangerous and not worth the trouble anyway. What is this boardroom equivalent of nuclear power? The consent agenda.

A consent agenda is a parliamentary tool that bundles a number of routine, but necessary, agenda items into one item that usually draws no debate and is quickly voted up or down. The board then moves on to more substantive issues that warrant the real discussion. Typically, consent agenda items are spelled out in detail in the mailing that goes to the board before the meeting, allowing full review of the material. When the vote is taken, questions or comments should be encouraged, but typically the items are ho-hum: renewal of loan covenants, pay raises, continuing to use the same audit firm, or unexceptional committee reports.

Many corporate boards find the consent agenda a valuable timesaver, and they are particularly popular with nonprofit boards, which often face a large number of standard approvals. But that doesn't mean consent agendas are loved by one and all. Eric Orlinsky, an experienced counselor with the corporate law firm of Saul Ewing Weinberg & Green, says, "I don't believe the time savings are all that critical," and other observers (especially on the legal side) fret over potential liability exposure.

However, Greg Varallo, a partner with the firm of Richards Layton & Finger, suggests stretching the idea even further and using consent *meetings*. "In lieu of [regular] meetings, they're a terrific way to accomplish routine tasks," Varallo says. Although he cautions against using consent meetings for major, sensitive issues, they can be just the ticket for board meetings with light agendas or when no one wants to fly in from the beach just to say "aye" to a standard stock option plan. If the "agenda is circulated to all the board members, and they unanimously agree, under Delaware law, it's okay," Varallo states.

Consent agendas can be a valuable board meeting tool, but make sure that any items waved through won't come back to haunt you.

Coping with Your Personal Boardroom

For too long, we've assumed that corporate directors know everything—so much so that they're afraid to ask when they *don't* know something. This is most apparent when a person attends his or her first board meeting, where even someone with the most solid of resumes faces a wholly new, unique power system.

How can you fit into a new board environment most smoothly? And what are the most common boardroom mistakes that could mark you as a governance amateur?

- "The first sign is stopping and asking about everything, but another is being afraid to ask *anything*," observes John Gorman, a partner with the Luse Lehman and Gorman law firm who works extensively in new director orientation. "The new director has to find a route in between. You don't want to be a silent partner for any period of time, but you have to use discretion to make your input without things grinding to a halt." As a new board member you need to be a quick study, but if you've gotten to this level, it's likely you already are.

- You've been named to this board in part for the past skills you've gained, but "be careful not to overdo the references to your prior experience," warns Gorman. "If you keep saying that this is the way we do things at my company, you can turn off the other board members." Instead, let the knowledge you've gained outside the boardroom shape specific suggestions targeting the situation at hand.

- To prevent novice boardroom fumbles, the new director should seek out (or the smart board should assign) a buddy to provide one-on-one director feedback and advice. Carter McNamara, president of Authenticity Consulting, which handles extensive boardwork, suggests assigning this mentor and then "at the end of the board meeting, he should set aside a few minutes to talk with the new director, critiquing his performance." If the new kid is making errors, McNamara advises not isolating the individual, but making his or her problem a cause for overall board support. "What I see working best is for the board chair to treat the new member's problem as an overall board problem."

- McNamara also advises making a general post-game review of the board's meeting a standard coda to *every* meeting. Even a few minutes of general discussion on how things went not only uncovers unspoken problems, but it can also gently hint at their solutions to all involved.

A business group called Women Connect recently sent me an article called "Boardroom Bound," which offered a solid first-person walkthrough on how to establish yourself in your first board seat. These ideas can help new directors, regardless of their gender. Here are some key points:

- Put courtesy first. The boardroom is like the U.S. Congress, where politicos may frankly view their fellow members as venal morons, but will always refer to each other as "my esteemed colleague."

- Respect authority and each other. Direct confrontation or ignoring seniority and titles in the board meeting is taboo, even if you know something being said is blatantly wrong. Save it for a personal chat after the meeting.

- Be visibly prepared. That means not just having studied the material in your board book in advance, but also making sure that everyone *knows* it, with such techniques as highlighted info or notes on particular issues. Make clear to your colleagues that you've done your homework, but avoid tossing off infobits or random questions just to prove how clever you are.

- Watch your seat. See if there's a power section of the board table and gravitate toward that neighborhood, but also try to rotate yourself around the group to build relationships.

- Appearances count, particularly for the new woman on the board. Cute micro-skirts went out with Internet Time and *Ally McBeal*. Even if fun, edgy, or sexy outfits are acceptable back at your office, they still lack gravity in the boardroom—where it's never casual Friday.

Though it's by no means a mega-trend, the number of corporate boards adding international directors is steadily growing (even at smaller, home-town companies where none of the staff ever used to need a passport). Tech firms, in particular, may have research and capital people from around the globe in their boardroom.

But multinational business collaborations add to the danger of culture clashes. Such miscues are especially common (and dangerous) at board meetings, where the stakes are so high and so much of the value added comes through personal interaction. How can you guard against "international incidents" in your boardroom?

First, learn what corporate governance really means in the director's particular culture. A U.S.-based firm added a noted Japanese national to its board as a director, but was disappointed when (despite excellent English skills), he sat silent as a stone through the first several meetings. The board chair took this director out for a one-on-one dinner and found him full of valuable ideas, yet the director was puzzled about the "odd" way U.S. board meetings worked. In Japan, it turns out, board members tend to talk out board business in advance of the board meeting, and the actual meeting itself is a quick legal affirmation of what's already been decided.

By global standards, the American boardroom is a pretty freewheeling place. "Americans have a style that combines informality with aggressiveness, and many cultures find that confusing," notes Pam Pappas Stanoch, chief of Minnesota-based culture consultants Window on the World. "The Scandinavians or Dutch, for example, find U.S. boards informal, but at the same time assertive and noninclusive. Americans tend to push their ideas, but the other cultures are more consensus based and inclusive." Some foreign directors may seem to acquiesce to the pushy Yanks, but in fact could be taking a passive-aggressive role that in the end sabotages the proposal. The moral is, don't assume that boardroom silence means consent.

Most world cultures find family and personal ties at least as important as business relationships. American directors tend to miss this cultural cue. "Three U.S. directors joined the board of a major Brazilian firm," recalls Stanoch. "They attended their first board meeting, but after 2 hours, the chairman called for an adjournment until tomorrow. His mother was going on a trip, and he wanted to visit her before she left. The other local directors saw nothing wrong in this, but the Americans were disappointed and even sarcastic about the delay."

The more mixed your board, the slower the pace should be, and the more interpersonal time you should offer for bonding. "Build in time for informal relations, with longer breaks and more time for directors to rest their minds and share information," advises Stanoch. Remember also that taking part in a board meeting held in a second language demands much more tiring mental effort for your international members. Speaking of languages, consider translation for some board materials to ease this burden and also to make sure no directors feel left out of the info flow.

Keeping It Legal: New Board Meeting Dangers

High-profile arrests and perp walks for execs at the scandal companies (along with shakiness in many of the world's stock markets) should prompt your board to take a fresh look at its liability threats. Rest assured that your board can expect director and officer (D&O) liability to attack from some new directions. Charles Demonico, chair of the Corporate Governance Practice at Pittsburgh law firm Dickie McCamey Chilcote, offers this view of what's on the liability horizon.

"A first concern is the new effect of corporate compliance oversight on the company itself, and the way it relates to directors, who can have personal civil liability," Demonico explains. This compliance oversight by the board will extend particularly to how closely it watches top management, says Demonico. "More cases are being filed on the board's general duty to exercise appropriate oversight of management." Recent cases of accounting and audit fraud by top managers have left many boards red-faced. But the SEC and investors have grown more demanding and are more likely now to put board members in the dock.

Keep a close eye on your corporation's subsidiaries. "The Supreme Court has traditionally limited the liability of a parent for a subsidiary, but this shield only held if the parent was not involved in the affairs of the subsidiary," says Demonico. "Some of these traditional barriers are falling, though." Two examples are dot-com and tech companies, which may be a maze of cross-holdings and shared management. For more information on subsidiary boards, see the following section.

Lou Kling, an attorney in the New York office of Skadden Arps, works extensively on parent/subsidiary issues and offers some advice. "The biggest mistake parent corporations make is not respecting the corporate formalities between the parent and subsidiary. Failing to maintain separation from the subsidiary creates a risk that someone will be able to claim in court that the parent should be on the hook for subsidiary actions." These formality breakdowns include not maintaining separate books, parent officers signing documents on behalf of the subsidiary, or even signing subsidiary documents in the parent's own name.

Such failings are easily avoided through rigorous internal policies of separation, but if some sort of breakdown pierces the corporate veil into the boardroom, the problem will already be out of hand. The board should respond to the issue up front by insisting that subsidiary issues be handled in the subsidiary's boardroom. "The mere fact that the board is looking at this helps," says Kling. "You want the subsidiary board to really function as a board, authorizing material transactions and such on its own behalf."

With busier, more dispersed directors having to confer more often, the number of telephonic board meetings has soared. But too often the unique legal and tactical issues that arise when a board meets over the phone are disregarded—until a legal blowup makes it look like the board was playing it fast and loose. J. Grant McGuire, a partner with the West Virginia firm of Campbell Woods Huntington, has seen a number of cases where a quick telephonic board meeting led to long litigation and offers these tips:

- Make sure in advance of your legal ground for board meetings on the wire. "Provide in your corporate bylaws for the validity of telephonic board meetings, and check your state laws to make sure that such meetings are allowed, or at least are not disallowed." Build into your bylaws things that will make telephonic meetings practical as well. Once you have a quorum online, state that the quorum is considered present, even if a director sneaks away from the phone for a minute. Votes should be taken the way NASA does prelaunch checks, with each member being identified and saying "yea."

- Speaking of geographic legal issues, Delaware corporations should have no problem with telephonic meetings, but, for example, it was unclear until recently whether West Virginia law allowed board action over the phone. Geography should only be a concern regarding the *state of incorporation*. Where the company headquarters is, where the board or committee chair is, or where the majority of directors involved is located shouldn't be factors—just where the company legally hangs its hat.

- "My advice is not to tape-record telephonic meetings," says McGuire. "Have a good professional notetaker like the corporate secretary making notes from the speakerphone. Otherwise, the things people say can always be taken out of context."

- Be aware that security is a bigger issue with telephonic board meetings and it could reflect badly on you if a leak occurs. The ideal is for everyone to be on a handheld, hardwired phone. Cell phones are subject to interception, and do you really want to discuss board business while walking down a street in New York? Speakerphones should likewise be avoided unless you are in your own private office. No speakerphone governance from poolside in Cancun, thank you.

- McGuire notes that, while telephonic board meetings are in most cases perfectly legal and binding, for some issues it may *look* better to convene a face-to-face meeting. "The board might be subject to later criticism if it handles serious business like interviewing a new audit firm or CEO candidate over the phone," McGuire says. As a backup, the board can approve a resolution validating its telephonic decision at its next face-to-face meeting.

We Don't Talk about That: Boards Do a Lousy Job of Handling Their Personal Issues

The boardroom itself is both a powerful symbol of and nexus for the board's deliberations. In the last chapter, I noted that board education is like sex education, but governance offers another family values metaphor: the boardroom as home. Like the traditional view of the family castle, the boardroom is a place that keeps its secrets from the outside world. What goes on in there stays there, and talking outside boardroom doors is considered a serious taboo, a betrayal that even the most sincere of good governance leaders avoid.

"It's almost a religious view, fervently held, that directors don't talk," observes Richard Koppes, a governance attorney with the Jones Day law firm in California and an Investor Responsibility Research Center board member. "They don't talk to the press. They don't talk to investors. They don't talk about what goes on in the boardroom."[1] As an editor of two governance publications, I've learned that the only way to pry information out of directors is to first assure them that you're *not* trying to get them to tell tales out of school.

Part of the reason for this reticence, I suspect, is that there is little open discussion to report on. A corporate board is a unique, if not bizarre, interpersonal field. By the time you are named to a corporate board, you've earned plenty of bones in dealing with subordinates, business meetings, negotiating with peers, and general politicking. You know how to handle power and get things done. But now you find yourself in a boardroom,

---

[1]"The Directors," *Fortune*, 14 October 2002.

gathered around a table with other people who are just as much savvy Type A's as yourself, and you're supposed to function as collegial peers.

Since even active boards may have full meetings just six times a year (and four is more common), little time is available to develop an effective boardroom chemistry. Further, most of the real work of a board doesn't happen around that mahogany table, but in hurried conference calls, one-on-one chats, or over lunch. Really difficult tasks (showing a CEO the gate, getting the skinny on a legal crisis, or sorting out a boardroom battle) typically happen over a hushed cup of coffee the night before a board meeting in scenes out of a spy novel. As Tom Clancy will tell you, not all of us are cut out to be spies.

Neither are directors the sort who sit around spilling their guts to each other, sharing feelings, or giving big group hugs. Even the idea of individual board members sharing concerns outside of the CEO's earshot is still somewhat subversive. Also, if a board member doesn't know some aspect of corporate governance, he or she is in no position to pop up with dumb questions. Directors are the pros; they're supposed to already *know* all the answers, right? So directors suffer in silence through such questions as how to challenge the CEO without destroying him or her, how to ease an incompetent director off the board, or how to sort out founder/family/venture-capital/board disputes.

Boards can and do evaluate themselves, of course, but if the system encourages you to repress your own concerns, imagine how effective it is in discouraging you from pointing out that others around the table are failing. Boardrooms, as noted, are the well-shuttered house that shelters its own corporate family. If that family is dysfunctional, the members have no way to seek help, and outsiders never, ever find out.

The Boardroom Newbie (and Wannabe)

Despite the growing workload and dangers, many of us would still like to add a board seat to our resume, but aren't sure how to proceed. How can you improve your "boardability?"

- Start with (and make wise use of) nonprofit board opportunities. "Nonprofits are always looking for directors, but be strategic in selecting among them," counsels Larry Stybel, the head of board search and advisory firm Stybel Peabody in Boston. Aim for boards that you can "grow into," Stybel says. "If you're the most experienced person on the board, it's probably not for you."

- Network wisely. Cultivate contacts among partners in venture firms and law firms, as well as banks. Let them know about your board interests. These are people in a position to bring you together with board opportunities.

- Take advantage of the growing corporate governance network. Along with the board search contacts already mentioned, more business schools in the United States and worldwide are offering governance courses, seminars, and degrees. (The Institutional Shareholder Services' "Corporate Governance Quotient" web site offers an excellent listing of these programs at www.isscgq.com/programlist.htm.)

Your Board Networking Strategy

With service on a corporate board growing more dangerous by the day, you need to make sure your board seat offers you the most personal value possible. One way is to make the smartest use of the boardroom's networking possibilities. Networking potential was one of the reasons you talked yourself into taking that board seat in the first place, but the rules are subtle. Networking professionals offer the following tips for making the best use of those Type As sitting at the table with you:

- Establish who you are and where you come from, and keep that in the context of your board discussions. However, Susan Roane, business speaker and author of the book *What Do I Say Next?*, asserts that "the boundary is the person who talks about his or her services and products, who really sells as part of the conversation."

- A key not only to good board networking, but also to effective boardsmanship overall is knowing the background of your fellow directors before you start working with them. "Do your homework on the company and the other board members first," Roane suggests. "[W]alking in with a blank slate is not a good idea." A good tip is to take a few minutes to log on and do a Google search on everyone else who'll be on the board with you. Learning about Joe's vitae is good, but discovering that he's an avid model train collector can be networking gold.

- Board meetings offer good mingling opportunities with breaks, lunches, and chats in the cab to the airport. Set yourself a goal of at least *one* brief conversation with every member of the board at each board meeting.

- Make effective follow-ups part of your board networking strategy. Be generous in sending emails or personal notes the day after the board meets to members who made an especially good point or contribution, or who offered you some useful advice.

Overall though, the rules of board etiquette are up for grabs. "The dynamics of the boardroom have major problems," says Cynthia Lett of Lett Group consultants. "People tiptoe around straight talk." Nothing quite prepares you for the etiquette of the boardroom, but here are a few rules of engagement from folks who've been there.

Listening in the boardroom is too often a lost art. "Outside directors are obviously high-level, successful people" says Barbara Pachter, president of her own business etiquette service. "But when they get to that level, they tend to be listened *to* rather than vice versa." A CEO may have gotten used to meetings with staff where his or her views are the final word, so brush up on your negotiating skills. In the boardroom, directors must not "assume their way is the only way," Pachter says. "[L]earn to confront peers in a positive way." Unless you own a good chunk of the company, power as a director is earned.

The board is a group, so treat it as one. "Everyone has to learn how to build a consensus in the boardroom," notes Cynthia Lett. "Work calmly on building common goals that everyone will appreciate." Legally, the board is a single entity, so each member is married to whatever the board approves. Use this legal idea as a litmus test for how your board decides. If an issue is divisive but still could gain a bare majority vote, maybe you should consider putting off the proposal. A divided board is a vulnerable board—vulnerable to bad choices, second guessing, and litigation.

The new company's first board of directors presents an incredible opportunity to start the firm off on the right foot, with smart oversight, well-defined roles, and a prejudice toward shareholder value. But it can also lead to a battling clique of underqualified, self-serving venture capitalists (VCs), buddies, and clueless founders giving the legal minimum of oversight—if that much.

Entrepreneurs in particular must learn to cope with the new idea of a board telling them what to do. However, there's more to this matter than the founder just learning to "deal with it" (as business advisors often suggest). Feuding founders and directors suggest deeper problems with governance that isn't working. Few startup boards give much thought to how their boardroom procedures can be designed to make them much more effective. Their committee setup is a minor, ineffective distraction, and board self-evaluation, if considered at all, is dismissed as a wasteful frill.

Worse, the young firm's governance can suffer from the very individuals who drive it. A hot myth of governance is that a director who owns a substantial chunk of equity in a business must make a better board member. No doubt the motivation is there, but this investor may still know little about the business involved or how to serve as an effective director. He or she may also have a personal agenda to pursue. Meanwhile, as discussed later, a founder may view the board as the other end of a tug of war rather than as a resource. Putting effort into good governance from the start is more than just a procedural frill. It can help draw a fractious board and its leadership together and point them in the right direction.

Q: I'm a woman entrepreneur with my own private company, and I've been invited to serve on my first outside board seat. Not only is this my first board, but I'll be the only woman director on this board. Any advice on preparing for this role?

A: Start out by making sure that you really want to take this board seat. As the need for talented leaders and diversity has increased, candidates with your background are in a seller's market. If you should pass on this board, another offer may be just around the corner. Madeline Condit, a senior partner in the board practice at Korn/Ferry in Chicago, suggests that you begin by asking one question: "Why me?" Condit advises sitting down for a candid talk with the CEO or board chair. "Do they want a woman on the board, or do they want your specific expertise? Either reason is acceptable, but it's important to know." Follow that up with a frank discussion (and your own instincts, since answers may not be forthcoming) on "the board's culture, background, decorum, and social setting." She also advises digging into the board's operating style: "How does the chair like to conduct meetings? Is most work done in committee? Is there much private discussion between meetings? and so on."

As the new kid in town, expect that you'll need to start by learning the board's culture before trying to change it, and if that culture is one you can't fit into, walk away. As a woman, Condit finds that, once she joins a board and establishes her professional savvy, "she's treated no differently than the men."

If you decide to say yes, candid insight on the board is important to women directors, says Pam Farr, president of the Cabot Advisory Group in Washington, D.C. "Engage a seasoned board member as your board buddy," she says, "someone who can fill you in on the board's dynamics, players, and history." Pick a lead director of the board, the one member who is respected and listened to by all, and make him your mentor. Farr agrees that gender proves less of a hurdle once you're in the boardroom than it does from the outside. "Once relationships are formed, and you demonstrate leadership, gender fades."

The CEOs of young, fast-growth companies are usually the folks with the most urgent need for good information on governance issues. But because they are busy, overstretched, and often isolated, they also have the hardest time getting these boardroom answers. For decades, international business support group The Executive Committee (TEC) has helped the CEOs of young companies form local networks to share ideas and problems, and to learn that they're not alone. I recently asked Ken Hamlet, chief executive of TEC worldwide (and an experienced CEO and director himself), to share the most common boardroom questions he hears from the chief executives of growing companies:

- "Our CEOs are often uncomfortable talking about governance issues," Hamlet explains. "A lot of them are self-made entrepreneurs who never really had a board or boss to contend with, so they go through fits and starts in learning. Most are resolved on this, though. They know that if they're going to grow, they need a board." In short, if you're the CEO of a growth company and having trouble getting "broken to harness" when it comes to a board, you're not alone—but the effort is worth it.

- Founders and CEOs are getting the word that they not only need a board, but a *good* board. "They used to put their accountant, lawyer, and friends on the board, but these days, they're trying to bring in the best talent they can."

- What are the major issues these CEOs tap into their boards for? "A lot revolves around capital growth structure, attracting and retaining human capital, and growth, particularly international and in new product lines."

TEC provides a valuable networking resource for younger CEOs who are looking for answers, with TEC chapters throughout the United States and in many foreign countries. Learn more at their global web site at www.teconline.com.

Ronna Lichtenberg, head of Clear Peak Consultants in New York and author of the book *It's Not Business, It's Personal*, is an expert on how personal issues shape business relationships. She finds the boardroom a hothouse of hidden but powerful interpersonal battles.

Every board is going to form networks and pecking orders among its members. Accept this and turn it into a strength. "Some directors will have more status than others, based on things like the size of companies they run, or how they handle themselves at the senior levels," Lichtenberg states. The informal "lead director" is just the most obvious sign of this ranking and is one of the keys to an effective board. "This is most apparent in times of crisis, such as pushing the CEO out. Whoever is strong enough to act as a motivator takes the lead by default."

The board differs from many other office structures because even the most active board spends relatively little time together as a group. This doesn't keep rankings from forming, but instead can make them arbitrary and volatile. A single *faux pas* can brand a business Alpha as a boardroom loser. "Directors don't spend much time together, so they tend to make judgments of each other quickly," says Lichtenberg. "This makes it important to give them as much face time with each other as you can." Lichtenberg notes that when boards *do* get together, however, they have opportunities for concentrated time sharing, with board dinners and long lunches.

Even though American boardrooms are among the world's most feisty, Lichtenberg finds that an in-your-face approach will backfire. "At the board level, importance is placed on gracious handling of interpersonal disputes," she explains. "You won't openly disagree with others around the table . . . things are worked out before the directors get there." Although some boards no doubt get raucous at times, in most boardrooms "a lifted eyebrow is the same as screaming elsewhere."

Lichtenberg offers another chemistry tip for the boardroom novice. "When people are new to boards, especially when they're women or minorities, they feel insecure and tend to talk too much, and make more judgments and pronouncements. This is pretty much exactly wrong. It takes a little while to learn when to talk." Just to complicate your life, board novices can also stay too *silent* for too long. Finding the right medium here is one more way to prove your boardroom status.

If you're new to the boardroom though, you can take a few active steps to build your ranking. "Fight to get on committees with real decision-making power, such as audit," says Lichtenberg. "Something like a 'social responsibility' committee shouldn't be your only one." Also, when working your way up in the boardroom, "try to form two or three particularly close ties on the board . . . get to know them personally, going for depth with a smaller group that includes the leaders of the pack."

Board Talent: Getting the Good Ones . . .

Every year boardroom burdens increase, more board candidates find themselves "boarded up," and the average director tenure grows a bit shorter. As a result, more boards are seeking talented director nominees at the same time as more of these A-listers are saying no to board offers. Board search consultants tell me that, as a rule of thumb, half of all top board prospects decline. Even a candidate who does ultimately accept a board nomination won't first respond by jumping up and down with joy. At the level of talent you're exploring, a board invitation is not a major event. Besides, the past year has made the burdens and dangers of joining one more board an honor many prospects can live without. What can your board do to improve the odds, and how can you turn a no into a yes?

- Realize that "no" isn't always the last word. Although execs with a half-dozen other board seats or who are battling through a major turnaround have good reason to say no and mean it, most prospects are surprisingly persuadable. "If they demur, or say it's difficult at the moment, or act coy," they may still be interested says Stephen Fowler, head of the Boardseat.com, online director matchmaking service. "Tease it out of them. Ask if they're happy with all the current boards they're on, or if they're thinking of dropping any. They may be firm now, but not so firm in 2 months. The best thing is to get them talking."

- The better the board prospect, the tougher the sell. If top candidates are "on three or four boards already, but feel they could squeeze in one more board seat, they get very selective," says Bob Shields, a partner in the Chicago office of SpencerStuart. "You have to persist with them a bit so they fully understand the business needs of the organization. Even if they first feel the fit is not right, giving them added info on the company and its situation, and what's sought from them, will usually interest them." A popular salesman's trick for this is to draw the prospect out for advice on what the company needs to do going forward and how its board should contribute. Once you coax the prospect to move beyond what "they" should do to what "we" should do, the battle is half won.

- The board itself is often your best salesperson. "Do everything you can to get the candidate to spend time with the CEO or someone on the board," advises Julie Daum, SpencerStuart managing director for U.S. board services. "Use personal chemistry and fit . . . the prospect may really like the CEO and feel these are people he or she can work with. Try to find a connection. One of the board members may bring some personal appeal." This combines the strength of the "old boy's club" boardroom with the talent needs of a modern board. Rather than tapping current directors' networks for "who knows whom," seek out some strong candidates and *then* use board member's networks to make a connection.

- Give active listening to a candidate's initial reasons for saying no. Between the vague demurrals you can overcome, and the solid deal-killers you can't, the prospect may have some valid concerns with your board that can still be negotiated or explained. "If the candidate has some concerns about the level of your director and officer [D&O] coverage, for example, those can be addressed," notes Stephen Fowler. Indeed, prospect concerns on issues like liability, current strategy, or company leadership offer a valuable outside take on how the company is viewed, and how it needs to improve to draw top board talent.

As the previous list suggests, the percentage of new directors recruited through professional search firms is steadily rising. However, putting a headhunter on the case can bring its own pitfalls if badly handled. When your board ventures into using an outside recruiter to fill a vacancy, what do's and don'ts should you keep in mind?

First, realize that a board search *is* different from an executive search. For starters, recruiters know they won't get rich doing a board search. Although the fee for a management search is typically a percentage of the executive's often hefty pay package, board searches will be a flat fee—and usually nothing that sets a headhunter's heart racing. Indeed, search firms often do director searches as a loss leader to keep their big executive search clients happy. This also means that you might get what you pay for in terms of research, scope, and background checking.

Firms that specialize in board searches or matchmaking are a growth market and may offer a more targeted job of finding the boardroom talent you need. Virtual-board.com, Boardroom Consultants' Board-search.com, Stybel, Peabody's Boardoptions.com, and Boardseat.com are a few of these newer board search specialists. According to Boardseat's Stephen Fowler, "You need to find a company that really understands what goes on at board meetings."

Be realistic in your director search. Some corporations assume that a search firm can do miracles. Dennis Carey of Spencer Stuart in Philadelphia finds that boards come to him and "assume we can get them Jack Welch . . . well, no, we can't, so part of the process is helping the board get a reality check on who might be available based on geography, industry, schedule, and other factors." Carey says that even the most savvy of search firms still averages an eight to one turndown ratio when approaching top Fortune 500 execs for board seats.

Use the search firm to help you winnow down to a final candidate. Carey says a major headache to recruiters is the client who "makes contact with more than one candidate at a time." The inevitability of backing off on one in preference to another "gives the impression that someone is more important to your board." Carey explains that "[t]his isn't an executive search, where everyone knows they're in a horse race." The result can be hard feelings among board prospects.

Finally, make sure the headhunter knows who's in charge at your end. Despite the growing power of boards, it's still usually the CEO who works with the search firm on finding a director. Today though, savvier CEOs want the firm to work in concert with the board's nominating committee or the committee itself may now be handling the search from the start. However you divide it, there should be no board/management battles on your side about who the headhunter works through. Any smart headhunter would view such squabbling as a good reason to warn his best prospects away.

Many of us recall jobs early in our careers that imposed a brief probationary period after hire, 30 or 60 days when the boss could judge how we were working out, and drop us if we weren't. By the time we're invited to serve on corporate boards, we're beyond such job tryouts. But isn't acting as a shareholder fiduciary now at least as tricky as being a junior clerk was back then?

Some boards are finding that a few months of probation for new directors not only shapes better board members, but also improves overall governance. Sarah Gerdes, founder of consulting firm Business Marketing Group, Inc. (BMG), in Seattle, has served on many boards and consults on governance. She has helped boards shape new director probation plans and sees them as an effective tool for improving the director's contribution.

Gerdes first saw the need for testing out directors at a fast-growing, privately held services company, where board recruits with excellent resumes in product-based companies "had a problem transferring their skills." To fix this problem, the board tried a three-part director recruitment process. First, a prospect went through an interview with the company CEO/founder. Next was an interview with the entire board. At this point, the successful prospect was named a director, but not quite a real director.

Gerdes explains that "for 6 months, the person attends board meetings, but receives no compensation." The director takes an active, constructive part in board discussion (the more the better), but has no vote and is legally not yet a member of the board. This "director without portfolio" is essentially an unpaid consultant on the board and faces no legal director liabilities.

So what's in it for her or him at the start? Stock options may be granted to the director from the get-go, but they do not come into effect until the start of the director's seventh month, at which point he or she is formally named to the board. At public companies, Gerdes suggests a small up-front cash meeting fee for a director, but again, any options don't vest until month seven, at which point the director is formally elected.

Director probation goes hand in hand with solid director benchmarks that both alumni and the plebe directors must meet. "If a board is smart enough to have a probation program, it's smart enough to set milestones," says Gerdes. Use solid deliverables such as a certain number of new business leads, new sales opportunities, or introductions, or new funding. This is a way director probation can work well for nonprofits, where directors are often expected to meet fundraising targets.

It's already hard enough to find good directors. Won't such an unpaid probation make board recruiting hopeless? Gerdes sees precisely the opposite effect. "There's been absolutely no pushback. When we've found board members with the right traits, there have been no problems."

. . . and Losing the Bad Ones

Q: I've recently taken over as CEO at our company, with a mandate for some restructuring and new initiatives. The board itself might be slowing down change, however. Most outside directors have been on board for years, and I frankly think some members contribute little. Also, the board contains 13 directors, which seems too large nowadays for the size of our business and our industry. What are some effective (but humane) ways to weed out nonproductive directors?

A: Gentle ways to ease out weak directors are always in demand (though little discussed). Your particular situation, with the board changes as part of a general board shape-up, allows you to bring some overall good governance exercises into play. Robert Lear and Boris Yavitz, cofounders of Lear Yavitz Associates governance consultants, have decades of experience between them on boards and shared with me their real-world advice on boardroom housecleaning.

Easing out ho-hum directors is relatively bloodless if you back it up with a solid evaluation program to first separate the sheep from the goats. "If you have a regular CEO evaluation, then it makes sense to also do the board," says Lear. "Then you suggest looking at the individual directors. If 12 out of 13 directors give negative ratings to Old Joe, then Joe is likely to decide he shouldn't be there." Lear suggests a nominating or specific governance committee for such evaluation, and that an outside facilitator guide the process. "That way, you can blame it all on the consultant."

Yavitz advises that this consultant should interface with the chair of the committee to process "director feedback on individual board members, but without the [raters'] names attached." The committee chair then meets with the chair of the board and with individual directors who were voted the weakest links. If you are also the board chair, though, "it's better that the CEO be insulated from this, so it won't look like you're blackballing a board member."

Directors still may be reluctant to point the finger at individuals, so another evaluation tool that Yavitz recommends is to have them "write down the four most effective and four least effective members of the board, and briefly state why." Common beefs include a lack of meeting preparation or a tendency to push a single issue. This technique spreads the blame, and when directors are privately told that they received the most negative votes ("taken out for a cup of coffee" by the committee chair or lead director), they often do the right thing on their own. Weak members decide not to stand for election. "You give them a big party and a plaque, and everyone goes away," says Lear.

With the ongoing use of such evaluations, you should be able to both slim down the size of your board and strengthen its value within a couple of years.

Ending the tenure of retirement-age directors can be particularly tricky on nonprofit boards. The board may need new talents or a member's contributions may be flagging, but sometimes these directors "just don't have a life, so they make it their boardwork," says Tom Tucker, a director affiliated with the Hughes Aircraft Credit Union (HACU) in California. "People can stay far too long. They're just not able to detach." Easing these seasoned directors off the board is not only politically dicey, but too often wastes the experience and counsel that they can offer.

Consider a *director emeritus program* such as the one Tucker helped evolve while on the board at the HACU. "Essentially, the CU recognizes the distinguished service of our volunteer while providing a transition between fully active board status and retirement." How does it work?

- Members are elected for a 3-year term to the emeritus board. Emeritus members can attend board meetings, but do not vote. They receive a budget to attend state and national CU conventions for the first year of their term, and take part in the usual board information programs.

- The nominating committee of the board selects nominees for the emeritus program, based on members' age, contribution, and their desire to stay active (which shows the value of a smart nominating committee). "We had one member who just couldn't disconnect, and when it came time for her reelection, the nominating committee said that they wanted to induct her into the emeritus program. She wasn't so happy, but said 'fine.' Now, she likes it."

- The emeritus program offers a number of other benefits to both the member and the board. "The beauty of this is that you don't just have to kiss people goodbye after they may have given 15 or 20 years to the board," notes Tucker. "[I]t offers an easy way to transition away from the board. Typically, [emeritus] members show up three or four times the first year, and then just drift away." Also, an emeritus program lets the board avoid inflexible retirement ages or term limits.

Tucker himself is now in the emeritus program and sees it as working well, though the board has made a few recent changes based on how effective the program has proven to be. "We no longer limit the travel budget for the last 2 years of the 3-year term. The emeritus directors weren't going anywhere by then anyway, so we just left it in for the full term." Note that several elements of this program could also be used on the corporate board as an effective say-goodbye tool.

Q: I'm CEO of a growing venture technology company with a boardroom problem. An equity firm with an investment in us has a member on our board as part of the deal. However, this guy just doesn't cut it as a director. He shows little interest in our strategy or needs, and spends most of the board meetings either distracted by outside issues or complaining about our results. Frankly, he knows little about our market niche and adds zero value, but, as you can tell, we're married to him as a member of the board. Any advice for turning this boardroom lemon into lemonade?

A: Being stuck with a bad director is not as hopeless as it may seem. Jim Drury, a former SpencerStuart honcho who now has his own board-consulting firm in Chicago, sees your problem as a common one with venture firm partners who "may have impressive vitae, and serve on three, four, or five boards, but still don't know their true role." The 1990s boom in venture capital firms led to lots of new folks who simply lacked the maturity needed to serve as good directors. "They may not know the importance of their roles besides just protecting their investments," Drury says. "They're prime prospects for some of the board conferences and programs that are growing more popular." Find out if your regional business schools are offering board education, bring the topic up at a board meeting, and drop a few subtle hints (Drury plugs the local board program offered at the University of Chicago).

Also, try to draft the talent already on your board to play a mentoring role. Typically, even a young, pre-IPO firm will have someone on the board with the age and resume to both know how a board really works and to gain the respect of your boardroom bumbler. Urge this Gray Eminence to act as an informal mentor. "The senior member should take this director out to lunch and help them learn about their role, that they need to be there not just in a financial sense, but to provide empathy to the firm," Drury states. This word-to-the-wise approach from a senior board member is also effective in dealing with problem directors at family companies and nonprofits as well.

If these tactics fail, a subtle phone call to a senior partner at the venture firm could be advised. "You may have to go to the principal of the firm to talk about this, but they're usually receptive." Drury's final word on the subject of coping with your doofus directors is "you don't have to just live with the problem."

Sorting out Your Boardroom Clashes

To paraphrase a business cliché, a board where everyone thinks alike is a board where no one is thinking. As boardroom risks have increased, so has boardroom debate, but this is also more likely to dissolve into boardroom conflict. Although good board leadership can help avoid and resolve boardroom battles, sometimes a bit of outside advice can make the difference. BoardSource, formerly the National Center for Nonprofit Boards (NCNB), offers a valuable booklet on cooling boardroom passions called *Keeping the Peace: Resolving Conflict in the Boardroom*. The 44-page publication is written by Marion Peters Angelica and, although targeted at nonprofits, it offers tips of value to any boardroom environment. It costs $20 per copy for non-BoardSource members. To order or for more information, call (800) 883-6262, or stop by the www.BoardSource.org web site.

Q: I was a director with a tech firm recently acquired by another company, and another former board member and myself joined the new, merged company's board as part of the deal. But I'm having some trouble fitting in here. I've walked into someone else's boardroom culture and feel a bit like a fifth wheel. Any ideas?

A: Being the new kid in the merged boardroom will be uncomfortable. Realize that "it's not just you feeling like a fifth wheel . . . such problems are normal," says Mitchell Mark, head of the Joining Forces merger consulting firm. But one thing that makes a difference here is to ask *why* you're feeling like a wallflower. Was the merger friendly or more hostile? Are you on the new board for your expertise and value, or through ownership in the acquired firm that mandated a board slot? Even if the acquisition seemed to go smoothly, Mark notes that often "the deal proceeds on wishful thinking," and unresolved postdeal issues can make you a boardroom reminder of what went wrong.

Make a fresh start by identifying the power centers on the board and by quietly lobbying them for governance improvements that will help the board overall (and also your own position). "Support some teambuilding activities and board education," says Mark. Perhaps take on the role of the board member who asks questions, "the one who stops the proceedings to ask a seemingly naïve question." Such "point of information" queries, handled reasonably, not only help the board member come up to speed, but force incumbent directors to explain why they've always done things that way.

Q: I'm an outside director of an established company with a growing governance problem. The company founder (also board chairman) is working toward retirement, and a while back we brought in a new chief executive from the outside. Although the founder supported this move and started out as a booster of the new CEO, tension seems to be growing between the two. Our results have been good, and our board doesn't have any serious issues with the CEO's job, but the chairman increasingly second-guesses him and is dragging his feet on retirement. Meanwhile, our chief executive is getting restive with the founder's unwillingness to cede power and is growing more abrupt with him. With the clashing style of these two, I don't know how long our good results will last. Is there some way our board can defuse this feud before it explodes?

A: Richard Hagburg, a California-based consultant who specializes in succession issues, was recently called in on a similar situation. "There was a real breakdown between the founder of the company and the new CEO," Hagburg explains. "They were the opposite in style. The founder was an evangelistic, entrepreneurial type, while the new CEO was a real manager, the tactical, disciplined sort both the founder and the other board members thought the company needed. But now the two of them weren't getting along.

"The board saw that the conflict was one of style and expectations, and they thought the founder/chair was wrong. The new CEO was doing what was needed, so the board called us in. We did evaluations and found that the CEO was above average, though there were some problems with his style. Also, one of the directors took the chair aside and told him that he was stepping over the line. The chair realized that there was a problem and wanted what was best for the company. The board then more closely defined the roles of the chair versus the CEO. We discussed these roles with the two, and this helped to clear the air."

Although Hagburg's example shows that outside help can be of real benefit in such a clash, it also shows how vital a strong board with an independent voice is. The directors could simply give in to an imperial founder and push out the CEO, or (in rarer cases) stick with their executive and battle the chair over control. But this board showed the leadership needed to talk tough with both sides —and to shape a solution that benefited everyone.

Q: I sit on the board of a growing, family-held company. Our founder and chairman is well along in years and has a general sort of succession plan for his son, but frankly the chair doesn't seem to be in any hurry to retire. He keeps pushing off any firm decisions, and I know that his son is expressing some frustration on the issue. I'm a friend of the founder, but I don't believe he should be letting the succession issue drift like this. What can we do at the board level to help move things along?

A: Being a board member on a family or closely held company can be the worst of both worlds. You're in a position to analyze the problem, but lack independent power with the chair to do much about it. Further, the board may share common structural faults of family business boards, with a makeup of the founder's old cronies and mentors, plus maybe one or two younger family members.

But this informal closeness can be put to work in your situation, suggests Mark Silverman, president of StrategicInitiatives.net and a specialist in family firm issues. "Sometimes Dad is very caught here," Silverman remarks. "The truth is, he doesn't respect the next generation's leadership, but he can't fire them. A board can be tremendously helpful by having an objective talk with the founder."

Every board has someone other than the founder who holds the respect of all players, maybe even a long-time board member who helped mentor the founder. This director needs to have a one-on-one meeting with the chair. Discuss what the strategic goals of the company are and subtly contrast this objective, well-planned vision with the lax, subjective job of assuring the leadership needed for its fulfillment. "No dad is objective," notes Silverman, but it takes a special attaché from the board to sell Dad on the need for this objectivity.

Another problem in such generation shifts is that often the board-room deck is too stacked with folks from Dad's age group. "Biology being what it is, Dad is usually in his 60s, while Junior is at least 20 or 30 years younger," notes Wayne Messick, CEO of online directory service Ibizresources.com. If the board is a kitchen cabinet with everyone Dad's age, the next generation will lack a real advocate in the boardroom. "I remember at one family business, the young successor CEO went through a long presentation to the board on expansion plans, and Dad, who was still on the board, cut him short with 'Not with my money, you're not,'" says Messick. If all directors are the same generation as Dad, they can all fear the new generation as loose cannons threatening their Florida condo plans.

As a response, Messick suggests the board add at least one new member from "the in-between generation, between the founder and the son." Such a member can value the viewpoint of Dad's concerns while still seeing the need for Junior to finally take complete control and serve as a liaison between both.

Of course, family firms aren't the only ones with generational conflicts. The past decade's tech boom and bust gave us lots of 20-something entrepreneurs who, though not quite as cocky as they once were, are still players in many boardrooms. But their style may well clash with the older generation of suits who make up the traditional board culture. Although this sounds like a swell sitcom plot, in the real world this boardroom generation gap can harm a board's effectiveness.

"They're a little more judgmental of management," observes long-time board pro Raymond Troubh of the dotcom age directors. "They're quick to judge events and situations . . . if you've been around longer, you tend to mull things over awhile before you have a reaction." This quick-draw background tends to shape the younger directors' boardroom style as well, says Troubh. "I think there's a cockiness . . . they know everything. They have to get accustomed to working with the chemistry of the whole board and seeing how it handles situations."

From the other side, situations may occur where "a director in his 60s or 70s may not appreciate the landscape of the new economy," observes Mike Frank, a general partner with the Advanced Technology Venture firm's Boston office. However, younger directors "may be very bright and analytical, but they have precious little experience," Frank says. "They tend to oversimplify and think there is only one right solution . . . they may not appreciate people, inertia, and the challenges involved." Frank even finds that "older directors are *more* open-minded." He says that strong experience with company operations and growth (both successes and failures) is vital no matter the board member's age.

Stephanie Joseph, who heads the Director's Network firm in New York, agrees that in the boardroom generation gap, the youngsters lose points for style. "The older directors may not be more conservative, just more thoughtful. They're more likely to see problems coming when the younger directors don't have a clue." To sum up, the young directors can probably learn more from their elders than vice versa.

Q: One of our outside directors seems to be a professional naysayer. Whenever discussion turns to a new idea or direction, he's always the pessimist, doubting its value, playing up the risks, and predicting doom. What can you do with a director like that?

A: Remember Eeyore, the gloomy donkey in the Winnie the Pooh tales? Sounds like he's moved into your boardroom. This situation came up in a recent program I conducted for CEOs of fast-growing companies, and several had their own boardroom Eeyores to discuss, as well as a couple of good strategies.

First, the pessimist is often opposed to ideas on which he has no ownership. Consider forming a board committee on strategic planning (not a bad idea anyway) and making Gloomy Gus the chair. If the guy who likes to rain on parades finds himself in charge of parade planning, you might see a distinct change in attitude—and if not, at least he stays occupied.

Route two consists of an attitude change on the part of yourself and the rest of the board. Someone at our conference asked the CEO with the resident naysayer, "Yeah, but how often has he turned out to be right?" The CEO had to admit that Eeyore might be gloomy, but that he was also often correct in his predictions. Maybe your problem isn't that boardroom pessimist, but instead too many boardroom optimists.

Q: I'm on the board of an NYSE manufacturing company, and our chairman/CEO is launching a strong acquisition program. He's worked out a deal to buy a certain target company, and I know that all the other board members are willing to approve the deal. I have some serious concerns with the firm though. We'll be voting on the acquisition at our next board meeting, and I feel I should vote no, even though I'll be the lone vote against. The deal will still go through, but would having a vote that isn't unanimous send up a red flag to potential shareholder plaintiffs?

A: You've read the situation well. A single no vote on a major corporate decision can indeed draw negative attention. In 2001, two merger suitors were pursuing Wachovia Bank. Wachovia chair Bud Baker favored a friendly (but less remunerative) offer from First Union and sought a formal board vote rejecting the richer offer from rival SunTrust. One Wachovia director voted against rejecting the hostile takeover bid though, and this lack of unanimity was newsworthy enough to grab an A Section article in *The Wall Street Journal*.

In your situation, a no vote "could very well give support to a plaintiff," notes Charles Demonico, chair of the Corporate Compliance and Governance Group at the Dickey McCamey Chilcote firm. "It can clearly be used to argue that the board decision wasn't appropriate when bringing a derivative action." Yet the ultimate "test will always be your fiduciary obligation." If you believe the deal is a bad one, you must vote no.

Agreed, these aren't the greatest of choices, but some alternative strategies exist. "I think in a situation like this there might be a problem with the supporting information," says Demonico. Put in extra time and effort researching the target company, its strategic fit, and potential problems. This might allay your concerns, but if not, it will help in the next step, a "sell me" session with the CEO. "Sit down with the chairman and express your concerns . . . make him satisfy you," Demonico encourages. If the deal still smells bad, you'll need to vote your conscience, but at least you won't be blindsiding the chairman.

By the way, a single no vote may not be as bad as it seems. If your board has a history of split votes on other issues, this can be cited as proof that a single is part of a pattern of overall boardroom independence (and this counts in your favor).

Q: Like many other boards, we have a policy written into our governance guidelines requiring outside directors to submit their resignation to the board if they have a change in job status. But I've never seen any solid rules on how this clause should be handled. Just what constitutes a real change in job status, and what standards should our board use in deciding whether it warrants a membership change?

A: Dealing with a change in the outside director's job status is one of those litmus tests of what really matters to a board. Since in even the most progressive boards dumping a director from the slate for no solid reason looks bad, the "submit a resignation" clause can give both the director and the board a graceful out.

For starters, ask why this particular director was added in the first place. Was his or her status as an active CEO the key? If so, retirement (the most common job shift at these levels) could lessen a board member's value over time. "A lot of boards are trying hard today to recruit active senior executives," notes Charles King, head of Korn/Ferry's global board search practice. "If the person retires or leaves that position, they are then not fulfilling one of the requirements."

On the other hand, boards are too often fixated on titles. In one case, the CEO of a smaller firm received many board offers, but these dried up when he left to serve as a mere divisional head at a much larger corporation. Worse, seeking only active CEOs on a board leaves it with directors who are often too busy and distracted to handle the nuts and bolts of networking or committee tasks needed for your board. In the long term, a retired CEO may lose the edge needed for active governance, but most retain great value for some years after their "sell-by date."

Of course, some job changes, such as a sacking or failure of the executive's company, are trickier and may even make your own board look bad (a top Enron executive in your boardroom looks a lot less impressive now than a couple of years ago). Here again, a resignation policy gives everyone a discreet out.

In sum, keep your resignation policy, but combine it with a regular, searching evaluation program that tells you just what you demand from board members. "What you're really weighing is the contribution of the director rather than the title," notes King.

The Exploding Job Description: We Have No Idea How to Evaluate, Motivate, or Pay Directors

ighlights for Children is a publication American kids have regularly encountered for over 40 years. The only times I recall ever seeing a copy were in a doctor's waiting room, which is enough to put any kid off the magazine right there. *Highlights'* best-known (and most often parodied) feature is "Goofus and Gallant," two cartoon boys who portray proper and improper ways of dealing with childhood issues. Goofus cuts in line, lies, cheats, grabs the biggest piece of candy for himself, and so on. Gallant is respectful of his elders, kind, honest, brave, and politically correct. Goofus and Gallant never seem to age beyond 12 or so, but if we extrapolate them into adulthood (and into the boardroom), we'll learn a moral lesson about boardroom motivators. These (often perverse) motivators are rarely understood but powerful reasons why boards suck.

Let's look at two outside directors on the board of Business, Inc. Director #1 is attentive, carefully reviews all information, stays in touch with the CEO between meetings, and asks insightful questions. He holds a substantial amount of stock in the company as a way to identify with shareholders and works to support the CEO, while still keeping an objective arm's length.

Director #2 doesn't open his meeting info pack until he sits down at the table, misses a good number of board meetings, and largely ignores the company in between. He approves whatever is put to a vote and waves through audit reports and CEO pay packages. He holds a negligible amount of company stock, and he exercises and sells any stock options as soon as he can. His snore is heard in the darkened boardroom during slide presentations, and his major governance concern is the lunch menu.

What are the results of such polar boardroom behavior? Although the danger of a fiduciary oversight is greater due to directors like Director #2, the *degree* of added danger is very debatable. Also, liability often seems to rain down on good boards as well as bad boards, and it drizzles equally on the individual directors. Should a disgruntled shareholder sue the board for a provable fumble, both our boardroom Gallant and Goofus face equal liability. Worse, under hostile cross examination, Director #2, yawning and looking distracted, says, "I dunno; I just signed what they told me to." The jury scowls. Earnest Director #1 tells how he was a careful, vigilant fiduciary on the board, but that somehow an Enron or Tyco scam seemed to sneak by him anyway. The jury still scowls. And, of course, boardroom Gallant's good-faith investment in the company is now worth pennies on the dollar.

Positive incentives are also vague. If Business, Inc. posts record profits and a high stock price, it's very hard to show any causal link between these and the quality of governance. Board pay based on company performance remains very rare. Directors may receive a hefty load of stock options as an incentive, but if they're feeling noble (like out boardroom Gallant), their ability to convert these into anything bankable is limited both by legal restraints and growing pressures to "show confidence" in the company. Further, those options work to make the board's outside, objective oversight increasingly subjective and "inside." Good directors should not hesitate to rock the boat, but what if rocking the boat pushes down the share price? Uh-oh . . . this brings us back to those boardroom contradictions discussed earlier.

Directors are increasingly expected to do a full-time auditor's job, but if we pay them like a full-time auditor, they lose their independence, becoming part of the problem. We try to motivate directors to provide good governance, but the upside motivators corrupt them into greedheads, and the downsides just drive the best and brightest away. In short, director incentives tend to consist of a few shriveled carrots, but some very threatening sticks—and both are wildly inconsistent in their usage.

How Do You Measure Corporate Boards?

Some of the most common questions *BoardroomINSIDER* readers ask concern what's normal in the boardroom. But an objective study of how (and if) corporate boards work is still a very new science, and tools for measuring boards remain uncertain. Even the best board evaluation programs still lack objective measures. Your board can decide that its communication is good, and its succession planning is average . . . but compared to what?

The movement to improve boards is still a decentralized cottage industry compared to the rest of business management. This business school/consulting infrastructure has greatly improved how businesses function, with common yardsticks for everything from financial controls to administrative systems. The boardroom, however, still potters along as a cottage industry, combining a few legal minimums with improvisation and informal networks.

The following section outlines a few simple measures that provide a rough take on how well your board compares to other corporate boards. They are not precise and are open for plenty of debate, but will give you some idea of how outsiders measure boards as a whole—including yours. Setting some common measures for what boards *should* do is the first step in expanding what they *can* do.

For starters, here are a few answers to the question, "If you had one tool to measure the value of a board, what would it be?"

- "How much equity does each director have in the company?" is a key test for Charles Elson, head of the Center for Corporate Governance at the University of Delaware. This investment shows, with the most direct of benchmarks, just what the director thinks of the company. But how *much* equity? "A benchmark of about $100,000 means something," Elson says. (He is also strong on attendance at board meetings: "100 percent is the target . . . 99 percent is just okay.")

- Here are a few boardroom measures I find telling: What is the average director age? (If the board average rises above the early 60s, start thinking young.) How many directors have "retired," "former," or "emeritus" in their titles? (One maybe, but two or more and the board is looking backward rather than forward.) How many directors are insiders or former insiders? (More than two nowadays makes it look like a management committee and may flunk new independence measures.)

- Len Simon, president of the Board Effectiveness Institute in Massachusetts, suggests that, during your next board meeting, someone keep tabs on how many questions outside members of the board ask the CEO or other managers. Forget the quality of questions for the moment. How many are asked *at all*? It's hard to give a target number for this, but if a 3-hour board

191

session draws one query per hour, assume that there is too much sleepiness at the table.

- Len Simon raises another point: "Board and CEO evaluation . . . is the board doing these at all?" If not, the board needs to launch a program for both, and start it yesterday.

- Cathie Linebach, a principal of management consultants Strive.com, sets a tough standard for board strategic leadership. "What percentage of strategic concepts for the company are coming from the board? What percentage of motions are coming at board meetings?" Her target for both: 90 percent. Although she admits this is pretty unlikely in the real boardroom, it remains a viable target. "The higher the percentage, the greater the value the board is bringing."

Although boards are figuring out that regular, pointed evaluation of themselves is vital, this doesn't mean that you're doing it right. What are some of the most common board evaluation fumbles?

- Selling the board on doing a self-evaluation is not enough. Spell out a statement of support for the entire process going in. Mark Akerley of Sigma Resource Group consultants urges you to "guarantee that the evaluation will be put on the board agenda again—evaluation is an ongoing process, not an event."

- Either name a governance committee to manage the whole evaluation process or make evaluation central to a current committee's mandate. "A governance committee can focus on these things," Akerley explains. "It's part of their job to ensure a follow-through." Although a downside of committees is that they never seem to die, they also guarantee an ongoing constituency for their role. This is crucial for something like evaluation, which the board may try to sneak out on.

- Doing too much too soon is another problem. "If you start with a 50-question formal assessment, most of your directors aren't ready and won't have enough data," warns Akerley. "Our experience is that you should start very briefly, say, with an hour of open-ended board discussion on how we did last year and what we want to accomplish next year."

- This leads to another failing with most evaluations: spending too little time on the critical things only a board can provide. "When the board asks itself what it does, it usually first answers with something like, well, we meet quarterly. Ask what things your board *needs* to do to add value. This can cover a lot of areas, like taking a long-term view or giving good counsel to the CEO, but narrow it down to half a dozen items, such as overseeing the strategic process or ensuring financial stability." Quantify items you can benchmark for 12 or 24 months.

- Don't rush into evaluating individual directors. "Once your board is comfortable with evaluation, the next step is to assess individuals," says Akerley. "But that stage is going to take at least a year—do the other pieces first."

- Although an outside facilitator can help you start the evaluation process well, remember that a facilitator can sometimes just give you the results, accept his or her check, and fly away. The board is then left to look at the report, nod their heads, say "Mmmm" a few times, and forget about following through. "The facilitator should help the board get into a long-term cycle of evaluation," says Akerley. Still, an outsider can't push the board to act on the findings. You'll have to build a system with a prejudice toward action.

  And after you evaluate? Boards can still blow it on the final step: putting the evaluation results to work. Boards are "absolutely falling down on this," says Akerley. "Discussion of the results can be very good, open and candid, but then the board decides to take a look at the issue next year." In short, all the effort, discussion, and research end up gathering dust.

- After the evaluation, "typically, not a lot gets done until the next quarterly board meeting or even until the next evaluation," notes Akerley. To ensure that issues are followed up, try assigning each item to an individual director for attention and reporting at the next meeting. "Say this is what we've got to do, and this is who's going to lead it."

- A common homestretch problem hits when the board and CEO disagree on a timetable for changes (or even the need for them). "I see varying expectations . . . one party may say we can make transitions in a few months, while the other is talking in years," Akerley says. Once again, spell out your implementation plan going in by passing a strong evaluation resolution at the start.

A strong evaluation process for your board is so valuable and helpful in improving board quality that I almost hesitate to mention a potential downside. Nevertheless, you must know about one possible drawback. Your directors try to do the right thing, sit down, and put together an honest, tough-minded read of their own and each other's failings. Could the results then be demanded as part of lawsuit discovery? You might be surprised to learn that they sure can.

"I don't know of any reason it wouldn't be discoverable," says Eric Orlinsky, an attorney with the firm of Saul & Ewing, even though governance pros have yet to see it happen. In researching this, the top legal and administrative people I talked to all said about the same thing. At first, they hadn't heard of a case where a board was forced to spill its evaluation dirty laundry . . . and then added, "but now that I think of it . . . "

The result could be plaintiff attorneys tapping into a mother lode of candid comments on directors who aren't pulling their weight, board weaknesses that haven't been addressed, or second thoughts about past board actions. This danger that hasn't hit yet should *not* persuade your board to give up on exploring self-evaluation; this threat may never occur, but you should consider a few moves that may ease the risk.

Start by bringing counsel into your evaluation early. Although legal work products and findings are usually privileged, assuming that your evaluation is protected just by having a lawyer sit in likely won't hold up. "If done in communication with counsel, you might be able to claim privilege, but I think you'd be pushing it," says Orlinsky. Charles Elson of the University of Delaware corporate governance center also says that the privilege claim may prove vulnerable. But it could add one firewall to discovery, and, should these cases pop up in the future, judges may be inclined to respect a legal shelter claim if they feel the value of good board evaluation warrants protection. In short, it can't hurt.

Also, keep it verbal. "A lot of the results are discussed orally, so there's nothing to produce," notes Amy Goodman, a counsel with the law firm of Gibson Dunn & Crutcher. Although a final report of the evaluation may be needed, raw evaluation instruments with salty comments are way too dangerous to keep around. "We had a policy of, after getting the initial comments, destroying the material," says Kathy Gibson, chair of the American Society of Corporate Secretaries (ASCS) Corporate Practices Committee.

You should also view potential discovery as an evaluation spur rather than a check. In case the big *if* should occur, and a director has to comment on evaluation shortfalls, the weaknesses uncovered likely won't be the issue. Rather, the company will face danger if failings are identified, but then *not* corrected. Consider this a goal to follow through on your evaluation and not just leave problems until next year. They could prove to be ticking time bombs.

Q: Our board is making a periodic review of our board charter and governance guidelines, and the issue of director age limits has come up. Do most boards have age limits in place for board members, and is there an average age for these? Also, do any have written policies on not naming someone to the board who is past a certain age (too few years available until retirement)?

A: Age limits as an element of board guidelines are quite common. The 2000 Korn/Ferry Board Study found 77 percent of the Fortune 1000 boards surveyed have age limits, with the average age ceiling being 71. The use of age limits varies by industry (just 38 percent of healthcare boards set a retirement age), but in most studies, the retirement age is set narrowly between 70 and 72. However, boards that impose age limits may hedge them with qualifiers, allowing the board to overrule the boundary in cases when a director with urgently needed skills is needed. Even then, though, the ceiling is usually respected.

The second part of your question has fewer hard numbers, but is vital for making the best use of your board members: Should we set a minimum amount of time between when a director joins our board and when he or she must retire? Even the strongest boardroom talent needs a year or so to get up to speed on your company, and if that takes up half the director's time until retirement, your governance payback will be minimal.

"The director tenure that will be available is a real factor in searches," says Roger Kenny of Boardroom Consultants in New York. "Clients tell us that they want a board nominee to be able to give them at least 10 years." Mike Nieset of recruiters Christian & Timbers says that in his company's board searches "clients want at least 5 to 8 years of availability" depending on the governance needs. I've found no company with a written policy on minimum age windows, and putting such a limit in black and white is unlikely due to age discrimination factors. However, board election policies need not be written to have an impact.

Board recruiters tell me that a distinct trend exists among boards to move away from naming retired CEOs to the board, in favor of tapping currently active executives. Such a policy in itself would widen the retirement window of opportunity for your board members.

Your Biggest Board Motivator: Stuff That Spends

It sounds so good on the surface: Provide your directors with pay incentives the same way you do top executives. But the idea remains very controversial. What do top governance and compensation experts say about offering performance-based pay incentives to members of the corporate board?

"Frankly, I think it's a very dangerous practice," says Mark Poerio, an attorney with the Washington law firm of Paul Hastings. "You want to manage for long-term value in the board. Short-term incentives are appropriate for those who need them, but that's not the reason directors serve. Stock awards tend to be delivered for short-term results, and you shouldn't set up your directors for criticism by adopting a formula that appears to encourage the short-term view."

George Sissel is chairman of packaging firm Ball Corporation, which offers several board incentive plans. "When I took over 7 years ago, I spoke with institutional shareholders who were concerned about what they saw as weak stock ownership by our directors and also by our board pension program," Sissel says. "We took the advice to heart and integrated both the programs by eliminating the retirement program and investing the proceeds in a director-restricted stock program. But we also extended an Economic Value Added pay incentive program we'd set up for management to the directors. They put half of their annual retainer into restricted stock. This puts a large amount of their pay at risk, but it gets everyone's attention. No doubt the board has a limited role in creating value—it doesn't manage. But the board's business is to select the managers who do, and most of the time they can add a bias toward thinking like shareholders."

Jim Reda, a principal with Buck Consultants in Atlanta, doesn't see board incentive pay as a good idea. "The typical amount at risk is maybe 10 percent of the retainer, and that's not enough," Reda asserts. "Also, directors can become too aligned with management, especially on accounting issues." That is, results can be "adjusted" to meet targets. "I don't think directors should be so closely tied to the structure of the company. The only situation where it might be useful is on the boards of private companies. There, you have limited equity reward options, and you're less tied into shareholder versus manager issues."

Carol Bowie, currently corporate governance director for the Investor Responsibility Research Center (IRRC), was formerly a compensation consultant and sees the director incentive issue from both the governance and pay angles. "This is really not a priority among institutional investors," Bowie explains. "Directors don't have the operational ability of management; directors are primarily responsible for monitoring strategy and the management team. It's not that widespread either." In 2000, the IRRC found that 32 of 1,163 top Standard & Poor's companies offered some form of incentive-based awards to board members. This compares with 39 in 1999, so the total actually declined. "About 5 years ago, this was predicted as being the next big thing in corporate governance, but it just hasn't panned out," Bowie concludes.

If incentive board pay remains tricky, how about *variable* board pay? Why should we pay directors the same committee fees no matter which committees they're on? The audit committee is a prime example here. Audit workloads, skill requirements, and liabilities have skyrocketed and will increase even more as the new reform rules are put into place. If one director serves on the audit committee and another on, say, the nominating committee, we know which one faces much greater burdens. Yet it is universal boardroom practice to make committee compensation, whether through retainers or meeting fees, the same across the board. Should we pay more to get more?

"I don't see this as a trend, but I see other ways it is being handled," says Rhoda Edelman of Pearl Meyer & Partners pay consultants. "Committee chairs are typically paid more than other members, and this can vary by committee. Also, if the committee meets more often, as audit committees seem to be, then meeting fees will add up. Also, boards can pay consulting fees to a particular director who is doing extra work."

Jay Lorsch of the Harvard Business School, remarks, "I could see why people would argue for a differential, but I see a reluctance to differentiate." He adds, "That could lead to different pay based on years of experience and so on. The only trend I see is toward the opposite—pay directors one big fee for everything they do."

Chuck King of Korn/Ferry pay consultants also addresses the question. "People are beginning to mull this over, especially related to the audit committee, but they're just talking about the fees paid to chairmen, because it's such a time-consuming job. As for the rest of the committee, I don't think you can have an imbalanced compensation scheme."

Options have become the coin of the realm for pay plans over the last decade, from the Fortune 500 to the latest tech startup. For corporate directors, this shift to equity has been particularly strong. A 2002 William M. Mercer survey of major companies found that 57 percent of director pay is now in equity (and equity had fueled a 60 percent jump in average board pay over the previous 5 years).[1] But this swing to stock raises some new issues for directors, who may be juggling stock pay plans from several board seats and who face unique trading and holding rules. Here are some fresh options for your options:

- Use your leverage as a director in striking a stock pay deal, aiming for flexibility. "The smart directors are trying to get their equity in a number of forms," says David Gumpert, author of the book *Better Than Money*. Combine stock with options and even restricted stock, if possible. "Try to build in some diversity," Gumpert emphasizes. Remember, he notes, that "typically, if a director is getting options, they're not qualified," which means different treatment in taxes and exercise choices. Strive for ease of early exercise, especially for that big lump of options you got in the beginning from a struggling startup.

- "Keep track of what you've got," counsels Gumpert. He sees too many cases where board members receive various grants from their various boards and "put them in a box and forget about them—it's incumbent on you to keep track of them, particularly when they vest." It's easy for active directors to lose track of these details, especially when you have a mixed nest of options hatching at different times.

- Speaking of vesting schedules, as a director you have the muscle to push for a liberal vesting policy. "If there is a special event, like acquisition of the company, your options may not automatically vest, so you'll only see part of their value," notes Gumpert. The solution: Insist on liberal vesting. "Everything is negotiable, and as a board member, you have a fair amount of clout."

- Another board stock negotiation point should be a flexible policy on transferring options. "This can be important for

[1]William M. Mercer press release, "Director Compensation: Stock Makes the Difference," 4 April, 2002.

198

estate-planning purposes," says Dale Krieger, head honcho at Stock-options.com. This site, by the way, has a terrific online calculator that lets you figure values and taxes on your options under lots of scenarios. (Note: This site may not work as well with Macs.)

- Here's another nifty online stock option manager. Mystockoptions.com offers a supermarket of info on your options for options. Calculators, tax guides, a glossary of option terms, tips, advice, chat boards, and tracking software make this a handy everything-you-wanted-to-know site for those who are waiting to vest.

Of course, the idea of juggling your paper option wealth has become a tasteless joke to lots of people over the past few years. Many board members of 1990s growth companies deferred a hefty share of their pay into options. Now these directors are expected to work harder than ever rebuilding shareholder value and retaining talent while sitting on a personal load of underwater options.

A study by iQuantic pay consultants found that over 80 percent of surveyed firms had at least some outstanding options underwater, and many were acting to address the problem. But what sort of action can your board take?

Simply repricing options won't work anymore. "Repricing has basically died due to changes in FASB [Financial Accounting Standards Board] rules," says Bill Witt, a principal at McDaniel & Associates consultants in Atlanta. Accounting treatments now demand that old options need to be canceled and new ones reissued, but you must wait at least 6 months for reissuance. "Six months and 1 day later new options are issued," observes David Broman, CEO of the Syzergy Group consultants in California. "Basically, you just ride the market until then."

Although this approach can work for top executives, directors face a higher standard in raising their own sunken options. "With these [repricing] programs, I see directors excluding themselves," observes Broman. "They see that they need to send a message to stockholders."

However, directors may be trying alternatives to take up the slack in their option nest egg. "Some have added dilution by making more grants to directors, with a new strike price and vesting schedule," says Broman. Note, though, that this dilution may bring its own problems. "[W]e may begin to see boards turning back to restricted stock or outright stock grants to directors," Broman suspects. "This used to be more common, but fell out of favor in recent years."

How about more cash pay for the board? Pay plans "treat the board more as executives today," says Bill Witt, which can mean upping the ante for pay. But cash has been at a premium for most firms lately, especially startups. In summary, most directors are dealing with underwater options by riding it out, coping, and betting that reappreciation is down the road.

The hurry-up corporate reform laws of summer 2002 featured one hurry-up provision that directors must bear in mind. The Securities and Exchange Commission (SEC) Section 16 rules on when and how corporate officers and directors disclose trades now take real-time notification to the extreme (within 2 days), and the last thing you as a director want is to be dinged for tardy trades. What do you need to know about the new turbo-charged Section 16 rules?

- First, the basics. Virtually every stock transaction you make as a director (including receipt of stock options) must be reported to the SEC within 2 days of the transaction. The only delays allowed are for gifts of stock, and you'd still better clear with corporate counsel what defines a gift.

- Directors have had varying degrees of cooperation with the company on stock trade filings, from letting corporate counsel know after the fact to telling the corporate secretary, "You handle everything." Look for more of the latter, says Ron Mueller, a partner with the Gibson Dunn Crutcher law firm in Washington. "Directors often precleared transactions, calling company counsel and asking if it's okay to sell some shares," Mueller explains. "Now, companies will say that's fine, but we need to know what day you place the order, and please give us your broker's phone number. Companies may even want power of attorney from the director." In short, directors will need to surrender some control over their trading to ensure that these vital disclosure deadlines are met.

- Most companies will be struggling to bring their filing procedures into compliance for some time. The 2-day disclosure rule was buried under some bigger, more urgent changes that must be sorted out first. "Companies are still struggling with the 10Q [certification] and unlawful executive loan requirements," says Mueller. Translation: If anyone in the corporation is going to worry about how you personally must deal with the trade filing rules, it had better be you.

- Here's an often-ignored trading issue that can come back to bite you. Companies that file trade information electronically through the SEC's Electronic Data Gathering, Analysis, and Retrieval (EDGAR) system give what's called a Central Index Key (CIK) code as an identifier for each director and officer. Know your code for each board you serve, and make sure that it's used for every trade report. If corporate staff slips up and files your trade without it, you'll be given a whole new CIK code, deactivating the record of your trades under the old code. It's sort of like making sure that your social security withholding is actually being withheld to the right account.

- Remember that the Section 16 filing rules "are your responsibility," says Mueller—*not* the company's. If a trade is not disclosed in line with the new deadlines, *you* are the one who suffers the penalties.

Before there was the Sarbanes-Oxley law and its SEC how-to's, there was the SEC's Regulation Fair Disclosure (FD). Earlier I discussed this 2000 SEC rule, designed to eliminate "whisper" numbers to stock analysts. What you *haven't* heard about Reg FD, though, could be a nugget useful to you as a director: new ways to structure officer and director stock-trading programs. "For the first time, the SEC has defined by regulation what constitutes insider trading," says Keith Bishop, a partner in the California law firm Irell & Mancella. "This allows insiders to set an affirmative defense policy for insider trading." Previous federal regulations forced insiders to fit their trades within shifting trade windows around various filings, results releases, and major company strategic moves. For companies in heavy acquisition modes, windows were almost always closed.

This has always been clumsy and risky for insiders, especially with the massive amount of stock and options many top execs and directors now hold. But the Reg FD rules permit insiders to set up advance trading plans that commit them to buying and selling stock on a set future schedule, disregarding the traditional windows. "The change is a response to the huge pileup of company securities held by insiders," notes Arnold Ross, president of the Ross Companies pay consultants. How can you put the new FD rules to work for you, and what is the downside?

- Be aware of how the rules work. "It's not as simple as saying that you're just gonna sell," says Keith Bishop. "The SEC rules still set specific conditions." Be aware of the new fast-turnaround SEC rules for reporting trades, for example. Your financial planner or broker can help you map out a targeted plan.

- Think about your financial strategy first. The new advance trading plans versus the previous trading windows are a bit like the stock indexing versus active trading debate. By setting and using a future trading plan, "Everything goes on a long-term average . . . you hope that selling high and buying low even out," observes Arnold Ross. The traditional windows approach may be riskier and more volatile. Aiming your stock trades at trade windows is still permitted and may in fact still suit your needs just fine.

- *Advance* means advance—sort of. FD requires that you file a trading plan in advance of your trades, but there's still gray area on the terminology. Although no SEC filing requirement exists, "somebody outside of you has to know about the plan, though it can be filed internally with the company," says Ross. How far in advance "advance" must be also is still up for grabs, but Ross says it should be "at least 4 or 5 months before the first sale under the plan." As noted earlier, giving your company counsel power of attorney on this may be an option.

- Check out other trading rules that may apply. Trading plans allowed under the federal Regulation FD in 2000 were not okay under California state law until the next year, notes Keith Bishop, but "even the jurisdiction where your insiders are located could reach out, so you need to look at all state laws." Also, you'll need to make sure your company's internal rules on insider trades are updated to meet the new options allowed under FD.

- Final note: If your company is closely watched by analysts, a trading plan filed in advance can ease concerns about big, sudden insider trades that could shake confidence in the company.

Deferred pay programs have become a staple for savvy directors over the past decade. With board pay an addition to already complex personal financial plans, board pensions on their way out, and complex tax issues, it often makes more sense to push director compensation off into nest egg territory. But deferral itself raises some tricky tax and planning issues, and your choices are constantly changing. What's the latest when it comes to deferring your board pay?

- The most common deferral plan with cash is for a director to turn a set amount of the pay into something like units of restricted stock, notes Peter Opperman, a senior board pay consultant with William M. Mercer in New York. Then the units are "turned back into dollars when the payout is made," according to Opperman. For example, 1,000 stock units are paid out at whatever price the stock pays at the time. Some volatility exists in this stock-price-based scheme, so Opperman says a trend is to give directors an added premium at the time of deferral. "Instead of 1,000 units at $50 a share, for example, the company might grant the director 1,200 units to make up for the volatility."

- Paying directors in stock options was a tasty trend back when the markets were booming, but doing so now creates a very different volatility problem for board members. Rather than pushing for more cash though, boards once again are giving themselves a boost to make up for wobbly stock values. "Many are getting a 10 to 20 percent premium . . . the premium is the trend," Opperman remarks.

- Although executive pay has seen enormous creativity in dealing with huge amounts over the past decade, Opperman says that director pay actually offers more room to experiment. "Directors generally don't look at what they make as a huge piece of compensation, so they're very willing to try new things."

Q: I'm looking ahead to retirement in a few years, and I also plan to make my current term as an outside director my last. What sort of board financial issues (options, pay deferrals, etc.) should I keep in mind in this countdown to retirement?

A: With board pay up, stock and options a much bigger factor, and board pensions almost extinct, lots of directors haven't kept up with the retirement planning implications. "The biggest emerging issue is stock options," says Mark Poerio, an attorney with the law firm Paul Hastings. "Termination of service will trigger the exercise period," and this can leave you with a ticking load of options, perhaps forcing you to forego exercising some to avoid bad tax timing.

Instead, you (and the entire board for that matter) need to plan out a fair, flexible postretirement option exercise program now. Right of exercise periods can vary all over the calendar, including 3, 5, or even 10 years. Further flexibility can be added by crediting retired directors as advisory board members for a period of time, suggests Poerio, with the option clock not ticking until the advisory status ends. Jeff Kanter, a partner with comp consultants Federick W. Cook, suggests that a simpler approach is to look at your top managers' postretirement options and deferral plans, and pattern your board setup on theirs. "Flexibility is the watchword," Kanter emphasizes.

Negative Board Motivators: Sticks among the Carrots

What are board members fretting over at the moment? Audit oversights? Sluggish results? Terrorist attacks? In the real-world boardroom, most directors are concerned about something a lot closer to home: their own personal board liabilities. Gyrating stock prices, the weak economy, and corporate scandals and subsequent lawsuits are sending director and officer (D&O) insurance coverage into one of its periodic "soaring cost, assuming you can find it" explosions. What D&O questions does your board need to be asking right now?

- Will coverage really be there when you need it? "The biggest concern is policy rescission," says Bernard Bell, partner in the insurance practice group at law firm Swidler Berlin. Your insurance carrier may try to invalidate the whole policy based on misstatements in your application, and they can interpret a misstatement very broadly. The company will then get its premiums back, "but that's cold comfort if you have a claim," says Bell.

- How is your coverage allotted? D&O policies provide several elements that enable you to better customize coverage. "What they call Side A coverage is for the individual officers and directors," says Bell, "while Side B coverage is for the company itself, for indemnification." By mixing these two elements, directors can ensure that they have coverage even if the corporation itself should lose out. This leads to a next question . . .

- Does your policy have severability provisions? With this, if a claim is made against one person in the company, or even a rescission of part of the coverage, "it's not imputed to others," according to Bell. Talk with your company counsel and risk manager about this, but the hard truth is that some of your directors and officers are more likely to face damages than others (and would you like to be in the same liability lifeboat as certain Enron staffers?).

- How healthy is your insurer? "The coverage you have is only as good as the provider," warns Bell. Although insurer failure (leaving you bare) may seem unlikely, it could become more common. Also, future mergers or underwriting changes by the insurer could force you to start shopping for a new policy sooner than you'd planned, leaving you vulnerable to market changes and coverage gaps.

- What are your coverage limits? Damages and settlements are soaring, while your D&O payout ceiling may still be stuck in the good old days. Your insurer will be more than happy to show you scary charts of liability claims going through the ceiling, and this time it might be wise to listen.

Asking your underwriter D&O questions is a good idea, but not enough. Ask some questions *internally* too by speaking to your company legal and risk management staff. Here are a few pointed questions to ask, questions so simple and yet wise that they could save your assets:

- What are the *specifics* of our D&O coverage? Stephen Weiss, a director liability pro with the Washington law office of Holland & Knight, encounters directors "who are very proud to tell me that before they went on a board, they asked the CEO whether the company had insurance, but then they never asked the coverage limits or how good the coverage is." Even in our present deadly liability climate, far too many of you still take a hear-no-evil, see-no-evil approach to protection.

- Who actually negotiated our coverage? Generally, the person on the company end who negotiates coverage knows little about the intricacies of D&O policies. "It's usually the CFO or corporate counsel's office," notes Weiss. "The CFO knows accounting, and the general counsel knows law, but risk management is usually dumped here. If it's the counsel's office, negotiation is usually handled by some junior birdman who doesn't know much about the SEC or class actions. Insurance is the Rodney Dangerfield of corporate work." This leads to the fruit of those negotiations. . . .

- Show me how you got us the best deal. D&O coverage is "the most negotiable insurance in the world," observes Weiss. "A good negotiator can double the value of a policy by eliminating exclusions or adding endorsements." Smart directors will demand proof that the company struck the best deal on the best D&O coverage.

Q: I'm an independent board member on a younger, venture-based firm. We're in a tech sector, and you know how the market has gone over the past couple of years. Revenues have gone from bad to worse over the past three quarters, and we're staring over the abyss by the end of the year, with all the potential liabilities and fallout. I'm considering resigning from the board, but what are the standards for this? How do you tell if you're a rat deserting a sinking ship or a prudent person keeping your name and reputation intact?

A: First, focus on what you can do: your basic boardroom role of hiring, firing, and evaluating management. If the CEO seems to be making the best of a (very) bad situation, you may need to accept that you set the course, so you have a duty to see the voyage through. Yet Tamara Davis, the managing director of the Corporate Governance Practice for Levin & Company in Boston, notes that, "If I no longer had confidence in the CEO, and the rest of the board did not support my position, or there was fraud involved, I would bail out. However, if I joined the board believing in the company's leadership and business model, and it's a case of the environment having changed, then I wouldn't."

Still, Davis, who has served on a number of boards in the biotech sector (which suffers a huge mortality rate), says that directors looking over the brink should learn to be more flexible in pursuing company alternatives. "There are many instances where poor clinical trial results or a regulatory finding suddenly kills the main product line," she explains. "The board responds by building its own strategy, looking for a strategic partner or an acquirer." Before you jump ship, consider that other ways may exist to turn this lemon into lemonade.

The Elephant in the Boardroom: Boards Don't Handle Bad News Well

Many voices today demand that boards offer active monitoring of management and the corporation. But this gives the board one more contradiction to sort out: that they *actively* handle a *passive* role. This overseeing, fiduciary board functions like a lifeboat, which is vital in case of an emergency but otherwise hangs patiently from its divots, waiting for something to go wrong.

In many ways, the board is the final firewall against corporate mischief, but this role is not as noble as it sounds. It means that all internal controls, all management's smoke and mirrors, and every attempt to salvage the situation will have broken down before the disaster makes its way into the boardroom. By the time the CEO tells the board, "We have a problem," the problem may already be in the terminal stage. The board will have few options at this point, and the ones presented will likely be unpleasant: a major restatement of profits, bankruptcy, asking a prosecutor for mercy, or sacking the CEO.

Asking tough questions of the CEO is what everyone tells you to do as a director, but hardly anyone does in reality (it makes you just as unpopular as it does anywhere else in life). Information flows into the boardroom (typically through the CEO's office), but the board is wholly unsuited to go out on its own, either individually or collectively, to dig for info. Special investigation committees of a board are a rare, fairly new creation, often formed when the corporation is already foundering in obvious scandal. Even then, the board doesn't do its own digging, but charges a legal counsel (often the company's own inside counsel) to investigate.

If the board is to hear bad news about the company, it must usually depend on the CEO (the person ultimately responsible for the news being bad) to deliver it. For some reason, CEOs are not eager to do this. Fortunately for the CEO, many ways exist to obfuscate, soften, delay, or redirect the bad news. The board, for its part, has many incentives to assist the CEO in this deception. Directors do not like headaches, especially ones they lack the time, resources, or expertise to do anything about. Further, if the CEO thoughtfully tells them none of the bad news, directors can maintain plausible deniability. And as they learned from watching director testimony at the Enron hearings, pleading ignorance, while maybe not blissful, is certainly safer than being a co-conspirator.

Bad News and Tough Calls

Company results are slipping, client orders aren't recovering from recession, and your business model looks ever more wobbly. Cash flow is tumbling, and creditors are grumbling. Talk of bankruptcy takes over your board meeting, and counsel presents a Chapter 11 scheme. What questions should you as a director ask *before* voting on the bankruptcy plan?

- How solid and workable is the plan? "I see a lot of Chapter 11 plans that should not have been filed," says Jim Burghardt, a partner with the Moyes Giles O'Keefe law firm in Denver. "They file on a wing and a prayer, and don't have an idea of what they hope to accomplish other than to buy some time. You need an objective going in." The result: A huge majority of Chapter 11 plans do not reach their ultimate reorganization and end up slipping into a Chapter 7 liquidation.

- How good is our advice? "Don't just rely on your corporate counsel . . . talk with a firm that does bankruptcies," says Burghardt. This search for outside advice includes the board itself, which should consider hiring its own counsel for the process.

- How good is your data? "Boards have to ask for sufficient info on the finances of the company," notes Craig Hansen, a partner in the Restructuring Group at law firm Squire, Sanders and coauthor of the book *The Executive Guide to Corporate Bankruptcy.* "What is the current liquidity? What are your alternatives, risks, and benefits? How will customers, employers, and suppliers react?"

- What are your *personal* liabilities? A company becomes a different animal once in bankruptcy, one that not only won't shelter the director anymore, but can even turn on you. Kmart, currently reorganizing in Chapter 11, has sought depositions from its directors for approving "retention payments" to top execs before the filing. "What protections can and can't be negotiated will depend on the jurisdiction and circumstances of the filing," counsels Greg Rayburn, a principal with restructuring pros Alix Partners in New York.

- Should you stick around? Board members may well wonder why they want to deal with the high-pressure, fishbowl atmosphere of a bankruptcy workout, but "It's always better to be part of the solution rather than exit the board," suggests Hansen, especially if you've been on the board for a while.

A board of directors is a collective human entity and is subject to the all-too-human issues of ego, sloth, impatience, and conflict. So why shouldn't boards also be prone to post-traumatic stress disorder after living through a particularly painful corporate event? Death of a founder, bankruptcy, a CEO firing, a legal investigation . . . these can all leave their mark on the people in the boardroom. Assume that the directors at scandal companies such as Tyco and WorldCom (even the new recruits) are waking up some nights in a cold sweat.

William Rollnick knows a thing or two about such post-traumatic stress in the boardroom. As a director on the Mattel board, Rollnick found himself pitching in as interim chairman when CEO Jill Barad was sacked. How does a board work its way through such trauma?

- "First, the board has to coalesce and become one," advises Rollnick. "Looking back, I don't think there were any leaders on the board at the time, but we all became leaders. This was a board I was very proud to be part of."

- For board members to work their way through a crisis as an effective team, it's crucial "to bring everybody onboard immediately, with no secrets," Rollnick says. "No segment of the board should feel left out, or that somebody else knows something they don't." Although this may seem to add time and hassles to the board's heavy burdens, such an open-boardroom approach actually speeds decision making and avoids infighting.

- Good communication lines between directors and key top staffers are crucial to working your way through a crisis. "This becomes very tricky . . . you know these people, but not well, and you don't have time to sit and discuss the business one on one," Rollnick explains. "But now you have to build these relationships, and very quickly. We were blessed at Mattel by having three [division] heads who were fabulous managers, and that made it easy for us." But assume that your board may not be so blessed when a crisis strikes, and some staffers may even be part of the problem. Build board links to a variety of key managers in advance.

- Especially when facing a tough CEO ouster, boards must have thought-out succession plans, both for emergencies and the long term. "Large Fortune 50 companies have succession plans, but for a company at our size, we didn't," Rollnick admits.

- During a major crisis, every second counts, and a board may have to make decisions first and worry about whether it was right later. "You have to move fast, be crisp, and make sure the board is unanimous—without that, you're dead." Finally, assume that a board crisis will trash your appointment calendar. "It's not a question of how much time you have available for this board, but how many hours are available for anything else. Weekends, Sundays . . . it made no difference. We just did it."

Q: I'm a director with the board of a fast-growing service company. We do a lot of acquisitions, but I'm concerned about some of the prospects that another member of our board brings to the table. He's a venture capitalist, with lots of projects in his portfolio, and most of his ideas seem to have his fingerprints on them. How does a board avoid such director conflict and self-dealing problems?

A: Director self-dealing is one of those problems that everyone denies, but they can also cite at least one instance of it occurring on a particular board they served on. As with most behind-boardroom-doors problems, some issues are a lot grayer than others. Sarah Gerdes, CEO of Business Marketing Group, Inc, (BMG), recalls when "the CEO of an e-company here in Seattle was all set to finish up a round of funding, but the board held up the transfer of funds. A lead member of the board was from a venture capital

(VC) firm and picked that moment to tell the CEO that they'd hold up funding unless the CEO left for another company the VC wanted to start. That's both a massive conflict and unethical." Another boardroom pro tells me of the time some hungry young entrepreneurs included the VC who had provided key funding on their board. One fine day he used his expertise on the company to lure away a key tech talent for another venture he was funding. What could these entrepreneurs do? "Grit their teeth," recalls this board expert.

But you *can* build a few protections against director self-dealing, especially if you get them right from the start. "Early on, insist on full disclosure from all directors," advises Gerdes. "Then you need to address what happens if the need arises, with penalties, performance measures, and incentives." Director conflicts are like bribery or any other form of corruption; they tend to wilt when exposed to sunlight. If push comes to shove, though, Gerdes knows of more than a few cases when the board sued its own members. Founders also need to be choosier when putting a big funding source on their board. "Select your board members very carefully . . . don't just get to know them over three lunches."

Family-held corporations generally have a bad rep for the quality of their governance. Too often, the boardroom is viewed as either a quiet collection of relatives and cronies or else a battleground of factions. Even though it doesn't have to be this way, one issue often becomes a flashpoint due to the unique chemistry of the family company: succession planning. How can your family board stay ahead of this issue?

- Start by getting the board in shape to handle succession. "The vast majority of family business boards have been nonfiduciary advisory boards," says Richard Narva of consulting firm Genus Associates. "They are essentially compliant, rubberstamp boards." Ralph Daniel, a principal at the Center for Family Business Dynamics in Santa Barbara, California, concurs, noting that "most family boards are poorly constituted and are all insiders. Unless you have two or more truly outside directors, it's hard to come up with good succession criteria."

- After you've brought the board up to speed, put some serious deliberation into company strategy and how succession can make it happen. "Come up with a strategic plan and a mission," says Daniel. "This gives them a road map." Company expansion, or even sale, can be part of this vision, but the family firm may well include keeping management in family hands as part of its vision statement for the company. In this case, executive development plans must be shaped to support this goal.

- Family business boards often approach succession the way humans view their own mortality: by not thinking about it. "Many CEOs who founded a company see themselves as immortal," observes Daniel. "They just can't fathom the company continuing without them. The existing CEO needs to step aside and, simultaneously, the board needs to handle passing the baton."

  But not *too* simultaneously. "The boards tend to think of [succession] as a one-time event, but they should allow at least 5 years to plan and implement the process." Set concrete benchmarks and dates for the process.

- Be sure that your succession plan is a real plan, rather than just collected assumptions. This way, your succession ideas will at least be subjected to some naked-light-of-day review that can bring out wrong presumptions. "I see a familial pull to assign the successor role to offspring, but sometimes the board or even the CEO is not sure that this is the right person," Daniel remarks. "This can create a real bind at the board level." By making a solid plan for who's next in line and why, any concerns with a candidate can be addressed early and often fixed.

Q: At our company, those of us on the board have always had fairly open communications with staff, but some of the things I've been hearing lately have me concerned. A couple of senior managers have mentioned that our CEO's behavior is becoming a problem. In the last few months he's started throwing temper tantrums at subordinates, grown withdrawn and defensive, is missing meetings, and making decisions that don't seem logical. I've known this man for a few years, and this doesn't sound like him. In dealing with our board, he seems reasonable enough, but I do know that he's had some personal traumas at home over the last year. I hate the idea of getting the board into this situation, but what should we do?

A: Such *Caine Mutiny* situations are not common in the boardroom, but when they arise they bring enough trauma to last a lifetime. As a first step, recognize that the board is likely the last to know about such a CEO problem. By the time anyone works up the courage to say something to a director, erratic CEO behavior is likely obvious to most of the top staff. Dr. Mortimer Feinberg, chair of the New York consulting firm BFS Psychological Associates, suggests that you begin by "speaking to another director on the matter or forming an informal committee, playing everything low key."

The next step is for the board to launch an inquiry, but *not* with the stated intent of profiling the CEO. "Go to the CEO and say that, in order for us to feel more comfortable, we'd like to do a morale study of management here. This needs to be nonthreatening, making it clear that you're not trying to lynch him."

Feinberg notes that the board can conduct these subordinate interviews, but it may be wiser to hire an outside consultant or a respected former board member who has good relations with the CEO. The CEO's reaction to such an inoffensive morale review by the board will give you a clue in itself. "If he's not defensive, [and] says he has nothing to hide, go ahead; that's a positive sign. But if he rejects it, gets defensive, and says the idea itself is crazy, that's a different indicator."

The board should study the results for signs of "irrationality compared to past behavior," according to Feinberg. "You're looking for deviations from the baseline, like now coming in late, or changing in relations with peers and subordinates, or even throwing things." A distinct negative change, noted widely by employees, will suggest that more is going on here than just a couple of disgruntled employees. In that case, a respected board member should privately suggest to the CEO "that he get some help or consider a leave of absence." Express positive concern rather than cold disinterest and offer the board's support. Still, as a board member, you must recognize that "you have a legal obligation to take this issue seriously." A CEO who's slipping over the edge is not only a human tragedy, but also a fiduciary responsibility.

Um . . . We've Got Some Bad Numbers Here

With corporate financials of the past few years now receiving a microscopic second look (and CEOs having to swear on their lives to them), financial restatements are in the news. Unfortunately, restating company results can bring all sorts of unwelcome attention. What can your board do to ensure that your statements get it right the first time?

Huron Consulting Group has surveyed almost 1,000 restatements filed with the Securities and Exchange Commission (SEC) over the past 5 years to find the most common reasons. The most popular error is revenue recognition, which accounted for over 20 percent. Errors in accruals, reserves, and contingencies were the second most common restatement problem (12.6 percent). The number of restatements more than doubled from 1997 to 2001, leaping 25 percent over those last 2 years alone. I spoke to Joe Floyd, a Huron managing director, to find out what boards can learn from this data to avoid restatement problems in the first place. His comments are as follows:

- Decisions to restate are never simple, and they may balance on the knife edge between dishonesty and simple misunderstanding. "Restatement involves a misuse of the facts, available facts that were improperly applied, or misuse of [Generally Accepted Accounting Principles] GAAP," says Floyd, "not about things like changing estimates or use of a preferential accounting principle." Some cases will not be clear-cut, and the audit committee should serve as arbiter by digging out all the facts. "All restatements are not fraud . . . often it's a matter of interpreting the rules."

- Restatement issues are very industry specific, so learn where pitfalls lie in your own sector. "In software, there are a lot of bill and hold and right of return problems," Floyd explains. "Understand your unique accounting policy risks."

- Restatements are often prompted by poor internal controls that allow errors to sneak by. This is a special problem with "subsidiaries that are far flung, so the control environment is not entirely adequate."

- The need for a restatement could also mean that your auditor is not doing enough testing going in, allowing control errors to slip by. "If the auditor is testing enough, the errors above should be getting caught," asserts Floyd.

The SEC is also cracking down hard on corporate earnings management—is your board? Everything from abuse of special charges to roundtrip trading to stuffing the sales pipeline is now under fire, and income accounting standards that were acceptable just a few years ago are today under a microscope. Since your audit committee will find itself on the spot (and maybe in court) for these revenue figures, what impolite questions should you be asking?

Earnings trickery tends to sneak in through gray areas, such as the subjective items on the balance sheet, according to Jim Roth, president of the AuditTrends audit training and accounting firm. "Look at unusual items that require significant judgments, such as reserves, accruals, and estimates . . . there is a lot of room there for manipulation," Roth remarks. "Reserves, especially, are most commonly used for income management." It's easier to hide voodoo numbers under headings that are already fuzzy.

Change is good, except in accounting. "Look for significant variances from prior years or from budget," Roth suggests. "Ask why we have this now. Look at the overall picture for unusual items." Changes in general accounting treatments of revenue are also a red flag. "If the auditor says that the accounting board changed a rule, and the company has decided to make the change, ask if it's required, what the effect on income and executive compensation will be, and, if the change is such a good idea, why the company didn't do it earlier."

Bringing income recognition policies into compliance with new SEC standards is also good, but examine what it does to earlier company figures. "Definitely look into changes this year to meet the SEC rules. It could mean that something was being done wrong earlier. Ask management and the internal and outside auditors why in their view it was done this way before, if they are comfortable with it, and whether it was typical."

When asking such questions, hold out for solid answers. "Beware any kind of explaining away without fully explaining," cautions Roth. "If accruals of income have increased by 50 percent in the last year, and the auditor says that this is just normal fluctuation, well, that's not good enough. Ask exactly why it was handled this way."

Remember when growing a business on "Internet time" was a matter of months, or even weeks? Ah, the good old days of nonstop initial public offerings (IPOs). Over the last couple of years, though, many IPO-track companies have gotten derailed, or at least sidetracked. If you serve on the board of such a startup, the shift from blitzkrieg to trench warfare requires some governance changes from the board. How do good directors respond when your IPO goes slo-mo?

For starters, be realistic. The frantic pace of taking young companies public that we saw up through 2000 was an anomaly, so accept that a long, hard slog to the IPO stage is the norm. "If everything is perfect, it should still take a year to take a company public," notes Charles Kaplan of Equity Analytics. "And things are rarely perfect." If your slowdown seems market driven, assume the market is trying to tell you something. "If you have a first-class underwriter who says he or she can't put away the deal, and it's in your best interest to wait, you'd better listen," emphasizes Kaplan. "It's probably good advice."

Can the company settle for half a loaf? "The other possibility is that you can put away the deal, but at a substantially lesser amount," says Kaplan. "Companies have had to make that call a number of times, and the decision can't be made by anyone but the board." This means a second look at your long-term business plan to see not how much financing you *should* have, but how much you *must* have to continue.

Make sure the board stays informed on why things are lagging. "Directors should get the investment bankers to make a presentation to the board, or should go to them, and ask questions," Kaplan advises. What are the specific problems? Can we get bridge financing? Also, management needs to keep up a running dialogue with the board, particularly if the CEO hopes to keep their confidence.

Operations are at least as important as financing during this stage. "This is probably the time for the board to spend more effort on operations," says Brad Feld, a principal of Softbank Venture Capital, who has seen many recent IPO slowdowns. "The IPO was a financing event, but now you need to focus on an operating plan that makes sense, on how the company is executing it, and on real customers." Feld expects directors to add more value rather than less when the IPO retreats. "If you signed up as a board member, it's because you believe in a company that has lasting value. An IPO is not an exit event, but a financing event."

Looking Your Liabilities Straight in the Eye

The federal Private Securities Litigation Reform Act of 1995 didn't quite make the boardroom safe from strike suits. Although plaintiffs must jump more hurdles on their way to the courtroom, once they get there the cost to your company has soared, and that was before the corporate outrages of 2002 hit the court dockets. Is your board prepared?

"There's been an enormous explosion in the magnitude of settlements over the last 18 to 24 months," says Dan Bailey, chairman of the Arter & Hadden law firm in Columbus, Ohio. In 2000, shareholder suit settlements over $100 million were unheard of, but by the end of 2002, at least 10 cases hit this figure, with some breaking $200 million. The biggest settlement so far was the Cendant case, with total damages reaching $3.3 billion, but even viewing this as an outlier, the average is up sharply. RiteAid, 3Com, and Informex ($142 million) were a few recent settlements, and just wait until Enron, WorldCom, Tyco, and so on are added to the damage sheet.

"A variety of developments have caused this," says Bailey. "Mostly, it's inflated stock prices. When those prices drop, the damage, in theory, is astronomical." As a corporate director, what do you need to know about this director and officer (D&O) danger (and how should you prepare)?

- Don't assume your industry is safe. "There's no pattern to it," warns Bailey. "People thought high tech would be the most vulnerable, but big damage awards are hitting all industries."

- Get ready for higher D&O insurance premiums. "Premiums are heading up. . .there have been 15 to 20 percent higher charges just this year, and even that won't be sufficient," Bailey says. Corporate counsel should give your board regular updates on your D&O coverage, what sort of increases or limits may be coming, and whether shopping around for new underwriters is wise.

- Check your D&O coverage limits. Sharp inflation in the "average" liability damage claim could leave your current coverage limits far behind (remember when $1 million in D&O coverage seemed generous?). With the current market, you may be stuck having to pay *much* more for *much* more coverage that actually covers far *less*, but it's still better than the alternative.

- Higher damage settlements mean that potential claims against individual directors (as well as their defense costs) will be higher as well. Be sure to double-check your policies on advancing defense costs to board members, particularly assuring that these will be advanced as incurred (not forcing directors to carry the costs until the last appeal).

- While you're chatting with counsel, ask for an update on where your company's liability exposures lie and how they might be shifting. A PricewaterhouseCoopers survey finds that, although the total number of federal shareholder suits has fallen, the number alleging accounting violations has climbed: 53 percent of the total as of 1999. Accounting accuracy is drawing more scrutiny now, and plaintiffs have learned that fraud allegations concerning financials are a strong tool for making initial complaints.

The need for a strong corporate risk management system has never been more urgent. But is your board closely involved in company risk management (RM) programs? If not, both your company and your directors themselves are in danger. First, review your board's role in risk management policy by asking these questions:

- How is RM review handled within your board structure? Most corporate boards now assign a review of risks facing the company and RM structures to the audit committee. Although this is a good fit for audit's mandate, make sure the committee looks beyond limited audit and financial risks to include legal, regulatory, information technology (IT), and operational risks as well (what are your terrorism vulnerabilities, for example).

- Where does the board fit into the company's RM policy and guideline process? Is it involved in the early stages of policy setting, or at the end, as a rubber stamp?

- How often does your board review the overall company control environment?

- Who gives your board its RM updates? Does your chief risk officer report directly to the CEO and the board, or to someone further down in the chain (CFO, treasurer, etc.)? How often are these updates given?

- Does the board prepare its own annual report on the company's risk and control environment?

- Does anyone on the board have a specific background in risk management and internal controls? Adding such talent to your board could dovetail nicely with the increased skills needed for the audit committee.

Finally, take a hard look at how much risk your board *itself* represents. Are there comments in meeting minutes that could come back to haunt you in court? Are potential director conflicts fully laid out? Have board members ever been the source of information leaks?

Corporate boards have been notoriously slow to adapt to new technologies, and that includes email. But given some of the legal and strategic problems that email can expose a board to, taking it slow may not have been such a bad idea. The outside director is privy to the most sensitive of corporate info, often discussing delicate issues like mergers and acquisitions in real time. But he or she is *not* a formal employee of the company (and is outside of its data networks), making the outside director an email disaster waiting to happen. What sort of boardroom email policies should you implement and how do you make them stick?

Make clear that, when a director emails an employee, that message becomes part of the company's email system and must meet its rules. "Whatever rules the company has for internal email must apply to the board as well," notes consultant Patricia Eyres. Most firms now have email policies regarding privacy expectations, personal use, and inflammatory language, but does the board know these also apply to them? Eyres has seen cases where directors forward jokes or cartoons to company staffers that are prime evidence of a hostile environment in sexual or racial discrimination cases. Although employees have gotten the word that they need to self-censor when sending such material on the company nets, directors too often view themselves as above the law.

Directors are privy to lots of highly sensitive financials and other information, but Eyres, who has served on several boards, has "received sensitive financials as an attachment to email, with no code, encryption, password, or anything." Such emails can easily be misdirected to the wrong mailbox and then opened by God knows who. Even if the email is properly routed, anyone on the director's own staff may be able to open it. "Directors need to set a policy at their offices that, if a board-related email comes in, it's to be opened only by the director himself," says Eyres.

Corporations must include email in their records-retention policies today, but make sure that the board is also up-to-speed on this policy, and living up to it. The Microsoft antitrust case proved that email is a fertile ground for lawyers suing a company, and in legal discovery today, "the single most sought after form of business communication is email," notes Eyres.

An advantage to email is that it enables us to dash out quick, sloppy notes to each other at the speed of light, but Eyres points out that this ease has a huge downside. "People tend to run off at the fingers and use lots of loose, unprofessional language. Remember that you're not just having a conversation, but creating a permanent business record." Directors are especially prone to such a "just between the two of us" attitude via email, sometimes with disastrous results.

The board of directors is an expert body that engages in highly professional, serious deliberation—except when it doesn't. The next time a foul-up in your boardroom leaves you feeling that things couldn't get any worse, mull over the following real-life boardroom headaches:

- Board and audit committee pro Barbara Hackman Franklin recalls a particular board meeting. "[W]e were discussing the status of the current CEO, and whether he should stay on the board after retiring," Franklin says. "We thought the CEO had left the room, and discussion was getting a bit pointed, when we looked up . . . and realized the CEO was still sitting there! After that, I think he politely excused himself and left the room."

- From a consultant and director who prefers to stay anonymous: "At a family company board meeting, a family director and the CEO had a disagreement. That turned into a shouting match, [and] that turned into throwing papers at each other, until finally the two attacked each other and we had to call in help to separate them. It was a shambles."

- Roderick Hills is one of America's most experienced turn-around directors and CEOs, but at one of his companies "our [audit] committee and internal audit set a formula for distributing indirect costs between our distribution and manufacturing divisions." Hills says that the company auditor reviewed the formula, "and it turned out we had the ratio exactly *backwards* —we managed to fool even ourselves!"

- Christine Comaford Lynch, managing director at hot California venture fund Artemis Ventures, recalls her entrepreneurial days. "[A] VC member of my board insisted that no one on staff be paid more than $75,000. Even then, it was impossible to get a good marketing person in their 40s with a house and kids for that price out here, and I argued that we could never hire the talent we needed. Finally, I started to walk out of the board meeting saying I was going to get my checkbook to give this investor his money back. He blinked first."

- From a noted West Coast board and consulting pro: "I'd just joined a company's board, and no one told me they had a strict policy of leaving all board book materials behind in the boardroom after meetings. So after we adjourned I packed up the board book and happily took off, only to have the company secretary, staff, and some other directors come running after me down the hall."

I realize that all this talk of how directors can't cope when disaster is staring them straight in the boardroom could be seen as discouraging. To conclude on a positive note, here is some advice given to me by one of America's most successful chief executives on how new CEOs should build shared, honest communications with their directors:

- "Communication with the board is the most important thing. Talk to them individually and build relationships with them through lunch or dinners, or inviting them to sports events. I try to spend at least an hour a month in contact with our directors, and make it a priority."

- "Make sure that the first time you tell directors about company bad news is *not* at the board meeting. This is where the individual communication is so important. As an outside director myself, my biggest frustration is to come to a board meeting and be surprised by some negative thing that's already been going on for several months."

Oh, by the way, this CEO was Dennis Kozlowski of Tyco. Or at least he *was* the CEO.

Conclusion

The danger is not that I should do ill,
but that I should do nothing.
—Michel de Montaigne

These failings in the corporate board model, as damning as they are, still miss what may be the ultimate reason why corporate boards do not work, as well as the greatest source of the damage they cause. From the points made in the previous chapters, you can see why we tend to approach the board of directors with a few distinct emotions—irritation, contempt, and disregard being the most common. We dismiss boards as weak, corrupt, out of touch, conflicted, beholden to management, and an institutional relic.

Yet the board is also something else, something far more estimable, but also somewhat tragic. Consider this benchmark board: a fast-growth, Fortune 50 company with a 14-member board of outstanding credentials. It contains only one inside director (the CEO/chair), and the committee structure is solid. Such star names as Wendy Gramm and Raymond Troubh are current members, and the long-time audit committee chair is emeritus accounting professor and dean of the Stanford Business School. This board deserves (and repeatedly received) accolades as one of the finest in the United States, a benchmark of fiduciary governance. This was the board of Enron as the company was accelerating into corruption and collapse.

The corporate board is a group of people who are typically seasoned chief executives, venture capitalists, proven achievers, and community leaders. When we rate these folks in any other context—by the businesses they've built, the advice they've offered, or the results they've achieved—we tend to rank them as our society's best and brightest. Further, I don't recall ever meeting a board member who didn't take his or her fiduciary duties very seriously. Rather, they tend to be aware, concerned, and often more frustrated about the failures of corporate governance than even their worst critics.

Consider the director's job description: "Highly important corporate position, with ultimate legal responsibility for company. High liability and reputational risk, meager pay, and too little time, support, or information to do the job." That sums up the role of corporate board members, and to make matters worse, the job doesn't even earn much respect nowadays. The consensus of government, investor activists, and the media is that board members are sleepy, corrupt CEO pawns who need to be cracked down on, forced to sign more papers verifying their work, and who deserve a good scolding.

Who would want such a job? Boards recruiting outside directors today go through more and more turndowns before getting to a candidate who says yes. Risky or young companies (the ones most in need of good directors) find it hard to draw outside board talent at all. No doubt the proposed board crackdown reforms will help drive out venal, lazy directors, but they also discourage the far greater number of competent, overburdened board members who just don't need the grief.

Now I doubt that anyone will actually feel sorry for those poor folks in the boardroom. They can and do fail to provide good oversight or to generate shareholder value. And in some instances they have been actively dishonest, allowing management to get away with murder for their own personal benefit. Further, given a choice, most of us would still prefer to be the director of a scandal company than an ex-employee, out of a job, with a worthless retirement plan and a scarlet letter on our resume.

Yet the board members of corrupted companies are still suffering. They are under an ethical and legal cloud that will track them for the rest of their lives, even if they are ultimately found blameless. Even worse, this cloud is one that they themselves still cannot fathom. This is well shown by the dueling postmortems on the Enron scandal. The internal report of the Enron board slammed management for perpetrating a scam on the directors. The Senate Subcommittee on Investigations, however, found that "the Enron board contributed to the company's collapse and bears a share of the responsibility for it."[1] I suspect that both sides are right; Enron's board (and

[1]"The Role of the Board of Directors in Enron's Collapse," Report of the Permanent Subcommittee on Investigations of the Committee on Governmental Affairs, United States Senate, July 2002.

those of other scandal firms) does bear guilt, but its members are still, sincerely, unable to see how they failed. They did their jobs according to the governance standards that they knew. Unfortunately, those governance standards no longer work.

Thus, even good people in the boardroom are trapped in a governance model that is almost designed to fail, and good people in the wrong job become bad people. Directors out there are using a huge number of boardroom innovations to provide more and better governance oversight with less time and effort. But these remain spread out among individual board pros, are anecdotal, and are too rarely shared with the boards that need this governance wisdom the most.

Throughout history, when good people have been trapped in failing, destructive, contradictory systems, while lacking the resources to make needed reforms, the results have not been pretty. There have been business failures, disasters, and death. Worse, the good people themselves become corrupted by the system, resigned to the status quo. They lower their standards, lower their heads, and cease to care. At times, they even cynically join in gaming the system. I suggest that this is the single most serious reason why corporate boards do not work. As it currently functions, corporate governance has neutralized the only people really able to reform it: the board members themselves. This book has collected some of these boardroom tools and offers them as effective counters to the major failings of our governance model. They are not panaceas; they're more like workarounds for built-in bugs of the boardroom system.

The American corporate board of directors as it functions at the start of the twenty-first century is a hugely responsible, powerful, yet burdened engine built upon the fragile old frame of an eighteenth-century joint stock company. Completely scrapping this corporate governance relic would be one *uber*solution. However, even the board's harshest critics have not proposed this, knowing that their next obligation would be to propose some better structure for governance oversight, and the critics have none. The corporate board, a creaky, ludicrous tool for fiduciary control, despite its failings and contradictions, has proven to be like Churchill's critique of democracy: It is the worst possible system, except for all the alternatives.

Index

Index

Index